THE LIFE OF MADAME NECKER: SIN, REDEMPTION AND THE PARISIAN SALON

The Body, Gender and Culture

Series Editor: *Lynn Botelho*

www.pickeringchatto.com/body

THE LIFE OF MADAME NECKER: SIN, REDEMPTION AND THE PARISIAN SALON

BY

Sonja Boon

LONDON
PICKERING & CHATTO
2011

Published by Pickering & Chatto (Publishers) Limited
21 Bloomsbury Way, London WC1A 2TH

2252 Ridge Road, Brookfield, Vermont 05036-9704, USA

www.pickeringchatto.com

BRITISH LIBRARY CATALOGUING IN PUBLICATION DATA

Boon, Sonja.
The life of Madame Necker: sin, redemption and the Parisian salon. – (Body, gender and culture)
1. Necker, Suzanne Curchod, 1739–1794. 2. Necker, Suzanne Curchod, 1739–1794 – Health. 3. Necker, Suzanne Curchod, 1739–1794 – Family. 4. Salons – France – Paris – History – 18th century. 5. France – Intellectual life – 18th century.
I. Title II. Series
944'.035'092-dc22

ISBN-13: 9781848930568
e: 9781848930575

Typeset by Pickering & Chatto (Publishers) Limited
Printed and bound in the United Kingdom by the MPG Books Group

CONTENTS

To Búi, Stefan and Tóbin, because you have all been part of this journey

ACKNOWLEDGEMENTS

This book could not have been written without the help, support, commitment and encouragement of many individuals on both sides of the Atlantic.

I thank Mary Lynn Stewart, who shared with me her fascination for the conceptual terrain of the body and was the best mentor and supervisor I could ever have asked for. To Kathy Mezei and Rosena Davison, thank you for your consistent encouragement, your probing questions and your care and support.

I benefited from the insights of numerous colleagues along the way, among them Lara Campbell, Catherine Dubeau, Stephen Duguid, Dena Goodman, Helen Hok-Sze Leung, Cindy Patton, Valerie Raoul, Betty Schellenberg and June Sturrock. I was also able to draw on the editorial advice and insights of numerous colleagues and friends, including Pamela Bry, Marica Cassis, Jean Guthrie, Heather Latimer, Helen Loshny, Byron Lee and Mary Shearman, and I am grateful for the assistance of graduate students, most notably Kira Petersson-Martin. I thank, too, Daire Carr and Julie Wilson at Pickering & Chatto for their insight, patience and efficiency.

The research for this book was conducted during the course of my doctoral study and was generously supported by the Social Sciences and Humanities Research Council of Canada and Simon Fraser University, and, later, during the editing and revising stages, by start-up funding from Memorial University of Newfoundland.

I also want to express my sincere appreciation to Mme Danielle Mincio and the staff of the rare books division of the Bibliothèque cantonale et universitaire de Lausanne, Mme Barbara Roth and the staff of the Salle Sénébier of the Bibliothèque de Genève, and to the cheerful and very enthusiastic archivist of the Archives cantonales vaudoises (Lausanne) for their welcome and assistance during my 2007 trip to Switzerland. To the staff in Simon Fraser University's interlibrary loan division: Nancy Blake, Mirfat Habib, Scott Mackenzie, Sonny Wong and Vera Yuen, my grateful thanks for processing the most obscure requests for a variety of seventeenth- and eighteenth-century works, for locating copies from afar, for discovering treasure troves of previously unknown electronic editions, and for never-ending patience and goodwill.

In Chapter 3, I draw on insights developed in an article published in *LIMINA*, 15 (2009). An earlier version of parts of Chapter 4 was published in the *Journal for Eighteenth-Century Studies*, 32:2 (2009), pp. 235–54, while parts of Chapter 5 appeared in *Eighteenth-Century Fiction*, 21:1 (2008), pp. 89–107. I thank the anonymous reviewers of these articles for their valuable feedback in the earlier stages of this project.

Finally, I could not possibly have undertaken this work without the support of my family. Thank you to Búi, Stefan and Tóbin for sharing laughter, sticky kisses, pinches, pokes and hugs, and for your unquestioning and completely unconditional love.

INTRODUCTION: ABJECTION AND DISPLAY

In elite society, it is theatre that presents itself first.[1]

Today, theatre is everywhere and everyone believes himself to be on stage for effect; this is the source of the corruption of both moral taste and taste in the arts.[2]

Madame Necker appears to have led a charmed existence. Her meteoric social ascension from impoverished orphan to esteemed socialite and philanthropist is the stuff of fairy tales. Suzanne had it all: beauty, brains, virtue and the coveted prize, a wealthy and politically powerful husband. It seemed almost too good to be true. Her precipitous flight from Paris during the early days of the French Revolution, followed by her tragic, premature death and spectacular burial, recall the final years of another otherwise charmed life – that of Diana, Princess of Wales – and would appear to be the only fitting end for a woman doomed to a life lived in the public gaze, a gaze she alternately courted and despised. Such indeed is the narrative outlined by her numerous biographers.

The bare bones of Madame Necker's life story, as we know them, are relatively straightforward. Suzanne Curchod was born in the Swiss village of Crassier, near the French border, on 2 June 1737. Hers was a family of modest means and moral rectitude: her father was a Calvinist minister and her mother a Huguenot exile who had fled France after the Revocation of the Edict of Nantes. From her father, Mademoiselle Curchod received a remarkable education, learning languages (including Latin and Greek), physics and mathematics, as well as the requisite feminine arts of music and painting. As one early twentieth-century commentator observed:

> She had been educated like a man destined to the career of science and letters, and was well acquainted with ancient and modern languages; nor was her knowledge superficial. Not withstanding almost masculine gifts and a powerful but well-directed will, she was essentially feminine.[3]

From her mother, meanwhile, she is said to have inherited her beauty. Once launched in Lausanne, she enjoyed success as a member of numerous social cir-

cles. Here, in 1757, she met Edward Gibbon, with whom she formed her first
– ultimately failed – romantic attachment.

Tragedy struck soon thereafter. The deaths of her parents, in 1760 and 1763,
forced her to rely wholly on her own resources. She took on paid work as a governess and later, at the encouragement of close friends, accepted a position as
the personal companion of a young Parisian widow, Madame de Vermenoux.[4]
Within a year of her arrival in Paris, Mademoiselle Curchod fell in love again,
this time with a wealthy Genevan banker, Jacques Necker.[5] The union produced
only one child, Anne-Louise-Germaine. Madame Necker dedicated herself
wholly to her daughter's moral and intellectual development, noting in a later
letter to her husband that she had almost never left her daughter's side during
the first thirteen years of her life.[6] Germaine Necker, later Madame de Staël,
flourished in her mother's salon and later developed into a woman of formidable
intellect and considerable charisma.

Even as Madame Necker supported her husband's political achievements
and encouraged her daughter's moral and intellectual growth, she, too, took a
prominent role within the French elite. She established her Friday salon soon
after her marriage, cultivating an environment that provided an opportunity
for her to engage in her literary desires, while at the same time developing it
as an effective vehicle for her husband's political goals and ambitions.[7] During
this time she also began to build friendships with other influential elite women,
among them the leading Parisian salon women, Madame Geoffrin, Madame
du Deffand and the Marquise de La Ferté-Imbault. In later years, she became
publicly active on the political front, directing an experimental charity hospital
and publishing a treatise against premature burial.[8] She died in May 1794 at the
age of fifty-seven. A treatise against divorce appeared later the same year.[9] Five
volumes of edited personal writings apparently never destined for the public
eye – the *Mélanges* and *Nouveaux mélanges* – were published posthumously by
her husband in 1798 and 1801.[10]

But Madame Necker's story is far more complex than such a simple retelling
might imply. Decades of profound psychic and somatic suffering recounted in
pages of intimate letters to close friends and family suggest a profound dissonance between the public façade and lived experience; in other words, between
the displayed or performed life and that intimately lived. A closer analysis, however, reveals a twinning of public and private lives rather than a contradiction
between the two. In this book, I argue that this linkage between public and private played itself out on Necker's body, which functioned both as a stage for her
public performance of self and, at the same time, as a site of deep psychic and
somatic suffering. Madame Necker's body not only displayed her elite identity,
but also manifested spiritual loss and psychic suffering, functioning as a symbolic reminder of human weakness and frailty. The relationships between the

culturally constructed body and the lived and experienced body are fundamental to my reading of Madame Necker's life.

Madame Necker's biography has largely been shaped by members of her family, from her husband, Jacques Necker, who meditated on his late wife's moral virtue in 1798, through to her late nineteenth-century descendant, Paul-Gabriel d'Haussonville, who, in 1882, published the two-volume work still recognized as the definitive biography of his illustrious ancestor.[11] Most subsequent biographical retellings have followed the path carefully laid by these two members of the Necker family.[12] But while Necker's biography might have been largely moulded by what Philippe Lejeune has identified as a nineteenth-century desire to recuperate virtuous ancestors,[13] there are nevertheless jarring dissonances. Madame de Staël, for example, in a tribute to her father's moral goodness, referred to her mother's profound physical suffering, a theme later taken up by Staël's son, Auguste.[14] Madame Necker's niece (by marriage), Albertine-Adrienne Necker de Saussure, exploring another facet of Madame Necker's character, hinted at her aunt's maternal rigidity.[15] More recent studies of Necker's activities delve further into the discordant aspects of her life. Dena Goodman and Valérie Hannin, among others, have probed the troubled relationship between gender, writing, ambition and publicity as they emerged in Madame Necker's writings, and Necker and Staël biographers have closely examined Necker's maternal narrative.[16] Others, among them Alexandre Aimes and Berthe Vadier, have taken an indirect route, focusing on Madame Necker's various charitable activities in an attempt to understand her life and motivations.[17] Léonard Burnand, finally, has examined her public image as it was propagated in libellous pamphlets of the period.[18]

The unpublished writings of Madame Necker, among them the extensive correspondence she shared with friends and colleagues in Switzerland, suggest that there remains at least one more story to be told. These letters, the majority of which are contained in two manuscript collections in Lausanne and Geneva, present a woman of profound religious faith whose internal moral turmoil functioned as the impetus for a life of physical suffering.[19] Even as these letters play into the principles of display so integral to eighteenth-century sociability and sensibility, they also attest to Madame Necker's deep ambivalence towards French moral values and social conventions, reveal the centrality of her cultural and religious heritage to her life and gesture towards an embodied sense of self that revelled in the deep sensibility and sensuality of corporeal suffering. While embodiment has been examined in relation to Madame Necker's treatise on premature burial,[20] to date nobody has examined the relationships between gender, piety and illness as they manifested themselves in her life and on her body.

At its heart, this book is about performance. Taking its cues from the elite eighteenth-century French culture of display and the myriad etiquette treatises that governed elite sociability during this period; the emergence of sensibility as an aesthetic and philosophical movement that transformed social, cultural and political understandings of mind/body relations and Madame Necker's veritable obsession with the intricacies of elite sociability – from her detailed analyses of French etiquette to the overt sensibility and sometimes maudlin sentimentality of her evocations of her body and its sufferings – this book seeks to understand the nature of autobiographical identity as it is mapped onto the body and performed and displayed on a social stage. More specifically, I examine the nature of Madame Necker's contradictory presentation of self and speculate on the possibility of corporeal autobiography, suggesting that identity can be read not only through autobiographical texts (both published and unpublished), but also through embodied experiences. At issue is the relationship between identity – the subjective experience of the self – and display – the public staging of that same self – and how this encounter might be mapped onto, and read through, the body. For Madame Necker, this relationship manifested itself most obviously in the form of the interminable psychic and physical sufferings that characterized much of her adult life and that she chose to share in intimate letters to close friends and family. But it also emerged in other forms. Madame Necker's public and political interventions, for example, demonstrated her commitment to the disenfranchised peoples of France. The sick, the poor, the imprisoned, the dying; each of these groups benefited from her close, thoughtful and careful interest to the extent that her own elite suffering body might be seen to have embodied the sufferings of these marginalized others. The commentaries of her contemporaries, which emphasize her social awkwardness and stiff posture, offer yet another window into Madame Necker's corporeal performances.

In this book, I explore the life and writings of Suzanne Curchod Necker from the perspective of what I have termed corporeal autobiography. In it, I posit the body as a stage upon which identity can be displayed and argue for an understanding of Madame Necker's body – as revealed in the correspondence, private writings, published works and public activities (and as assessed by her contemporaries) – as an agentive entity that has the capacity to take an active role in the construction and presentation of the autobiographical self. I operate from the premise that the body has stories to tell and that its speech – marked in tears, shivers, sufferings, languishing and other states – can offer important insights into the nature of the autobiographical self. I suggest that the workings of the body function as a stage, even as they speak in a language that is opaque, contingent and difficult to discern.

Madame Necker's body's meanings emerged only through her engagement with them; that is to say that her body's stories became meaningful only through the care and attention she showed them. For Madame Necker, the suffering body, as she wrote it into her correspondence and lived it through her political endeavours, was the canvas that displayed her emotional states. This body confirmed her allegiance to her homeland even as its sufferings evoked her deep psychic malaise. From Madame Necker's perspective, the fluxes and flows of her body revealed her self-conscious awareness of herself. In the process, bodily frailty was not only part and parcel of Madame Necker's lived experience, but also a stage upon and through which she could present and perform her identity.

This book is mainly concerned with identifying corporeal contradictions; that is, in understanding how Madame Necker's different bodily selves played in and through one another. More specifically, it is interested in identifying manifestations of corporeal dissonance as *loci* for the performance and presentation of self. By corporeal dissonance, I gesture towards the ways in which Madame Necker's performances of her body both conformed to and troubled conventions of her time. Looking at the performance of illness and suffering in particular, I draw on eighteenth-century understandings of sensibility, suggesting that physical debilitation can function as a barometer for an individual's psychic perceptions. I further suggest that in Madame Necker's case, suffering – and the detailing of suffering in narrative form – can be consciously deployed as a strategy for managing social, religious and cultural exile.

My work identifies a number of interlocking themes in Madame Necker's life: sociability, religion, illness and motherhood, all of which revealed themselves in a range of embodied practices; that is, through the writing and performance of the body's psychic and somatic suffering. At a meta-level, Madame Necker's embodied identity can be divided into five distinct and yet overlapping entities: the elite body, the Calvinist body, the maternal body, the sick body and, finally, the divine body. Each of these embodied identities reveals a different aspect of Madame Necker's subjective experience of self; at the same time, each acts on and through the others. Thus it becomes important to consider the broader picture that emerges when these five 'bodies' are put into play with one another. I suggest that the contradictions between the social body (as represented by the irreligious worldliness of the French elite) and the Calvinist body (understood through Madame Necker's moral stance) played themselves out in the maternal body, which functioned not only as the site for the realization of true virtue and happiness in a Rousseauist sense, but also, from a Calvinist perspective, as a locus of human weakness. I argue that the relationships between elite, Calvinist and maternal bodies converged in the sick body, an entity marked by psychic and somatic suffering that was finally memorialized – in the form of the embalmed cadaver – as the divine body. Ultimately, I assert that the externally visible corporeal sufferings of Madame Necker's sick body might be conceived as highly theatrical instances of narcissistic display, evidence of an understanding of the symbolic power of the corporeal as a prime site for the performance of abjection and the longing for absolution. These ideas – theatricality, display, abjection, longing and absolution – are present throughout Necker's published *oeuvre* as well as in her unpublished epistolary output. These concepts are also key to my analysis of Madame Necker's life and serve to anchor the chapters that follow.

The raw material for this project is extensive. Madame Necker's previously mentioned published *oeuvre* – her posthumously published private writings together with her work in hospital reform and treatises on premature burial and against divorce – has provided a rich foundation for this research. Her correspondence with various members of the European intelligentsia, among them Rousseau, Voltaire, Gibbon, Thomas and Buffon, is also readily available.[21] In addition to this, some 250 unpublished letters remain in archival collections in Lausanne and Geneva. Finally, there is much contemporaneous contextual material. As a well-known member of the Parisian elite, Madame Necker is mentioned in many of the personal memoirs dating from the period, appears in such periodical literature as Grimm's *Correspondance littéraire* and Bachaumont's *Mémoires secrets* and was the subject of a series of libellous pamphlets.[22]

This material provides ample evidence to sustain the biographical telling propagated by the Necker/Haussonville cohort: Madame Necker was, without a doubt, a central figure of the French Enlightenment and her public concern for the welfare of the poor and indigent in her society can be seen as a testament to what they perceive as her innate and irrefutable feminine virtue. It also reveals something more: a woman consumed by mental and physical torment and suffering. References to Madame Necker's continual sufferings are scattered throughout her correspondence. Over 60 per cent of her letters to Etienette Clavel de Brenles and almost half of the letters to Henriette Réverdil make direct mention of her illnesses, as do more than 40 per cent of her extant letters to Antoine Léonard Thomas.[23] Madame Necker also represented her torments indirectly: numerous letters are penned by a secretary. While she may well have called on secretarial services in order to handle more efficiently the extensive correspondence required of her social position and political status, she offered another explanation, suggesting in letters to friends that her physical weakness and frail health sometimes made it impossible for her to write letters herself. As she remarked in a letter to her close friend Madame de Brenles: 'Please excuse me, Madam, for employing the services of a secretary. An inconvenience, less dangerous but more unwelcome than the previous one, does not allow me to hold a pen.'[24] This approach is also evident in her formal correspondence. Four letters dating from the early 1790s and obviously written by a secretary still include Madame Necker's frail, thready and unstable signature, thus providing further evidence of her physical distress even in the absence of direct textual references.[25] Physical and psychic suffering are directly mentioned by Madame Necker, her family or her friends in at least one letter per year, almost without interruption, between 1764, the year of her arrival in Paris, and 1794, the year of her death.[26] The inclusion of letters written by secretaries further expands this total.[27] Thus, Necker's sufferings were ever-present in her life, even as her close friend Antoine Léonard Thomas was to exclaim in a 1785 letter:

> If I did not know, Madame, all of the activity of your mind, even in the midst of all of your weakness and suffering, your letter of 11 February would almost have made me doubt that you were sick at all! Health and life vibrate through each line.[28]

It is worth nothing that illness was a common trope in the correspondence of sensibility, a philosophical, literary and cultural movement that venerated the passional nature of the body and celebrated physical manifestations of emotional transport. Writers of the time – notably Voltaire – frequently resorted to recitations of their various ailments.[29] Madame Necker's case, however, is somewhat different. Not only are her words confirmed and reinforced by the concern of close friends, the observations of her family members – particularly her daughter, Germaine de Staël – and the recollections of her contemporaries, but they are further highlighted by her decision to become actively involved in French hospital reform and her accompanying interest in the sanctity of the dying body.[30] The prevalence of illness in her correspondence, combined with the testimony of her family, friends and contemporaries and her public work with the suffering poor of her community, suggests – even demands – further examination.

Women, Autobiography and Epistolarity

My reading of Madame Necker's corporeal autobiography emerges largely through a close analysis of her correspondence and private writings, considered in conjunction with her salon and philanthropic activities. All of these activities might be seen as elements of what Jeanne Perreault and Marlene Kadar have referred to as 'traces of autobiographical self-representation'.[31] The primary insights, however, come from her correspondence. As many scholars have noted, epistolarity emerged as a prime vehicle for women's self-presentation during the eighteenth century. Motivated in part by the rise of the novel, which placed the concerns of the domestic directly in the public sphere and the emergence of autobiography – as exemplified by the posthumous publication, in 1778, of Jean-Jacques Rousseau's immensely influential *Confessions* – the eighteenth-century art of epistolarity was also powerfully shaped by the posthumous publication of the letters of Madame de Sévigné in 1725. This correspondence, spanning almost fifty years of Sévigné's life, was lauded for its 'informal style, the wit, the maxims, the instruction in the ways of polite society, the models for polite letter writing and the moral values of the actions described'.[32] It also proved highly influential, such that from about 1750 on, subsequent letter writers directly referenced Sévigné in their own correspondence, building on and extending her approach as they shaped their own epistolary relationships.[33] But the publication of Sévigné's letters performed another function: it contributed to the emerging image of women as (letter) writers. Madame Necker emphasized Sévigné's influence on women's public reputations, noting that: 'it has been endlessly repeated, since Madame de Sévigné, that women write better than men and that they are more sensitive than men; just as one has believed, since the time of Locke and Newton, that the English are a philosophical people'.[34]

The association between women and epistolarity cannot be overstated. According to Dena Goodman, letter writing became an indispensable tool designed to inculcate into young women the conventions of normative femininity.[35] It was also, however, a vital conduit for the presentation of self. Women had few authorized avenues for self-expression during this period. While a select number rose to prominence as novelists and others would later claim posthumous fame as memorialists, most women of the elite had no recognized literary outlets for their thoughts and ideas. Through the art of epistolarity, women were able, quite literally, to write themselves into existence. As a result, letter writing enabled what Béatrice Didier has referred to as 'a vast staging of the self'.[36] In the words of Marie-Claire Grassi, the intimate letter gave women the opportunity to express the most personal aspects of their being: 'through her confidences, woman spoke of the difficulty of being a woman in the eighteenth century'.[37] Dena Goodman would concur with this assessment, observing that:

> Writing helps individuals who are socially embedded to reflect on themselves, their relationships, their society, their world, and to make choices based on their own standards or values, even as they may acknowledge the limits placed on both their autonomy and their choices ... For women in the eighteenth century, such choices were always constrained, and autonomy was always an achievement, always a matter of degree, and always relational. Writing letters and engaging in correspondence helped women to achieve moments and degrees of autonomy within the context of human relationships – from family and friendship to social and gender systems, systems that were becoming modern as they were themselves.[38]

Scholars have observed that correspondence, even the most intimate exchange, is as much about display as it is about intimacy. As a dialogic genre, letters were conversations in writing and, as such, enabled the development and maintenance of relationships between absent correspondents, presenting their writers with numerous opportunities to craft selves and identities to be shared with colleagues and intimates. Each letter, then, might be considered a conscious iteration of the self in and through the gaze of the other.

During the eighteenth century, letters were both public – meant to be shared among a broader audience of colleagues and associates – and intimate, designed for personal and introspective reading. Others still took the form of formal missives between official bodies. Madame Necker's extant correspondence spans all of these forms. From the formal letters she exchanged with regard to her various philanthropic activities to public letters shared with Enlightenment luminaries, among them David Garrick, Denis Diderot and Voltaire, and the intimate epistles she shared with close friends in France and Switzerland, her letters provide unique insights into the ways in which she chose to fashion her private and public selves in the context of elite eighteenth-century social practices and behaviours.

Necker's public letters reveal a woman obsessed with the requirements of elite sociability, determined to present herself as a woman of charity and sensibility and fully committed to the needs of her contemporaries. Sometimes stiff in tone, these letters belie her deep desire to conform to the narrow tenets of elite social practice, demonstrating an awkwardness that appears to confirm the critical opinions of her Parisian salon colleagues, who found her salon demeanour formal and, sometimes, intimidating. But in her intimate letters she let down her guard, presenting a very different persona to her readers. Here she touched on topics closest to her heart: faith and family predominate in letters to Henriette Réverdil, while childlike enthusiasm, delight, innocence and wonder characterize her correspondence with Etienette Clavel de Brenles. There is, however, one constant in all of these letters: throughout her correspondence, Madame Necker takes great pains to present herself as a woman of sensibility. Revelling in the emotional power of the workings of her body, she shows a propensity for deep and sometimes maudlin introspection.

Indeed, Madame Necker's letters illustrate her thorough engagement with the culture and language of sensibility. Popularly conceived during this period as a tendency to emotional excess and instability, sensibility manifested itself in the physical display of sentimentality. Tears, weeping, swooning and suffering were requisite elements for its successful performance. They were also regular features of both published literature and private correspondence of the period. But while sensibility was, in the words of Anne C. Vila, conceived as a 'creative force' fundamental to all human activities,[39] it was also, as Madame Necker herself suggested, construed as a hallmark of feminine weakness.[40] Women were understood to be particularly prone to over-sentimentality, a dangerous condition that could profoundly and inalterably threaten both their moral and physical constitutions, a concept I discuss in greater detail in Chapter 4.

Like many of her contemporaries, Madame Necker was keenly aware of the power of sentimental autobiography. As a close friend of Paul Moultou, the Swiss pastor entrusted with Rousseau's manuscripts after his death, she was one of a very few people to read the *Confessions* in manuscript form prior to their publication. And while it has been stressed that her own private writings were never meant to be published, it seems likely that she did consider this possibility. As English Showalter Jr has observed, '*after* 1725 every literate French man or woman writing a private letter would have been aware of the possibility of publication, intended or not'.[41] Indeed, Necker's self-conscious approach, particularly evident in her elegiac correspondence with Antoine Léonard Thomas, appears to suggest some sort of awareness of posterity, or at least of the importance of memory and memorialization.

It is equally clear that Madame Necker was influenced by Madame de Sévigné. A lengthy unfinished homage to Sévigné, published in the final volume of her *Mélanges*, cites not only the previously mentioned strengths of wit, grace, charm and moral instruction – Sévigné's demonstrated skill in the elite art of pleasing – but also stresses her tact, elegance, purity and, more importantly, a seemingly innate depth of sensibility:

> I respect Madame de Sévigné too much to compare her work with the large number of gallant letters that our century has produced and which, under the pretext of painting the true sentiments of the heart, instead demonstrate its corruption; as it is possible to mimic everything but sensibility; this is the only law that nature has never ceded to art.[42]

Given all of this, a critical engagement with epistolary theory and practice must be considered crucial to any analysis of Madame Necker's life story.

Autobiography and the Body

Madame Necker's correspondence, steeped in the sensibility of her era, is deeply embodied. By this I mean to suggest that her body is written directly into the text. Necker wrote her body's stories, placing great value on corporeal experiences as a way of displaying her mastery of the art of sensibility, while simultaneously calling attention to the suffering body that was ever present not only *in* but also *around* her texts. The body and its moods figure prominently in her letters; her tears, illnesses and sufferings part and parcel of a self-presentation that was intensely corporeal in nature. To a certain extent, this is to be expected, given the prominence of the cult of sensibility during her lifetime. But such a superficial reading makes it all too easy to dismiss her letters as the overly sentimental ramblings of a woman of sensibility. I suggest that Necker's sentimental letters, when read in conjunction with her published works and public acts, which further emphasize the body and its failings, offer another perspective.

In this book, I argue that embodied epistolarity must be seen as an integral part of a larger project of corporeal display: a staging of what might be termed a 'fleshy' autobiography, a self crafted by and through a body that physically manifests the sufferings and anguishes of a tormented psyche. The work of Anne Hunsaker Hawkins and G. Thomas Couser has been influential in this regard. Hawkins's pathography and Couser's autopathography – 'autobiographical narrative of illness or disability'[43] – allow for the integration of body and mind in the form of a collaborative life writing that acknowledges the workings of the suffering body as intrinsic to constructions of self and identity. This is of particular importance in the case of extended illness, such as that experienced by Madame Necker. While dis/ability scholars such as Susan Wendell rightly point to the limitations of this framework, which can problematically elide the dis/abled or dysfunctional body with a similarly 'dis/abled' self, this model does contribute to a growing discussion that considers illness and suffering as productive sites of identity formation.[44] In other words, as the editors of a recent collection entitled *Unfitting Stories: Narrative Approaches to Disease, Disability and Trauma* point out, suffering is not 'necessarily always bad'.[45] In Madame Necker's writings, consciousness and corporeality are not antithetical to one another; nor do they slide into one another. Rather, the relationship between the two is symbiotic: psyche and soma work in, through and against one another in constantly mobile ways. What this entails is close attention to the language of the body, listening not only to the body's narratives – in the form of clearly discernible physical symptoms – but also to how these stories are then interpreted and lived by sentient, social beings.

Staging the Self: Theorizing the Performative Body

Such corporeal stories were performed in the context of the salon, the performative playground of the French elite. As I discuss in the first chapter, the mirror functioned as the ideal metaphor for the staging of self during the eighteenth century. In etiquette treatises of the period, mirrors were both intimate and reflective; in other words, they revealed the inner self even as they reflected the gaze of their audience. Etiquette treatises and conduct books suggest that both letter and body might be conceived as mirrors that enabled elite individuals to craft selves in the face of, in relation to and also through, their audience. By conforming to the accepted models of elite sociability, the elite body mirrored the seemingly innate beauty, balance and 'rightness' of polite society as a whole, offering a pleasing, reflective surface that confirmed the cohesion and authority of the aristocratic class. The letter, meanwhile, expanded the sphere of elite sociability, extending it across geographic space to include relationships with absent friends and colleagues. Indeed, just as the aristocratic body mediated between performer and observer, at once revealing its inner workings and reflecting the expectations of its audience, so too did letters facilitate a dialogic relationship between sender and receiver, thus functioning as stages for the presentation of a relational self. Offering a reflective surface that both revealed and produced identity, the mirror acknowledged the contradictions inherent in the staging of self; namely, that identity could not be crafted in isolation. The self, defined by and through its borders, was always a product of the gaze of its others. Such was the principle that governed the practice of elite sociability during the eighteenth century, requiring its adherents to sublimate the self in the service of the larger whole.

At a theoretical level, I am deeply indebted to frameworks put forward by Julia Kristeva, Luce Irigaray and Hélène Cixous.[46] All three of these thinkers operate from the perspective of radical sexual difference, an approach which, I believe, most closely aligns itself with the cultural models proposed within the eighteenth century itself. As scholars such as Thomas Laqueur, Londa Schiebinger and Lieselotte Steinbrügge, among others, have pointed out, the eighteenth century was a crucial period in the development of modern understandings of sexual difference.[47] Laqueur and Schiebinger, working in the history of medicine and the history of science and influenced by the work of Michel Foucault, argue for the emergence of a two-sex model of human relationships during this period. Steinbrügge, operating through a Marxist lens, demonstrates the ways in which scientific rationalism colluded with cultural assumptions in order to create a 'naturalized' female other who was wholly dependent on – and subservient to – the whims of a capricious biology: 'woman is not an *homme manqué*. Instead, her membership in the female sex shapes her entire physical and psychic constitution, which differs in every respect from man's.'[48] Eighteenth-century thinkers identified women with domestic concerns of home and family, attributing to them such characteristics as humility, piety, grace and charm. Women were also perceived as volatile, capricious entities whose unstable tendencies, left unchecked, could pose a threat to social stability.[49]

The theoretical model propagated by Irigaray, Kristeva and Cixous offers clear possibilities for resistance to – and subversion of – the premises of hierarchicalized sexual difference promoted and practised during the eighteenth century. Just as illness and suffering might be considered from a productive rather than limiting perspective, Kristevan abjection, Irigarayan mimesis and Cixousian laughter all rely on the claiming of corporeal alterity as a site of possibility and transformation. Each of these theorists posits the female body, and in particular the reproductive female body, as the site of such alterity, a positioning that has enabled a recognition of the inherent value of an otherwise marginalized and stigmatized body.

This transformative potential of alterity is critical to understanding Madame Necker's life story. As a woman marked by her gender, class, religion, nation and suffering, Madame Necker experienced stigma on numerous levels. Not only was she physically incapacitated as a result of her extended illnesses, but she was also branded by her inability to conform to elite Parisian social convention, stigmatized for her Protestant faith and set apart as a result of her nationality. There is no doubt that the experience of stigma limited her life. At the same time, her letters also contain clear evidence of what Hélène Cixous asserts as the revolutionary power of stigmata. As Cixous observes:

> Stigma stings, pierces, makes holes, separates with pinched marks and in the same movement distinguishes – re-marks – inscribes, writes. Stigma wounds *and* spurs, stimulates.

Stigma hallmarks, for the best and for the worst: stigmata on the body are as noble as
they are ignominious, depending on whether it is Christ or the outcast who is marked.[50]

It is, ultimately, the disruptive and volatile agency of alterity that informs this
work. The research of a group of Swiss medical historians, who argue strongly
and convincingly for the authority of both patient and ailing body, has also been
particularly influential in this regard.[51]

The stigmatized body is located in a culture of display; its stigmatized state
emerges from the fraught encounter between spectacle and gaze. Such a body
must be considered, as Judith Butler has argued, a performative entity, whose
actions both mimic and resist the contours of cultural and social convention.[52]
It is precisely the possibility of mimetic parody or citation that makes the work
of Kristeva, Irigaray and Cixous possible; it is, equally, Butler's postulation of a
tense but symbiotic relationship between *pre*-formance and *per*-formance, that
is, between acquiescence and resistance to established cultural scripts, that enables us to understand the nature of performativity and the performative body.
Following theoretical understandings put forward by Irigaray, Cixous and, in
particular, Kristeva, the performative enables the taking on of a masquerade and
the claiming of alterity – or stigma – as a space from which to speak.

Kristeva's understanding of abjection serves as an organizing premise for this
book. The abject, which Kristeva has defined as the point of splitting, might be
best understood as the moment of suspension between life and death, an instant
associated with intense loss and, at the same time, overwhelming desire. For
Kristeva, the abject is a point of horror, an encounter with the sublime which
reveals not only its profound potential, but also the abyss of nothingness that is
its mirror. The abject dissolves previously immutable boundaries: between self
and other, desire and horror, life and death, even as it relies on the presumed
stability of those same binaries. As Kristeva writes: 'I expel *myself*, I spit *myself*
out, I abject *myself* within the same motion through which "I" claim to establish
myself.'[53] Located at the interstices, abjection is described in profoundly visceral
terms. Kristeva's evocation of the corpse, a material artefact of death, as a marker
of the abject, offers one example of this:

> The corpse ... is the utmost of abjection. It is death infecting life. Abject. It is some-
> thing rejected from which one does not part ... The corpse remains, even in death. It is
> thus not lack of cleanliness or health that causes abjection but what disturbs identity,
> system, order. What does not represent borders, positions, rules. The in-between, the
> ambiguous, the composite.[54]

This understanding of the space between life and death as both a site of ambiguity and a source of infinite potential is highly appealing in the case of Madame
Necker, a woman who struggled with moral quandaries, who desperately wanted

to fit into French society even as she was repelled by it, who sought redemption but felt that she was unworthy of it and who ensured her body's preservation well after death. In this book, I suggest that Madame Necker's stigmatized body served as a site of critical abjection, a space in which Madame Necker performed her alterity and confronted her personal demons, but also a mirror through which Parisian elite society was forced to confront its own limitations.

The performance of abjection requires both a stage and an audience. During the French eighteenth century, that stage was, indisputably, the salon. A gathering place for intellectual debate and theatre for the display of elite sociability, the eighteenth-century salon was the institution *par excellence* of elite sociability and identity formation. Led by a woman of means and peopled by members of the aristocracy, intelligentsia and cultured and connected foreigners, it was an intensely performative space governed by a detailed code of behaviours and practices that sought to define the parameters of the elite body. The salon itself was embedded in a broader culture of display, a social environment in which every action was measured, every behaviour observed and assessed. Analysing the nature of salon practices is, however, a daunting task, particularly when one considers the inherent transience and intangibility of salon conversation and the cultural and historical specificity and nuance of elite social behaviours.

Conceptual frameworks provided by scholars in the interdisciplinary area of performance studies offer useful entry points into this world. Marvin Carlson, drawing on the work of Erving Goffman, has observed that 'The recognition that our lives are structured according to repeated and socially sanctioned modes of behaviour raises the possibility that *all human activity could potentially be considered as "performance"*.'[55] Erin Striff concurs, noting that culture is 'unthinkable without performance.'[56] Drawing my inspiration from these comments, I argue that all autobiographical acts – in Madame Necker's case her writing, salon activities and political engagements – were negotiated on a public stage in full view of an audience. In this sense, performance might be most fruitfully understood, on a broad level, as a collaborative venture between audience and performer, as read through the lens of culture. As Carlson observes, performance 'is always performance *for* someone, some audience that recognises and validates it as performance even when, as is occasionally the case, that audience is the self'.[57] Such an argument suggests a need to reconsider the traditionally hierarchical relationship between performance and audience, spectacle and gaze. Specifically, this perspective gestures towards a more fluid encounter, in which authority is constantly shifting and power relationships are never certain, but instead, always in process and always being negotiated.

But this argument also suggests something more. The relationship between Butlerian performativity and Kristevan abjection, as read through the lens of performance, enables a significant repositioning of the elite social mirror.

Madame Necker's contradictory behaviours fundamentally troubled social conventions. By actively resisting the lure of the elite mirror even as she acquiesced to its seductions, Madame Necker transformed reflection into specularity, thus destabilizing the internal coherence of ideals of sociability. The specular abjection of Madame Necker's Calvinist, maternal body completely reshaped the salon stage. In complicating the elite mirror, Suzanne Necker was able to claim the specularity of her sick body and, from there, to reflect what she perceived as the moral sickness of French society as a whole. Appropriating the salon for the performance of excess within the contours of the mimetic masquerade allowed her both to perform the roles laid out for her and, at the same time, to resist and refuse them. Thus Madame Necker rendered both her own body and the elite social body abject, forcing a confrontation of critical self-reflection. These are the insights developed and analysed in the chapters that follow.

In Chapter 1, I argue for an understanding of the salon as an inherently performative space. I define elite propriety in terms of language, dress, tone of voice and physical presence. I also introduce the idea of stigma by examining Madame Necker's contradictory relationship with Parisian aristocratic behaviours. On the one hand, Parisian social practices were seductive, introducing her to a world of individuals whose interests and beliefs fuelled her personal literary ambitions and desires. On the other hand, however, she perceived these behaviours as inherently dangerous and actively cultivated her outsider status as a way of maintaining her distinctly different cultural and religious identity. Central to this discussion is an examination of the mirror and its role in revealing and reflecting elite identity.

Chapter 2 examines Madame Necker's cultural and religious alterity more closely. Situating Madame Necker's religious background and beliefs in the context of a broader history of Calvinism – and particularly Genevan Calvinism – this chapter introduces the idea of religious abjection. I am particularly interested here in the abject position of the body in Calvinist thought. The site of the believer's performance of her faith, the body was also the symbol of the believer's original sin; in other words, an indefinable purgatory where redemption remained eternally uncertain. In this chapter, I also develop concepts central to the work as a whole: display, exile, longing and communion. Each of these concepts emanates from Madame Necker's lived experience of Calvinism; namely, the inherently troubled nature of the divided Calvinist body.

In Chapter 3, I consider Madame Necker's practical application of her religious beliefs, looking closely at her uncomfortable self-positioning as both daughter and mother. Examining the ways in which Calvinist exile manifested itself in the form of the abject maternal body, I suggest that Madame Necker's filial longing, a futile quest for virtue inextricably linked both with the death of her mother and with her own religious desire, and conceived within the parameters of Calvinist moral failure, lies at the heart of her subsequent salon-based maternal practice. I argue that the salon, consciously claimed as a stage for the double performance of maternal duty and religious devotion, enabled a corporeal enactment of her intense psychic and moral struggles. The letters Necker exchanged with Madame Réverdil, a close family friend and maternal surrogate, are central to making this argument.

In Chapter 4, I examine the nature and purpose of Madame Necker's various nervous illnesses and argue that these illnesses constituted a corporeal manifestation of her psychic malaise. In other words, I contend that Madame Necker's extended and largely indefinable physical illnesses were the result of extreme moral alienation and isolation. In this sense, her nervous ailments can be seen as evidence of her experience of exile: both the externally imposed exile of physical dislocation brought about by the deaths of her parents and her self-imposed moral exile, the result of her perceived failure to fulfil her filial duty towards the memory of her mother. In addition to looking at her own illnesses, I also consider her public initiatives in support of hospital reform, situating my analyses in a broader context that looks not only at the development of public health, but also at the medical theory of vitalism, emergent interests in the concept of hygiene and the culture of sensibility.

Finally, Chapter 5 considers the ritualistic nature of Madame Necker's dying, death and burial. Considering her treatise on premature burial through the lens of her decision to be embalmed and in the context of her perception of her Calvinist duties, I assert that the conservation of her frail human machine (through the process of embalming) might be seen as symbolic of humanity's innate moral weakness and spiritual failure. In the process, Madame Necker's body, marked by suffering and physical incapacity, is transformed into the mark, or stigma, of human moral failure and the embodiment of Calvinist culpability.

1 'SHE WILL NEVER ACQUIRE THE ART OF PLEASING'

Madame Necker had none of the charms of a young French woman. In her behaviour and in her language there was neither the air nor the tone of a woman schooled in the arts, trained in the ways of the world. Lacking taste in her appearance, ease in her manner and attactiveness in her social graces, her character, like her attitude, was too studied to have any grace.[1]

Here, I am forced to hide the most natural movements in order to avoid the criticism of pedantry; I continuously enact a sort of assault against my heart and its emotions and at the very instant when I feel free, I find that it has lost its usual elasticity.[2]

Buried in the memoirs of the Scottish lawyer Archibald Alison is a touching scene. A young girl, her hair falling in ringlets around her shoulders, enters the family drawing room to say good night. In the presence of her parents' closest friends and colleagues, she kneels down at her mother's feet to pray, a touching picture of filial devotion and religious piety.[3] The scene itself, set in Paris sometime during the 1770s, is wholly unremarkable, save for the social and political status of the characters involved. The young girl was Germaine Necker, daughter of Suzanne Curchod Necker and her husband, the Genevan banker-cum-French finance minister Jacques Necker. Alison, here recounting a story apparently oft told by his mother, Dorothea Gregory, does not appear to note anything curious about the scene. Instead, he seems to use it as a way of marking social allegiances and laying claim to his family's authority and presence within the bastions of the European elite.

At first glance, Alison's reading is correct. The scene, in which a daughter shared her prayers with her mother, was a common one, doubtless replayed in many homes. Mothers were seen as natural teachers and moral guides who carried full responsibility for their daughters' spiritual development. Educating girls in the teachings of the saints and the practices of the church, Catholic mothers inculcated in their daughters habits of piety and religious devotion practised in the quiet isolation of the domestic sphere.[4]

On closer inspection, however, the scene appears far less predictable. While such an image of domestic felicity was conventional, indeed approved, its staging within the contours of a salon environment was not. Alison's image of touching maternal and religious devotion does not at all accord with the function of the Parisian salons, the regular weekly gatherings peopled by members of the French social, cultural and philosophical elite. Not only were salons theatrical spaces, sites of display governed by intricate rules and coded behaviours, they were also inherently secular spaces, in which opposition to religious belief and practice was much more common than allegiance. As such, salons were hardly the expected site for the display of domestic or maternal virtue.

From this perspective, Alison's recollections take on an entirely different cast. No longer evocative of cultural conformity in the realm of female moral education, they function instead as evidence of social and cultural discord in that they recall an instance of cultural and social alterity; that is to say, they illuminate domestic practices at odds with the acceptable conventions of the space in which they were performed. Indeed, Madelyn Gutwirth has referred to Madame Necker's maternal claim to the salon stage as 'daring'.[5] While this seemingly innocent tableau is relegated to a minor footnote in Alison's two-volume work, it nevertheless highlights the fact that Madame Necker and her family were outsiders, perpetually stigmatized by their nationality, moral values, religious beliefs and social class.

Madame Necker's social nonconformity has conventionally been read as failure. Indeed, Catherine Dubeau observes that Madame Necker, Swiss, Calvinist and *bourgeoise*, 'accumulated derogatory images and epithets, assuring greater longevity to her failures than her successes'.[6] But, as I propose here, it is precisely in the dissonant encounter between apparent social failure in the drawing room and ostensible virtuous success as mother and wife that we might more productively read the contradictions that marked Madame Necker's life. By examining her conflicted relationship with practices of elite sociability through the lens of her understandings of duty and responsibility, I argue that her failure might be more fruitfully reconceived as resistance. From this vantage point, Madame Necker's curious social practices did not signal an *inability* to conform, but rather an *unwillingness* to play the role assigned to her as a woman of means in elite French society. Madame Necker's lack of conformity emerges as a conscious act of self-stigmatization – or marking – and is ultimately symptomatic of a far deeper malaise. At the same time, Necker's willingness to engage with the practices of elite sociability and her obvious delight in many facets of her Parisian life suggest that she was uncomfortably, and indeed abjectly, positioned between two disparate worlds: the strict and morally rigorous Calvinism of her childhood and the carefree *élan* and fantasy of elite French society.

Such an analysis complicates conventional understandings of Madame Necker's life, but also provides unexpected insight. Necker's predominantly domestic sociability, a term I use to refer to the private activities that governed women's socially accepted roles as wives and mothers, was founded upon principles of duty and religious obligation. By contrast, prevailing ideals of French aristocratic sociability demanded allegiance to a wide array of coded courtly behaviours and practices. The troubled encounter between the two approaches provides a revealing look into the relationships among religion, filial duty, maternal responsibility and corporeal suffering as they played themselves out in Necker's life and through her body. Indeed as Sainte-Beuve noted already in the nineteenth century: 'The obligations and practices of elite society, a constant vigilance of self and of one's surroundings, and a sensitivity often repressed in silence and pain – all of this contributed to ruining Madame Necker before her time'.[7] By positing this discord as evidence of deeper undercurrents of religious isolation and cultural dislocation, I set the stage for the more detailed study that follows. In so doing, I engage the very performativity that defined not only the space of the salon, but also, and more importantly, eighteenth-century elite identity itself.

In the sections that follow, I outline the nature and scope of Madame Necker's social experiences in the French capital, situating her behaviours in the context of elite eighteenth-century social ideals and practices. More specifically, I argue for a corporeal understanding of elite sociability, suggesting a species of physical marking that served to identify proper and improper social bodies. Of particular interest is the slippage between Madame Necker's obvious desire to assimilate into the Parisian intellectual and cultural sphere and her concomitant need to distance herself from its temptations. My analysis depends on a detailed discussion of eighteenth-century conduct books, Madame Necker's posthumously published personal writings and her correspondence with two Swiss friends. This discussion ultimately suggests points of tension between elite understandings of such concepts as *politesse*, *bienséance* and *devoir* – which might be roughly translated as refinement, propriety and duty – and Madame Necker's own interpretations of these same ideas. Before getting to those terms, however, an overview of the historiography of the French salon may function as a useful contextual entry point.

The historiography of the French salon and its culture dates back to the early years of the nineteenth century, when writers such as Laure Junot, Duchesse d'Abrantès, and others, eager to capitalize on a general nostalgia for the *ancien régime*, published intimate and personal works that recalled the behaviours and practices of the French aristocracy.[8] The various writings of Sainte-Beuve and the Goncourt brothers, dating from the mid-nineteenth century, offered another interpretation of the salon. Firmly identifying salon culture with literary expression, they placed salon women on a pedestal, presenting them as embodiments of the eternal feminine.[9] Later nineteenth- and early twentieth-century studies focused on single salon women. Drawing on surviving correspondence and published memoirs, writers such as Paul-Gabriel d'Haussonville and Pierre de Ségur penned extensive and detailed biographies of illustrious women such as Madame

Necker and Madame Geoffrin, and offered titillating insights into the private life of Julie de Lespinasse.[10] Somewhat more recently, other writers positioned *salonnières* as successful social convenors firmly ensconced in the private, domestic sphere.[11]

The extensive scholarship of Dena Goodman, dating from the 1980s and '90s, inaugurated a new era of research into the nature of the salon and its hostesses. Building on the theoretical frameworks proposed by Jürgen Habermas, Goodman posited the sociability of the salon within the idea of democratization, suggesting that the practices of elite sociability, in particular those of mutual respect and deference, were essential to crafting a society of equals in the face of glaring and sometimes almost insurmountable class differences.[12] In Goodman's research, the salon emerges as a subversive force which countered the hegemony of the state-controlled public sphere through the enlightened interaction of rational beings. The *salonnière* hereby gained an independent voice and the authority not only to be heard, but also to play an active role in the conception and dissemination of public opinion.

More recent scholarship on French *salonnières* would suggest, however, that such a neat move from public sphere theory to the actual practice of elite sociability might not so easily be accomplished.[13] The work of Jolanta Pekacz, for example, stresses the dominant role of social propriety and contends that the salon was a theatrical space in which each actor played a prescribed role: 'the individual was expected to incarnate characteristics considered appropriate for his or her social position, gender, age, marital status and circumstances'.[14] Pekacz understands the salon space as a static environment in which spontaneity was discouraged and little social mobility was possible. Catherine Dubeau, while echoing some aspects of Pekacz's analysis, nevertheless stresses the possibility of mobility.[15] In this inherently exclusionary environment, the rules of the game demarcated the boundaries of acceptable behaviour and defined the parameters of proper bodies and proper objects.

The case of Madame Necker offers a significant example of social and cultural impropriety. Madame Necker's domestic actions, in particular her decision to mother her daughter in the salon, fundamentally reimagined the space of the salon. By inscribing it in domestic – rather than public – terms, Necker's maternal salon reveals another layer of eighteenth-century sociability. It reminds us that the salon, as a physical entity, was more than an extension of the public sphere; it was also at the same time an intimate, domestic space. Located inside the home, the salon was a space governed not by the king, but rather by the *maîtresse de maison* – the woman of the house – most often a wife and mother fulfilling a socially sanctioned cultural role.[16] In addition to this, the salon was, as Sherry McKay has observed, an architecturally gendered space, imprinted with cultural associations of ideal femininity.[17] As a space both socially and physically marked by gender, it existed as much outside the public sphere as within it.

The hybrid nature of the salon made it a difficult space for women to navigate, requiring them to negotiate contradictory personal impulses and paradoxical cultural paradigms. Questions surrounding feminine ambition, maternal authority, civic responsibility and religious duty were read not only against the ever-shifting backdrop of eighteenth-century ideals, but also through the lens of physical space and display; in other words, within a framework that recognized not only the troublingly indefinable nature of the salon stage but also the complex positioning of the salon hostess on that stage.

Setting the Stage

Suzanne Curchod was twenty-seven years old when she arrived in Paris as the guest of Madame de Vermenoux, a wealthy French widow who introduced her to elite Parisian society. Thrust into the limelight almost from the moment of her arrival, she found herself ill prepared for success in the French capital. As she admitted in a letter to a family friend in Switzerland, life in the aristocratic milieu was expensive and involved social performances for which she felt poorly equipped.[18] Mademoiselle Curchod possessed none of the effortless, spontaneous and suggestive *galanterie* which accompanied elite social exchanges. Her 1764 marriage to Jacques Necker positioned her even more directly in the public eye. No longer a salon guest in the homes of others, she was now mistress of her own home and soon became hostess of her own social circle. But being keenly aware of her limitations, Madame Necker felt significant pressure in this environment. As she observed in a 1766 letter:

> Imagine that for two years I have been alternately a housewife and a woman of society, that I was so ignorant regarding the first of these things that it exhausted all of my faculties, and so awkward regarding the second that it held all of my attention; if you add to this an [affectionate] attachment and new duties, you will see that I was able to salvage nothing but my heart from the shipwreck of my thoughts.[19]

Necker's new role was challenging and she frequently felt out of her depth: 'I have had not a single moment to myself. The details of [running] my house are enormous for a mind as inept as mine and if I did not put things in order we would be ruined'.[20] Nevertheless, she made concerted efforts to fit in by paying careful attention to Parisian social practices.

Central to her efforts was the establishment of a salon. When Madame Necker officially opened her doors to the French cultural elite in 1765, the Parisian salon schedule was already quite full: Monday and Wednesday were dedicated to Madame Geoffrin; Tuesday to Helvétius; Thursday and Sunday to the Baron d'Holbach; and Saturday to Madame du Deffand. Mademoiselle de Lespinasse welcomed company every evening. But Madame Necker, drawing on early salon experiences in Lausanne, had prepared carefully for her endeavour.

Assembling a group of close friends – among them Jean-François Marmontel, François Morellet and Antoine Léonard Thomas – to act as advisors, and seeking out the sage counsel of her mentor, Madame Geoffrin, she settled on a Friday afternoon gathering and began developing the exclusive guest list that would be necessary for her salon's development.

On the surface, Madame Necker's salon was an unqualified success. In addition to cultivating an international membership which included Enlightenment luminaries such as Grimm, Diderot, Suard, Thomas, Marmontel and Morellet, and foreign guests including Benjamin Franklin, Edward Gibbon and Ferdinando Galiani, her salon also witnessed some important cultural happenings, among them the initiation of a subscription project to erect a statue in memory of Voltaire and, in 1787, the first reading of Jacques-Henri Bernardin de Saint-Pierre's *Paul et Virginie*. Nevertheless, the impressions of her contemporaries offer a decidedly different picture. While Madame Necker was solicitous and attentive, her salon lacked the *élan* of those of her contemporaries. Necker's guests commented on her pedantry, overt religious practice and bourgeois social habits and found her stiff formality intimidating. In the words of her niece:

> We don't dare speak. Mme Necker intimidates the most fearless ... It seems that [Madame Necker] has imposed a daunting role upon herself, one which she is unable to relinquish; she speaks of virtue, of decency, of feeling, not from an outpouring of her own heart, but through the notions that she has formed of what *must* be; and I think that her own character is completely unknown to her, and that she has never enjoyed ... a moment of abandon.[21]

Horace Walpole, less subtle, was singularly unimpressed: 'I am not so transported with N**** cock and hen. They are a tabor and pipe that I do not understand. He mouths and she squawks, and neither articulates.'[22] Jean-François Marmontel, one of the founding members of Madame Necker's Friday salon, was similarly critical in his assessment of her social skills: 'Madame Necker had none of the charms of a young French woman', he observed.[23] She had little taste in fashion, little spontaneity in her carriage and little social appeal. In short, Madame Necker lacked the requisite social graces to succeed in polite society.

The most vehement criticism of all came from Henriette Louise de Waldner de Freundstein, the Baronne d'Oberkirch, who observed that:

> Mr Necker did not please me at all ... Madame Necker is even worse still. In spite of the grand positions she has held, she is a governess and nothing more. Above all else, she is pedantic and pretentious ... She is pretty, and she is not at all agreable; she is beneficent, and she is not well-liked at all; her body, her spirit, her heart, [all] lack charm. God, before creating her, dipped her both inside and out in a bucket of starch. She will never acquire the art of pleasing.[24]

Even more disturbing to Oberkirch, however, was the relationship between Madame Necker and her husband, Jacques. As she complained: 'They never bore [each other]; but they bore others and endlessly adore, compliment, and sing each other's praises'.[25] Oberkirch, an Alsace-born aristocrat now known primarily as a result of her posthumously published memoirs, encapsulated the essence of Madame Necker's crime: she was, for lack of a better word, a *poseur*, whose airs and affectations threatened the internal cohesion of the aristocratic class. A short entry in Bachaumont's *Mémoires secrets* confirms this impression. Stressing her simple beginnings as the daughter of a village minister, her erudition and her background as a governess, the author plainly suggests that Necker could never escape her background. Rather, her social endeavours were indelibly marked by her social, religious and cultural alterity.[26]

To a certain extent, the same could be said of Madame Necker's famous colleague, the great Marie-Thérèse Rodet Geoffrin, who, as the almost illiterate child bride of a wealthy manufacturer, hardly qualified as a proper member of the French elite. The difference, in terms of their reception by their guests, lay in their respective approaches to their *métier*. Geoffrin succeeded by never pretending to be more than she was. Direct, forthright and overtly *bourgeoise*, she acted her part well. In other words, Geoffrin knew her place in the world and deferred to it. Necker, however, marked by cultural, social and religious difference, would not play by the rules of the game and so alienated her contemporaries.

In part, the criticisms levelled against Madame Necker can be attributed to the xenophobic response of a self-congratulatory French elite accustomed to vaunting its superiority in matters of social skill. As Pierre d'Ortigue de Vaumorière wrote:

> Paris is not only the Capital of a flourishing Monarchy, but is even respected as the predominant City of all *Europe*. People come here from all parts, some to polish themselves, others to get Employments, others to see the finest Court in the World, and the greatest King on Earth.[27]

The fabled French art of sociability implied a strict adherence to a set of written and unwritten rules of conduct and propriety to which foreigners could never hope to aspire. Eminently desirable and deeply seductive, its inner workings, it seemed, would never be accessible to the likes of Madame Necker.

Madame Necker's biographers have generally dismissed such criticisms. While they acknowledge that she was socially maladroit, they contend that her memory should be founded upon 'her deep affection for all men of distinction, her charity, her goodness [and] her humanity, for which she was named mother of the poor',[28] rather than on a catalogue of minor faults observed, detailed and disseminated by less worthy contemporaries. Indeed, nineteenth-century biographical readings are almost unanimous in their praise of Madame Necker's

domestic virtues, in particular what they perceive as her 'worship' of her husband.[29] Sainte-Beuve, while acknowledging her social missteps, nevertheless
placed the spotlight on what he perceived to be her remarkable virtue. And Lairtullier, while mentioning Madame Necker's lack of naturalness, still paints her
as a successful social ornament, thus emphasizing the moral goodness that led
both to the conjugal devotion that characterized her marriage and to her work in
the area of charitable reform.[30] Such an appraisal, emphasizing Necker's 'devoted
love, truth, and purity' and evoking the image of laudable and seemingly infinite
and irrefutable domestic virtue,[31] is nonetheless selective, and runs counter to
the concerns and perspectives of many of her contemporaries.

This is not to suggest that Suzanne Necker was wholly reviled in her time.
On the contrary, the testimonials of some of her colleagues suggest that they
found her approach a refreshing change from the prevailing social norms. The
Marquise de La Ferté-Imbault, daughter of the famed Madame Geoffrin and
noted *salonnière* in her own right, warned Necker *away* from the very people
who could guarantee her social success, expressing her satisfaction at Madame
Necker's virtuous behaviour in the following passage:

> But ... your conduct was very good and very wise ... you did not attract the least bit
> of public condemnation nor the smallest bit of ridicule and moreover, Madame, every
> time that I have had the honour of seeing you, you have shown me friendship, respect
> and confidence; all of this is more than enough to have erased the poor impressions that
> your excessive love for the mind stripped of reason and virtue had made upon me.[32]

Edward Gibbon, too, highlighted the positive attributes of Necker's heritage
and background and encouraged her to remain true to her upbringing: 'I know
that your stay in Paris, by introducing onto a larger stage your taste and your
talents, did not at all suppress your Helvetic straightforwardness.'[33] Nevertheless,
outside of a small group of intimate colleagues and friends, Madame Necker's
social behaviours were seen as curious at best.

That the pious, religious and conservative Madame Necker would associate
herself with the irreverent worldliness of Parisian salon culture certainly seems
contradictory. But there is more at play. Haussonville and Antoine Lilti, drawing on the commentary of Madame Necker's contemporaries, have asserted that
her salon was expressly designed as a vehicle to support the political aspirations
of her husband, a position supported by the commentary of Marmontel, who
observed that for all Madame Necker's attentiveness, it was clear that the guests
were only there for Jacques Necker's amusement.[34] If this is the case, then Madame Necker's management of the salon space and her careful cultivation of an
impressive guest list can be seen as concrete evidence of her fulfilment of her
conjugal duties, a reading which accords neatly with Madame Necker's conservative moral stance. While her salon may have failed to live up to Parisian

standards of sociability, it served her principles and beliefs, thus enabling her to manage – if somewhat awkwardly – her cultural assimilation into the largely secular environment of the French elite.

At the same time, it is worth observing that Madame Necker was deeply drawn to her new cultural environment and seduced by the intellectual pleasures it afforded. In many ways, the environment of the Parisian salon represented a natural extension of her first social successes in Lausanne and Geneva, in particular her membership in the Société du printemps and her leadership of the Académie des Eaux de la Poudrière, a fanciful gathering that seems to have drawn its inspiration from the seventeenth-century literary world of Mademoiselle de Scudéry. Through the Parisian salon, she could further cultivate her intellectual interests, develop her skills and fulfil her literary and intellectual ambitions, ambitions clearly in evidence in her correspondence with Etienette Clavel de Brenles.

But Madame Necker appears to have had a deeply ambivalent relationship with the literary sphere: she embraced writing as a form of expression and a conduit into the public arena, but she was fully aware that such ambition was in conflict with her duties as wife and mother and knew that her husband was not supportive of women writers.[35] This tension highlights Suzanne Necker's complicated relationship with Paris and the French people.

Paris was a city that offered significant potential for self-realization through encounters with intellectually brilliant *philosophes*, opportunities to attend stage performances by some of the great actors and actresses of the day and the possibility of assuming powerful political roles. In letters to Swiss friends, Madame Necker recounted her adventures with obvious delight, revelling in the fact that she could consider so many enlightened individuals as close acquaintances.[36] In Paris, Madame Necker met and became fast friends with Jean-Baptiste-Antoine Suard, Antoine Léonard Thomas and Madame Geoffrin. She visited the opera and the theatre and witnessed the performances of the great Mademoiselle Clairon. In her letters to Etienette Clavel de Brenles, she announced the publication of new books, offered short vignettes of her experiences and wrote amusing portraits of the great men she encountered, all the while keeping her intellectually-oriented friend abreast of the cultural happenings in the French capital.

But while she seized the opportunities for social advancement and enjoyed innumerable hours of entertainment, she remained an outsider to the elite world of Parisian society and its social conventions. Her efforts to fit in often compromised her sense of self. In a letter to a friend, she wrote:

> Since I have been in Paris, Monsieur, I have been unable to surrender myself to the freedom of thoughts and feeling that your so precious correspondence gives me. Here, I am forced to hide the most natural movements in order to avoid the reproach of pedantry; I continuously enact a sort of assault against my heart and its emotions

and at the very instant when I feel free, I discover that it has lost its usual elasticity. I cannot stop myself from judging this country harshly.[37]

Not only were the rules of elite social behaviour intricate, arbitrary and almost impossible for an outsider to adopt, but they also conflicted with many of her own values and beliefs. 'Ah! Madame, how different were the times I spent close to you, the memory of which continues to compensate for the triviality of my current occupations', she sighed in a letter to Madame de Brenles. 'The only advantage of this country is to develop taste, but it is at the expense of genius; we express ourselves in a thousand ways, we compare ideas ... We discuss endlessly, and finish by saying: "That is in poor taste".'[38]

For Madame Necker, Parisian mores and conventions were completely foreign and entirely superficial. She suggested that if Madame de Brenles only knew what it took to excel at the art of pleasing, she would be appalled.[39] This opinion did not change with the passage of time. If anything, her sense of alterity only increased over the years. Writing to Thomas in 1785, for example, she observed that the elite social sphere had something of the fantastic to it; it was a dream that could never be realized: 'I cannot easily convey to you the impression that Paris gives me; it is nothing more than an illusion, an imaginary world populated with fantastic beings.'[40] In the face of such a vision, Madame Necker was forced to maintain her distance:

> It was twenty years ago, if you recall, when, finding myself amidst the most beautiful minds of Europe for the first time, I heard all of the ideas on which I had based my happiness, as well as the explanations of the phenomena of this world, treated as pipe-dreams. In the midst of this overwhelming incredulity, I carefully kept my opinions to myself.[41]

Madame Necker's letters suggest that her sense of alienation went even deeper: she found Paris not only foreign, but also dangerous. Her letters to Madame de Brenles refer to the 'whirlwind' and 'chaos' of Paris.[42] The city's frenetic energy was destabilizing and she became increasingly agitated by the constant bombardment of new sights and sounds: 'My soul [is] endlessly electrified by new objects and by new tastes'.[43] In such an environment of constant, restless – and, in Madame Necker's opinion, superficial – activity, repose and rest were impossible to find.[44] To Necker, Paris was a city out of balance, poised on the brink of ruin and potentially unable to recover from its excesses. 'We resemble those greedy individuals whose jaded palate is disgusted with all food and cannot, therefore, return to simple and healthy dishes', she wrote to Madame de Brenles in 1773. 'The refinement of taste is as magnificently perfected for the body as it is for the mind, and mentally and physically we bring to life the story of Sybarite, who was kept awake by a fold in a rose petal.'[45]

In response to this relentless clamour, Madame Necker consciously chose and cultivated the position of the exiled outsider. Throughout her life, she referred to her French colleagues as 'Parisians' or 'the French' while marking herself as indisputably Swiss. Reading national identity and the ideas of nation – *la patrie* – in terms of sociability, she used broad gestures to stake her claim to alterity. Clearly delineating the cultural differences between the two nations, she remarked: 'That which we call frankness in Switzerland became egotism in Paris; negligence of little things is here [understood as] a lack of propriety'.[46] From this perspective, her correspondence with Swiss friends appears to have served as a lifeline, a way of maintaining her connections to the morals, values and practices of her youth, particularly during periods when the endless frenzy of Parisian social life threatened to overwhelm her. Throughout her years in Paris, Necker continued to find solace in the past and experienced a gentle melancholy in the recollection of her youthful life in Switzerland:

> At the moment, my position is quite different. I was poor then, uncertain of my destiny, but I had access to joys to which I am no longer susceptible and I search the most brilliant gatherings in vain [for] some traces of the vivid impressions which I felt then.[47]

A letter written just four years after her arrival in Paris expands further on this theme:

> I live in a country, Madame, where we cannot respond but from the heart ... you have taught me a practice a thousand times more valuable and when this whirlwind in which I live begins to overwhelm my sensibilities, your charming letters quickly remind me of all the pleasures of friendship.[48]

Madame Necker's letters suggest that she felt profoundly torn between the social duties related to her new role within the Parisian elite – duties which brought her into contact with an intellectual sphere whose ideas and discussions she cherished – and her moral and religious duties to the nation and identity of her childhood, duties which compelled her to maintain a position of alterity, even in the face of the myriad seductions of the French capital. To understand her conflict, we turn to a discussion of the art of pleasing, as it was practised by the French elite during the eighteenth century.

The Necessity of Pleasing

Eighteenth-century elite ideals and practices of sociability were propagated through a wide array of conduct books and treatises, many of which, such as Nicolas Faret's *L'Honneste homme, ou L'Art de plaire à la cour*, retained their currency well into the eighteenth century.[49] Madame Necker's *Mélanges* and *Nouveaux mélanges* also offer extensive, almost obsessive, reflections on the nature of polite

society. Read as a whole, these texts offer detailed insight into the contours of
the elite social body as it was understood during the French eighteenth century.
They make it clear that four terms are central to understanding the nature of
elite sociability during this period: *bienséance, politesse, honnêteté* and *plaire*.
Together, these elements laid the groundwork for the successful practice of elite
sociability in polite society.

According to the *Encyclopédie, bienséance* – agreeableness or propriety –
encompassed both moral and practical concerns.[50] At a general level, it referred
to an individual's ability to behave according to accepted social conventions
and behaviours within any given social environment. In this sense, *bienséance*
was spatially oriented: any body or object that added to the balance and pleasing quality of the social environment could be said to adhere to its principles.[51]
Within the larger matrix of social comportment, *bienséance*, a general characteristic of sociability, can be understood as a backdrop to more detailed and
complex social behaviours such as *politesse*.

Politesse – or refinement – was a form of *bienséance* that enabled individuals to please and show their respect for others.[52] Related to the idea of civility,
it was directly linked to social class and manifest in both language and corporeal practices. Through the practices of *politesse*, elite individuals added polish,
refinement, beauty and finesse to their social circle, thus reshaping the social
environment. Like *bienséance, politesse* encompassed physical and moral attributes; in other words, the elite individual could also be understood as an elite
body '[clothed] with the softness, modesty and justice that the mind seeks and
that society needs in order to be peaceful and agreeable'.[53] The physical body,
defined by Jaucourt as a mirror of the internal soul, was transformed in such a
way that it could more accurately reflect 'man on the outside as he should be on
the inside'.[54] The act of polishing was, therefore, not just a social act, but also an
intimate and reflective act in which the social body reflected not only the inherent harmony of the elite social environment as a whole, but also the internal
beauty of the individual.

Elite individuals, now more broadly conceived within the parameters of
elite bodies, had an obligation to fulfil the social needs of their colleagues.
Indeed, the art of pleasing was the nucleus of the practice of sociability. Comprising *bienséance* and *politesse*, its successful enactment was intrinsic to crafting
the *honnête homme* – the true gentleman – the properly socialized individual
who, in fulfilling the requirements of *bienséance* and *politesse* through the art
of pleasing, was a model individual and a credit to his society. Paradis de Moncrif, for example, envisioned the art of pleasing as a tool for social cohesion
and mutual understanding. Positioned midway between indifference and true
friendship, it was a flexible gesture that enabled social individuals to acknowledge their own emotional needs for recognition and appreciation and to fulfil

the very similar needs of those around them. As he observed: 'The desire to please thus contains within it the desire to be loved'.[55]

In general, Madame Necker's thoughts followed the parameters of elite sociability laid out in the conduct books. She noted that in order to be an ornament to polite society, an individual needed to observe the basic principles of moderation, humility, decorum and subtlety. Social success, she argued, was founded on a supreme awareness of self. The successful salon hostess paid careful attention at all times.[56] Intimately aware of the social status of each of her guests, she was a good listener who ensured that every guest had an equal opportunity to speak, carefully but adroitly interrupted when necessary and treated everyone with deference.[57]

Like the authors of the conduct books, Necker addressed the use of language and stressed the significance of non-verbal cues such as dress, demeanour and posture. Offering a dictionary definition of *bienséance*, she observed: 'Propriety consists not only in clothing or well chosen furniture, but it appears in the total arrangement of the things which surround us. This order informs the mind that nothing has been neglected.'[58] In order to fit in, the properly social being needed to ensure that she followed fashionable trends. Large gestures, loud and shrill voices, sudden movements, excessive curtsying: 'all of this is unpleasant, in poor taste and poor grace', she counselled.[59] Madame Necker's writings describe a social environment of subtlety and moderation in which physical gestures were coded and catalogued and in which one's intrinsic worth was calculated not on one's moral or intellectual character, but rather, determined on the basis of external markers.[60] Impressing upon the reader the power and importance of the proper elite social body, Necker's comments serve to highlight the essentially performative nature of the salon.

Central to the conceptions of *politesse*, *bienséance*, *honnêteté* and *plaire* was the idea of display: the social body was, as Paul Goring has observed, an eloquent body upon and through which were enacted not only the behaviours intrinsic to social cohesion, but also the desires and seductions of the elite.[61] Eighteenth-century sociability, inherently performative, relied on the metaphor of the mirror, a device whereby the social individual could be both observing and, at the same time, observed, a position memorably evoked by Jeremy Bentham's panopticon.[62] The relationships between observer and observed, as read through the metaphor of the mirror, are clearly in evidence in seventeenth- and eighteenth-century conduct books. René de Bary, in his 1662 work *L'Esprit de cour, ou Les Conversations galantes*, includes a flirtatious dialogue between two would-be lovers, Théodate and Ariane, on the nature of the reflected self. On the one hand, Ariane extols the virtues of nature, drawing her inspiration from fountains and streams, 'moving mirrors' which, she feels, accurately represent her imperfections.[63] Théodate, on the other hand, praises civic virtues, suggesting that Ariane can reveal her true self only through social reflection; in other words, by mirroring herself through the gaze of others. Mirrors, he argues, exist as spaces of projection, through which one is able to realize one's deepest passions. It is through the mirror that Ariane is able to discover and project her understanding of her own worthiness, and also, able to receive the estimation of others: 'You should not consider yourself worthy because I hold you in high esteem, you should consider yourself worthy because you are worthy of esteem ... it is time that you [knew] through your own observations that you are worthy of being noticed'.[64]

Bary's *conversation galante* demonstrates the relationship between sociability and display. Functioning as both reflecting and reflective entity, the elite social body incarnated the inherently reciprocal nature of social exchange. More importantly, the metaphor of the mirror highlighted its necessity within the social framework: reflection could be successful only if every individual consented to participate. The refusal of the mirror fundamentally undermined the art of pleasing. Taken a step further, the refusal of the mirror could be interpreted as a very personal refusal of the individual who initiated the process of mirroring. If Ariane did not wish Théodate's eyes to reflect her brilliance, then this was because she had convinced herself that they were not proper for this purpose, or, more damningly, that they were not worthy of the function.[65] The act of mirroring was, therefore, more than a useful metaphor, it was a social obligation required of all participants.

Mirroring enabled social perfection, a fact of which Suzanne Necker was well aware: 'It was said of Madame De Lauzun: she modelled herself on the character that she was first given in the world, and this is why she is perfect'.[66] Eyes played a powerful role in this process. As reflective surfaces, they glittered and shone. Mirroring the brilliance of the observed, they acknowledged the social individual's veneer of *politesse* and assessed the individual's moral goodness. At the same time, eyes are porous and function as points of entry into the heart: through the observation and acknowledgement of others, social individuals were able to acknowledge and take stock of themselves. In this sense, the mirror enabled a process of mutual recognition without which the elite individual, as a social entity, would cease to exist.

In the early twentieth century, Maurice Merleau-Ponty would define this reciprocity as essential to his understanding of phenomenology:

> To see is to enter a universe of beings which *display themselves* ... In other words: to look at an object is to inhabit it, and from this habitation to grasp all things in terms of the aspect which they present to it. But in so far as I see those things too, they remain abodes open to my gaze, and, being potentially lodged in them, I already perceive from various angles the central object of my present vision. Thus every object is the mirror of all others.[67]

Madame Necker's correspondence with the renowned British actor David Garrick offers one instance of the practical application of the mirroring imperative. 'You have written me a delightful letter', she wrote in 1776:

> Through your pen you express the passion that animates your stage roles; for you, everything is the material of life. I have read this letter in private, first with tender feelings; next I presented it with pride to all of my friends. I found myself constantly surrounded; they said to me, 'Tell us more of this great man, How did he play Hamlet? King Lear? Sir John Brute?' I tell them and we laugh or we cry.[68]

By using the letter as her mirror, Madame Necker was able not only to present a self surrounded by the adulations of her colleagues – in other words, a self rendered more worthy as a result of her highly desirable friendship with Garrick – but also to provide a space through which this glory could be reflected back onto Garrick himself. There is an inherent theatricality to this exchange, one which overtly acknowledges the performative nature of the discourse of elite sociability. The audience is not just quietly assumed, it is an overt participant in a process of identity creation.[69] Such a performance demonstrates Madame Necker's deepening awareness of the purpose and function of the social mirror. Each of Madame Necker's activities enhanced her personal social capital, and through them she was able to cultivate her cachet in the public sphere. Her burgeoning social life was intrinsic to her development as a highly visible woman in the public eye and functioned as a platform upon which she constructed her Parisian identity. Madame Necker's embrace of her role as salon hostess, as we shall see, offers one window into understanding her evolution from simple Swiss maiden to member of the French elite.

Secrets of the Successful *Salonnière*

Women played a central role in the cultivation and dissemination of elite social practices. As social ornaments, their perceived physical and moral beauty enhanced the *bienséance* of the social sphere and offered demonstrable proof of the promise of the social endeavour; it was through women that civilization itself was possible. Women's bodies – the ideal proof of Nature's divine beneficence and glory – offered physical manifestations of ideal sociability.[70] In addition to this, as teachers of virtue, women were the perfect foil for men: 'Woman was created to charm Man; this she does and nature is pleased'.[71] Assumed to be naturally sensitive, emotional, modest and delicate beings, women provided a balance for and counterpoint to men's greed, avarice and ambition.[72] François de Grenaille, for example, suggested that women enabled the reflective and reciprocal function of the mirror, arguing in a very Platonic move that: 'we find that her face is the Mirror of her mind and that Beauty itself is nothing but the image of her body'.[73] Physical beauty was not only a concrete manifestation of moral beauty but also, through the metaphor of the mirror, a reflection of the beauty of the project of elite sociability as a whole. These ideals were manifest in the person of the *salonnière*, the hostess who initiated and managed the sociability of the salon.

Most *salonnières* learned their art as protégées of senior salon women. Madame Geoffrin, for example, began her 'training' in the salon of Madame du Tencin. Geoffrin, in her turn, acted as a mentor for the next generation of salon women. Not only did she advise Suzanne Necker, but she also financially supported the endeavours of Julie de Lespinasse upon the latter's break with her aunt, Madame du Deffand. Closer to home, she raised her own daughter, Marie-Thérèse Geoffrin d'Estampes, Marquise de La Ferté-Imbault, in the salon. However, even as salon women developed their skills under the tutelage of successful mentors in a culture dedicated to the principles of the art of pleasing, these apprenticeships were not designed to develop carbon-copy replicas. Each *salonnière* was unique. Just as Madame Necker was known for her moral rectitude and her disavowal of irreligious talk, so too was Madame Deffand known for her acerbic wit, Geoffrin for her organizational skill, and La Ferté-Imbault for her parodic approach.

Of all the renowned salon women, it was Julie de Lespinasse who most successfully embodied the ideals of elite sociability. Lespinasse was thirty-three years old when, with the financial help and political intervention of Geoffrin and other colleagues, she started her own salon. Her salon lineage was exemplary: not only had she served a lengthy apprenticeship at the side of her aunt, the formidable Marquise du Deffand, but she also received significant financial assistance and moral support from Madame Geoffrin, who invited her to attend her own salon. More importantly, she was able to poach many of Deffand's regulars. Lespinasse's salon, located in her apartment at the corner of the rue Belle-chasse and the rue St Dominique in the Faubourg St Germain, became a second home to such luminaries as Jean le Rond d'Alembert, the noted economist and statesman Anne Robert Jacques Turgot, and the thinker and mathematician Marie Jean Antoine Nicolas de Caritat, Marquis de Condorcet.

Lespinasse's salon was extremely successful, a feat due in no small part to her skill. Her guests, a somewhat motley assemblage of persons drawn from a range of social classes, were nonetheless – through Lespinasse's mediation – ideally suited to work together. As Jean-François Marmontel observed:

> [Mademoiselle de Lespinasse] gathered her guests from here and there in society, but it was such a fine assortment that, once they had arrived, they found themselves in harmony like the strings of an instrument assembled by a skilful hand. To continue the analogy, I would say that she played this instrument with an art that touched on genius; she seemed to know which sounds would create the chord she was going to touch; that is, she knew our minds and personalities so well that, in order to put them into play, she had only to say a single word. Nowhere was the conversation more lively, nor more brilliant, nor better regulated than at her home.[74]

Marmontel's description not only outlines Lespinasse's aptitude for social management, but also encapsulates the nature and scope of the elite social endeavour. The evocation of harmony suggests the power of the group over the autonomy of the individual and stresses the idea of elite sociability as an instrument of social cohesion. At the same time, by promoting musical harmony, which can result only from the combination of two different notes, Marmontel recognized that difference was essential to the ultimate harmony of the whole. Most significant, however, is Marmontel's equation of the *salonnière* with both composer and performer. In so doing, he explicitly identified sociability as a performative project governed by the aesthetic inclinations of the *salonnière*, cultivated through the varied conversations – or harmony – of the guests and developed and performed within the space of the salon.

Marmontel's analogy suggests that salon dialogue occurred on many levels. As the creator of the harmony, the *salonnière* was the author of the musical performance; in other words, she initiated the dialogue between the performer and the individual notes. First of all, the *salonnière* had to enter into an internal dialogue in order to decide which notes to put into play. Having reflected upon this, she then initiated a dialogue with the notes themselves, creating harmony – or sound – from a judicious blend of single notes. This is where her authorship, as performer and instigator of the dialogue, ended. The final dialogue could occur only between the harmony and the resonating space, or salon. Each step in the process was integral to the whole. As a virtuoso, the *salonnière*, though not actively involved in the dialogue between harmony and space, necessarily responded to it. The relationship between the original harmony and its resonance affected all of the *salonnière*-as-musician's subsequent decisions; after all, she was as capable of creating discord as she was of creating harmony. Marmontel's metaphor provides crucial information about the reciprocal roles of the salon, *salonnière* and guests and outlines their respective functions, rights and obligations. His homage to Lespinasse's skill as the orchestrator of salon conversation provides evidence of the formidable power and talent of the salon woman.

Even so, Lespinasse's skill was born from her self-denial: the success of her salon rested on her complete sublimation of her individuality – through the practices of elite sociability – to the good of the social unit as a whole.[75] As Paradis de Moncrif observed, the practice of elite sociability was conceived as a way of managing social relations; it was a force specifically designed to foster social cohesion and a method whereby aristocrats could define themselves and demarcate the boundaries of their existence. From this perspective, the art of pleasing can be understood as the art of exclusion. This, certainly, is the motive that lies behind the criticisms of Madame Necker's social skills. She did not fit in, commentators suggested, because she was of the wrong class and religion. Because of this, they asserted that she would never succeed at the art of pleasing and, therefore, could never be accepted as a full member of polite society.

However, the conduct books also tell a different story, arguing that the desired social cohesion was a result of *politesse*; in other words, they suggest the necessity of acknowledging – at least superficially – the inherent worthiness of *every* individual, regardless of class or rank. Jacques Delille, for example, a member of Geoffrin's salon, waxed poetic about the salon environment:

> A gathering of spiritual and refined persons, united to discuss and to learn together in pleasant conversation, through the mutual communication of their ideas and their feelings, has always appeared to me to be the happiest portrayal of mankind and of social perfection. There, each brings his desire and ways of pleasing, his sensibility, imagination, experience, all embellished by courtesy and contained by decency; there, appears a mutual instinct of benevolent affections ... there, without regulation, without constraint, is exerted a gentle discipline, founded on the respect that a gathering of individuals inspire in one another out of a need they have to work well together.[76]

Such an approach is intimately tied to ideas of democracy and equality. As Madame Necker observed:

> We have viewed refinement as a form of servitude; but its origin, to the contrary, can be found in the attentions of the strong towards the weak, the elderly, women, children and so on. Refinement conforms to this principle of equality of which we speak so often; it is the rampart of those who cannot defend themselves, and it is also that which garners praise and merit.[77]

The non-verbal manifestations of the art of pleasing, however, suggest that while diversity was tolerated, cohesion and homogeneity were valued. The social body was inextricably linked with the aristocratic body, a corporeal presence able to manifest virtue through the practice of courtly appearances and behaviours. The corporeal aspects of the social body: physical gestures, dress, comportment and so forth, were a sort of 'second language'[78] which outsiders could never fully master. In this system, the socially inferior body, while still tolerated, was inherently less able to manifest social virtue. Such, in essence, was the nature of Suzanne Necker's exile from elite sociability. As she concluded: 'No one has felt more than I that one must be born in this country in order to succeed in it through social grace and charm'.[79] Here, Necker's comments and concerns reflect the criticisms of her salon guests and, as such, appear to indicate a species of social failure.

The Seductions of Paris: Resisting the Elite Social Imperative

However, even as Madame Necker sought acceptance within the Parisian intellectual and social sphere, she nevertheless remained deeply ambivalent about the mores and values of this environment and actively cultivated a position of alterity. Intriguingly, such a stance on her part appears at once to confirm *and* threaten the social cohesion promised by the practices of elite sociability. This interplay between acquiescence and resistance must be taken a step further, and it is in taking this step that I situate my research as a whole. One of the intriguing aspects of this study has been the subtle interplay, interaction and tension between differing understandings of broader cultural and religious themes. Of particular interest are the slippages between French elite understandings of duty and those espoused by Madame Necker. These tensions not only appear in the texts defining elite sociability – in this case, the conduct books and Madame Necker's writings – but also, by leading to very different understandings of the art of pleasing, directly affected social practices and behaviours. At the same time, these competing understandings complicate our understanding of Madame Necker herself. A woman poised uncomfortably between two very different conceptual worlds, she exemplifies the ambiguity and opacity of abjection. Indeed, it is Madame Necker's positioning of herself within the space of the abject that has had profound resonance for this study.

An understanding of divergent, and indeed competing, meanings of the word 'duty' is integral to understanding Madame Necker's story. According to the *Dictionnaire de l'Académie françoise* (1762), the word *devoir*, or duty, can be understood as that which one is obligated to do by law, custom or propriety.[80] The individual could, for example, owe duty to her family, her church, her sovereign or her nation. The specific duties with which one engaged functioned as external markers of social identity; in other words, they were specific to the community with which one identified oneself. The realization of one's duties, then, could be seen as integral to the individual's perceived social and cultural roles. The fulfilment of one's duties signified the individual's acceptance of the requirements of one's position, socially, legally, emotionally, spiritually or otherwise. In this sense, the practice of one's duties could be said to operate on two levels: not only were duties externally imposed by the dictates of the social group of which one was a part, but they could also be consciously claimed in order to identify oneself publicly as a member of a particular group.

In aristocratic circles, the idea of duty was inextricably linked with the responsibilities that the individual owed to his or her social class; in other words, it was a duty owed to aristocratic sociability, in which the cultivation of the elite identity was paramount. Madame Necker, however, had an entirely different relationship with the idea of duty. While she acknowledged the duties she owed to elite society, her sense of identity was directly linked to the practice of civic duties; in other words, to the responsibilities she owed to society as a whole. This understanding of duty is laid out explicitly in one of her unpublished journals. After observing that God had given her twenty-four hours a day, she outlined her main responsibilities, which included not only the expected duties towards family and friends, but also direct responsibilities towards the poor.[81] Madame Necker's approach, which transformed social duty into civic duty through the vehicle of domestic maternal sociability as practised within the salon, suggests a fundamental repositioning of the art of pleasing. While the French elite, who quite literally nursed their way into elite propriety, understood the art of pleasing as a species of facile gallantry, Madame Necker perceived it as a way of giving meaning to her life. *L'Art de plaire* was much more than just the art of pleasing; it was the art of serving. To give, suggested Necker, was 'une jouissance' – a sensual pleasure.[82] In order to live virtuously – and thus, to attain happiness – one had to give: of one's time, of one's wealth and of one's self. As Madame Necker observed: 'To fulfil my duties, this is my first passion and my first concern'.[83]

Necker's repositioning is extremely significant. Not only did it subvert the exclusionary nature of the aristocratic art of pleasing, but it also fused courtly French manners and elite sociability with her strongly Protestant upbringing, thus creating a model which was far more relevant to – and compatible with – her own conception of self. Such a reformulation did not necessarily need to be fraught with contradictions. In fact, as Necker observed:

> One of the great principles of social custom is to appear happy with everyone one encounters, whether we like them or not; because if we are careful, it is possible to link the maxims of courtesy with the precepts of the Gospel; the first are the image and the second, the reality.[84]

In this passage, Necker demonstrates that moral and social duties were not at odds with one another. This excerpt also provides confirmation of her attempts to reconcile what could otherwise be seen as disparate gestures of civic responsibility. From this perspective, Madame Necker emerges as a hyphenated cultural hybrid. Influenced as much by the conventions of her adopted Parisian society as by the morally rigorous foundations of her upbringing, she crafted a method of social conduct that maintained the form of French propriety while at the same time substantially manipulating its content in accordance with her own deeply held beliefs.

This tension between moral duty and the elite social imperative suggests that it might be necessary to reframe the comments and criticisms of her contemporaries. Could it be that the discomfiture and criticism on the part of Madame Necker's guests emerged not from an awareness of her limitations, but from a recognition of her resistance? Certainly, the Baronne d'Oberkirch's previously cited commentary seems overly critical, defensive even, as if to suggest that she felt insulted and disturbed by Necker's behaviour. Oberkirch suggests a species of wilful defiance on Madame Necker's part, ascribing to her actions both a conscious refusal to play the role assigned to her as a result of her birth and upbringing and an equally audacious determination to infiltrate and infect the upper classes with what might more properly be perceived as bourgeois social values.

Pamphlet literature of the period reveals yet another layer of complexity.[85] Madame Necker was pilloried in a number of pamphlets dating from the 1780s; that is, during the period of her husband's political controversies and her own increased visibility on the public stage as a result of her charitable endeavours. The pamphlets attacked her on the very grounds upon which she founded her identity – her virtue and, implicitly, her religious belief – painting instead the image of a woman who would go to any lengths to protect her public image.[86] These libellous works presented their readers with the image of a scheming wife who sought further grandeur for herself and her husband through a variety of underhanded actions. Among the most disturbing allegations to emerge as a result of these defamatory pamphlets was that Madame Necker had plotted their removal – and therefore, the silencing of her critics – through direct intervention: by descending into town *en travestie* and falsely gaining a bookseller's confidence.[87] This damning indictment suggests that Necker's behaviour destabilized social relations in a number of ways. The image of the disguised – and possibly cross-dressed – woman not only undermined her performance of properly feminine virtue, but also subverted the masculine authority of the public sphere itself. Madame Necker, celebrated in her husband's infamous *Compte rendu* of 1781 as a paragon of feminine virtue and the epitome of felicitous domesticity, was here revealed to be nothing more than a social and cultural interloper, a deceitful woman whose very presence threatened the harmonious coherence of the French social and political sphere. Furthermore, these works suggest that Madame Necker's moral stance was itself the result of her performance of *travestissement*: the staging of virtue was precisely that, a masquerade that masked her less-than-honourable intentions.

The previously cited comments of Madame d'Oberkirch and the vitriolic criticisms of the pamphleteers are certainly worth considering. For if *l'art de plaire* was founded upon a necessary integration and sublimation of the self into the larger project of aristocratic identity as a whole, then Madame Necker's conscious resistance would have been understood as tantamount to betrayal. As a social mirror, she did not reflect back the requisite social identity; instead, she presented and performed an alternative identity informed by a wholly different set of values. In contrast to Julie de Lespinasse, for example, the supremely successful salon woman who sublimated herself entirely to the cause of elite sociability, Madame Necker performed her autobiographical self by laying claim to her alterity, using elite salon sociability as a stage from which to launch a counter-performance of domestic sociability based on a moral understanding of duty and directly informed by the values of her Swiss childhood and the theological tenets of her Calvinist faith.

From this perspective, Necker's performance can be read as a fundamental breach of salon etiquette and a powerful statement of nonconformity. By refusing the mirroring imperative so integral to the practice of elite sociability, she threatened the cohesion of the elite social project itself. More significant still is her political positioning. Unlike interlopers like Rousseau, whose behaviours and writings could be summarily rejected or officially banned, Madame Necker, as the wife of the politically powerful Jacques Necker, could not so easily be dismissed. Indeed, her idiosyncracies, while troubling, had to be tolerated. Not only did her husband ascend to the highest echelons of political power, but he had his devoted and loving wife as an intimate ally. Hence, the Necker salon must be conceived, as Antoine Lilti has observed, as an important political venue: 'It is impossible to separate "Madame Necker's salon" from the political career of "Monsieur Necker".'[88] In other words, Madame Necker's salon should be understood as the direct conduit to Jacques Necker's inner circle. In this sense, Madame Necker's mediocre social performance, glossed over by so many of her biographers, must be seen as intrinsic to understanding her autobiographical presentation. In order to explore this further, I turn now to the relationships between duty, desire and display as they played themselves out in the context of Madame Necker's spiritual heritage and beliefs.

2 EMBODIED FAITH: MADAME NECKER'S INTIMATE THEOLOGY

> As for me, I vow to you that I do not recite, *I think, therefore I am*, like the philoso-phers do; I say, *I think, therefore God is*. This idea is inextricably linked with the nature of my being; it is everything for me, it satisfies all of my tastes, it fulfils all of my desires. I have no more curiosity, the mystery has been solved: I have no unrequited desires, all of my wishes have been fulfilled; I no longer have any uncertainty; rather, my path is clearly laid out for me.[1]

> There are in man, so to speak, two worlds, over which different kings and different laws have authority.[2]

Madame Necker's mediocre social performances stemmed from her experience of profound religious alterity. Hers was not an elite social body; rather, it was a Calvinist body, whose contours bore witness to the principles of the reformed faith. Necker's religious beliefs were central to her life. She made a regular point of acknowledging her spiritual duties to a variety of Swiss friends and acquaint-ances, displaying her faith to close friends such as Henriette Réverdil and Paul Moultou, as well as to the celebrated Swiss physicist Georges-Louis LeSage and the geologist and meteorologist Jean André De Luc.[3] With them, she shared her belief in God's grace and provided evidence of her submission to his will, even in the face of the powerful temptations and seductions of the irreligious, elite Parisian social sphere.

She assured Moultou in writing of her religious fidelity by invoking God and her responsibilities to him:

> My dear friend, can you suspect me for an instant? My feelings were born with me when I came into the world, and you think that I can throw them over now when my whole happiness depends upon them ... I live, it is true, among many atheists, but their arguments have never crossed my mind; and if they have ever reached my heart it was only to make me shrink back from them with horror.[4]

The presence of such passages in her letters suggests not only Necker's desire for public devotion, but also her need for spiritual confession. As she observed, every day was a gift of Providence and needed to be lived as a whole life in and of itself:

'our first consideration must be to consecrate [our lives] to God'.[5] Madame Necker's comments can be read as confirmation of her religious piety and fidelity. She envisioned her role as that of a spiritual witness, whose beliefs and actions stood in diametric opposition to those of the society in which she found herself. The belief systems of certain philosophers, she contended, threatened the moral foundations of Calvinist belief: religion, piety, filial respect, conjugal love and patriotism.[6]

As we have seen, Madame Necker felt the tension of competing duties – those owed to elite society and those owed to her religion – deeply. In order to understand the nature of this struggle, I turn now to the religious, cultural and historical context of Calvinism and examine how this background guided and shaped her beliefs and actions. Of particular relevance are four interlocking concepts: display, exile, longing and communion. In the final section of this chapter, I suggest the possibility of self-imposed exile, whereby a positioning of submissive abjection – understood here as a conscious claiming of the sinful alterity of the exiled believer and a giving over of the sinful self to the dictates of divine will – might be deployed as a panacea for longing and considered a conduit to redemption.

Central to this discussion is the essential impropriety of the abject Calvinist body, an entity suspended between the potential of divine grace and the irrefutable reality of human weakness as understood through the Fall and the subsequent exile of Adam and Eve from the Garden of Eden. Indeed, William Monter has argued that Calvinist suffering emerges from this first sinful act.[7] Madame Necker, a devout Calvinist transplanted to the Parisian salon, was divided, torn between the social duties of her corporeal, earthly existence and the spiritual duties required to achieve full communion with God. This intersection of exile, longing and desire – as manifest in the abject Calvinist body – is integral to understanding Necker's contradictory and conflicted performance of self on the Parisian salon stage. Such a conceptualization necessarily placed her in a tenuous position. Continually beset by competing, yet equally essential, duties, she was finally forced to confront and negotiate the complex relationship between duty and desire in a struggle that would be played out no longer on the salon stage, but rather, as subsequent chapters will demonstrate, within the space of her own body.

Childhood in Crassier: Reflections on a Calvinist Girlhood[8]

Louise Suzanne Curchod was the only child of Louis Antoine Curchod, a village pastor at Crassier, a tiny community near Geneva, and Magdeleine Albert, a Huguenot refugee originally from the city of Montélimar, in the Dauphiné region of France. She was baptized on 2 June 1737 and instructed in Calvinism at home. 'La Suzete', as her mother called her, came by her Calvinism naturally. Her father, born in the Vaud region and descended from a French Huguenot mother and Vaudois father, had studied theology under the renowned liberal Calvinist reformer Jean-Alphonse Turretin at the Académie de Genève, matriculating in 1720 with a thesis on a text by St Paul. He took over the pastorate at Crassier in 1729 and remained in this position until his death in 1760. Mademoiselle Curchod's maternal heritage was equally informed by Calvinist belief. Her mother, born in 1698 to Jean Albert and Magdeleine Répara, was descended from a long line of faithful Protestants that could be traced back to one Jean Albert, 'Protestant and merchant, town councillor in 1585 and consul in 1588'.[9]

Mademoiselle Curchod appears to have enjoyed an idyllic childhood surrounded by deeply loved – and loving – parents and relations and the company of good friends. As her childhood friend, Elie-Salomon-François Réverdil, noted, 'In some ways, my relationship with Madame Necker preceded our birth, since our parents had already fulfilled all the reciprocal duties of friendship towards one another during their time together'.[10] From her mother, Mademoiselle Curchod inherited the singular beauty that enabled her early social successes and earned her the nickname 'la belle Curchod', while from her father she received her remarkable education. Along with the requisite feminine accomplishments in the fine arts – in Suzanne's case, harpsichord, tympanon, violin and painting – and a solid foundation in Calvinist morality and theology, she studied Latin, Greek, physics and geometry. In addition, she developed a strong affinity for literature, which she explored and articulated as a member of numerous social and intellectual circles in Lausanne and Geneva. Her friendships with such influential individuals as Jean-Jacques Rousseau, Georges-Louis LeSage, Paul Moultou and Samuel-Auguste Tissot all date from this period.

As a young woman, Mademoiselle Curchod was fêted for her beauty and her virtue, but her intellectual prowess took some of her contemporaries by surprise. As one of her admirers pointed out: 'You are – dare I say it? – yes, you are clever. Should we be surprised after this if the fairer sex sounds the alarm?'[11] Another of her early suitors put it this way:

> While I was studying literature in Lausanne, our professor, Monsieur Darney, told us that your intellect made you an exception to your sex and he suggested you as our role model. When you walked through the streets, always surrounded by admirers, I heard the [gathered] public say: 'There she is, the beautiful Curchod!' And I ran as quickly as possible along your route, where I stayed as long as I could.[12]

Calvinism in Geneva: Calvin, Turretin and Lullin

Mademoiselle Curchod's childhood activities and experiences appear to have conformed to the conventions of eighteenth-century Genevan social and religious culture. Geneva had developed into a thriving metropolis of 20,000 by the early eighteenth century. It was an international city with a flourishing economy that relied heavily on banking and international trade.[13] Increasingly influenced by the social practices of the French elite, the wealthy class constructed large mansions and cultivated interests in the arts and sciences. Learning flourished in such a cosmopolitan environment and Geneva produced a fine complement of scientists and scholars, among them Horace-Bénédict de Saussure, the eminent scientist recognized for his Alpine research; Georges-Louis LeSage, a physicist perhaps best known for his theory of gravitation, and the controversial political theorist, philosopher and novelist Jean-Jacques Rousseau, whose early work, as Helena Rosenblatt has argued, was directly influenced by his Calvinist upbringing in early eighteenth-century Geneva.[14]

The liberal theological approach promoted by Louis-Antoine Curchod's tutor, Jean-Alphonse Turretin, a leading Genevan pastor and professor of theology, revolutionized the practice of Calvinism by asserting the essential compatibility of reason and faith. In order to explain the nature of Turretin's theological revolution, I turn briefly to the early history of the Protestant reformation, particularly Jean Calvin, the most influential of the second generation of reformers.

Calvin accepted the reformed faith sometime between 1527 and 1534. Just two years later, in 1536, he wrote and published the first version of his foundational work, *The Institutes of the Christian Religion*. Upon his arrival in Geneva that same year, he quickly became an active leader in the Genevan Reformation. Geneva proved a strategic location for the international propagation of the reform and would continue to play a central role in the rise of Protestantism, functioning as a gathering place and beacon for persecuted believers until well into the eighteenth century. As a reformed pastor, Calvin undertook a far-reaching system of religious and civic reform which affected every aspect of everyday life. In addition to developing a thorough theological doctrine, he also envisioned a complete overhaul of social and civic relations.

At its heart, Calvinist belief extended the trajectories of those of his influential predecessor, Martin Luther. Central to the Calvinist reconceptualization of the Church was Calvin's belief in the gospel as both the guide to Christian life and the essential text on Christian duty and law. He insisted on the cultivation of a personal and individual relationship with God and defined the family as the key site of the reformed doctrine. This can be seen in his repeated exhortations to married women, urging them to maintain the marriage bond even in the face of continued marital transgressions on the part of their husbands.[15] Unlike Luther, however, Calvin did not preach salvation by faith but, rather, encouraged believers' active engagement in their own salvation. Within the Calvinist polity, civic duty was an extension of religious duty in that it was understood as a way of acknowledging and serving the glory of God. The fulfilment of civic duties contributed to divine grace.

Reformed Christian believers understood themselves to be fully subordinate to the will of God, who was the sole reason for their existence and from whom all goodness flowed. Calvinist doctrine defined an active religious role for civil government in the realization of divine justice and looked to religious individuals for the propagation of the faith. Within the damaged, impure world of man, believers were to craft an earthly space of religious purity, working together with other like-minded individuals to build a community of grace that could light the way to those who had not yet accepted the reformed faith.

Calvin's moral and civic reforms had a profound impact. The actions of reformed believers, governed by a belief in absolute submission to divine will, were supervised by the disciplinary power of the Consistory, a juridical body that enforced moral discipline by ruling on larger issues such as adultery and divorce and examining instances of moral weakness, such as laggard church attendance or failure to pray.[16] The Consistory was controlled by a series of ecclesiastical ordinances that sought to regulate every aspect of moral and civic activity. The five articles of the reformed faith professed at the Synod of Dort (1618–19), and reconfirmed in 1675 by the Helvetic Consensus Formula, further enshrined Calvinist doctrinal beliefs such as 'total depravity', which held that all humans were born in sin and could not escape their sinful state, and 'arbitrary redemption', which posited that mercy and grace were bestowed only by God, who as the creator of the world was also its final arbiter and judge.[17] These concepts – from the power of the Consistory to the doctrines of the faith – are, as we shall see, key to understanding Madame Necker's psychic and somatic malaise.

Turretin's approach was very different. Impressed by the rationalist principles of the Cartesian method, he sought to prove the nature of God through the use of reason.[18] Central to his theological approach was a fundamental belief that reason and faith were not inimical to one another: 'Since both are sources of truth they should not contradict each other. In addition, since God himself is the author of both the light of reason and the light of revelation, one should use them both jointly.'[19]

During his tenure, Turretin was responsible for moving the Genevan church away from the rigid strictures of the Helvetic Consensus Formula, which was finally struck down in 1725. Turretin's reforms also resulted in a substantial reshaping of the curriculum of the Académie de Genève, the traditional training ground for Calvinist ministers. Along with Cartesian natural philosophy, coursework at the Académie soon came to include natural sciences, mathematics and natural law.[20] Through the ideas of Turretin and his successors, strict theological conformity gave way to a broader world view in which religious belief came to be understood as a way of maintaining society's moral framework. It seems that Turretin's approach also influenced Jacques Necker, since similar ideas underpin his *De l'importance des opinions réligieuses* (1788), a largely deist work that conceived religious belief as central to the success of a strong government, essential to societal peace and well-being and integral to individual happiness.[21]

The 'reasonable reform' that reshaped eighteenth-century Calvinism is evident in the movement's increased interest in promoting the civic responsibilities of the reformed believer. Good citizens, Turretin argued, were good Christians; indeed, the two were inseparable from one another.[22] Sociability, the cornerstone of French elite behaviour, was revived as the wellspring of Calvinist community. According to the words of the Swiss jurist Jean-Jacques Burlamaqui:

> SOCIETY ... is not the work of man: it is God himself who is the author ... [Society], which by the help that men draw from one another, provides all of their knowledge, all of their conveniences and the pleasures that make up the safety, happiness and the charms of life! It is true that all of these benefits assume that men, far from harming themselves, live on good terms with each other and maintain this union by mutual offices.[23]

Social relations also changed on another level. In the face of an ever-growing patrician class and a proportional increase in religious leaders drawn from that class, the Calvinist Church revisited its perceptions of wealth. In the eighteenth-century Genevan framework, wealth was no longer evil in and of itself, but could be positively combined with virtue.[24] The acknowledgement of social and economic disparity carried with it the responsibility to act, a process whereby the redistribution of monetary wealth could be considered a step to ensuring the individual's salvation.

This more liberal approach, which stressed the value of a well-rounded rational education and deployed the principles of elite sociability in support of charitable initiatives and integrated them into ideas of public service, most certainly shaped the context in which young Mademoiselle Curchod was raised. Indeed, her broad educational background and later social debuts in Lausanne and Geneva suggest her family's adherence to Turretin's principles. Her training also recalls ideas put forward by Ami Lullin, one of the leading figures of eighteenth-century Calvinism. A Genevan pastor and professor of ecclesiastical history at the Académie de Genève, Lullin was the son of a wealthy manufacturer, merchant and banker, and heir to the greatest fortune in the city. He was also a writer, whose *oeuvre* includes four manuscript notebooks dedicated to 'La femme de mérite', or 'woman of merit', unpublished writings which apparently circulated throughout elite Genevan society.[25] In these notebooks, Lullin developed the definition of the ideal wife for a well-born man. Drawing on both his theological training and his elite social status, Lullin crafted a womanly ideal whose contours evoked the grace, charm and *esprit* of elite society while at the same time celebrating the modesty, humility and service of the good wife and mother. In addition, the woman of merit would possess a broad education, to include geography, Greek and Roman history, modern history, logic, poetry, language and algebra, as well as a thorough grounding in Calvinist moral precepts and teachings.[26] With this moral education, Lullin's *femme de mérite* incarnated virtue:

> We find in her the sensitive woman, the true Christian woman, the enlightened woman, the Wife, the Mother, the Relative, the Friend dedicated to her duties, the Woman of organization and action, the strong and courageous Woman; the Woman of Society whose noble and engaging manners serve as a model; and, all said, [the woman of] modest Virtue; who, content to have completed her duties, flees the spotlight, seeking much less the approval of society than that of her own heart, and to deserve the tenderness of a dignified husband.[27]

In Lullin's framework, wealthy Calvinist women embodied the promise of the Calvinist faith. As guardians of elite sociability in the public sphere and guarantors of the faith at a domestic level, their role was central to the actualization of Calvinist practice in the earthly sphere. On a corporeal level, the female body was no longer domestic only, but came to be reimagined in social terms, and, more broadly, in terms of *patrie* – or nation – an idea that will be revisited in subsequent chapters.

Practising the Faith

It is easy to recognize the youthful Suzanne Curchod in Lullin's portrait of feminine virtue. Pious, well educated and charming, Mademoiselle Curchod was a young woman who fully merited the attentions and accolades of her contemporaries. Her behaviour and beliefs promised a virtuous future and a life of happiness. From these beginnings, what then, can we make of the struggle between social and domestic duty that dominated Madame Necker's Parisian existence? Lullin's liberal vision, and Mademoiselle Curchod's successful actualization of it, would appear to serve as ideal preparation for her subsequent social roles. Why, then, did her contemporaries question her abilities? Why did her social performances fail to live up to the standards of the Parisian elite? Furthermore, why did Madame Necker feel a need to distance herself consciously from the value systems of her French counterparts?

The answers to these questions can be found in a period of loss and rupture that immediately preceded her arrival in Paris. Louis Antoine Curchod died in 1760, and his wife, Magdeleine, in 1763. The deaths of her parents fundamentally altered Mademoiselle Curchod's previously carefree existence. After her father's death, she was forced to put her educational background to practical use as a governess to members of the Lausannois and Genevan elite, managing to eke out a meagre existence upon which she and her mother could survive. Families she had once counted as friends were now employers who demanded her committed engagement to their children, her pupils. Likening her new situation to a form of slavery and regularly teaching for seven hours per day,[28] she had neither the time nor the energy for frivolity and the pleasures of conversation.[29] In response, she directed her resentment towards her ailing mother, whose material needs were a burden, the weight of which she began to resent: 'I blamed you for all of my life's vexations because my happiness depended on you alone'.[30]

Her mother's subsequent death was a shock that forced Suzanne to re-evaluate her relationship with her parents. In response, she began to develop a profound sense of filial guilt. To Gibbon, she confessed that her father had given up his health in order to support her. To Élie-Salomon-François Réverdil, meanwhile, she acknowledged the heavy burden of filial neglect, writing: '[there is] nothing that can take the place of duty or compensate for the fear of having diminished the happiness of the person who has given us life'.[31] The impact of her losses was exacerbated by her subsequent decision to leave Switzerland to seek her fortunes elsewhere. After considering possibilities in Germany, England and even Denmark, she ultimately took a position as the personal companion to a wealthy French woman, leaving Geneva for Paris in early June 1764. The dissonance between what she now perceived as petty resentment and the irretrievable rupture and finality of death was to haunt her for the rest of her life.

This period of trauma and instability – from the deaths of her parents in 1760 and 1763 to her subsequent emigration to France in June 1764 – offers considerable insight into the moral stance Madame Necker cultivated. Irrevocably marked by loss and overcome with guilt, she turned to her religious belief for sustenance. In 1768, she wrote to Madame Réverdil, 'I assure you that despite the charms that elite society and my situation present to me, <u>I seek God as the supreme good</u>, just as you have counselled me'.[32] For Madame Necker, Calvinist belief became inextricably linked to her experiences of loss. The losses of her carefree childhood, her parents and ultimately her nation manifested themselves in the form of corporeal exile, a gesture of submissive abjection through which she sought to acknowledge and atone for her failings.

Over the next thirty years, Madame Necker developed what might be understood as an intimate theology of abjection founded on four interrelated themes: longing, exile, communion and display. These four ideas blend seamlessly into one another in Madame Necker's writing. Her yearning for God, for example, was manifest through her longing for her dead mother and duty to her memory. In a letter dated 25 February 1765, she sought comfort in imagining her mother looking approvingly on her actions, writing: 'May she, from her heavenly vantage point, be able to see my heart, still filled with the desire of pleasing her'.[33] The letter, with its language of religious benediction, appears to have become a vehicle for superimposing her belief in the all-seeing gaze of the 'Supreme Being' on her moral responsibilities towards her mother, an approach she also adopted in a later, undated letter from the same collection: 'God, bless our cares; it seems as if my beloved mother approves of them from heaven above; and that I would dare to appear before her at that moment when I will meet her again'.[34] These moral obligations, realized in the form of charitable endeavours towards 'the unfortunate members of this [Protestant] communion who are isolated in the midst of Catholics',[35] enabled her both to seek communion with God and publicly to display her fidelity to the reformed faith and, in so doing, expand the network of Protestant belief, thus contributing to the ever-evolving Calvinist understanding of spiritual *patrie*.[36]

Spiritual longing and the quest for divine communion were central to the Calvinist experience. Belden C. Lane suggests that Calvin relied heavily on theatrical metaphors in order to strengthen his rhetorical persuasion and constructed the whole world as a stage upon which believers could enact their praise. Lane articulates the relationship between display and longing in the following manner:

> Spirituality, in Calvin's thinking, is a performance of desire shared by the whole of the universe, a deliberate practice of delight that echoes through every part of the created world ... All created reality, extending each moment from the hand of God, is shot through with longing.[37]

Calvinist longing emerged from the innate human propensity for sin, which both limited human existence and damaged the wonder of divine creation as presented in the theatre of the world.[38]

Each of these concepts – display, longing, exile and communion – must be examined individually. In the section that follows, however, I begin with an overview of the public activities that confirmed Madame Necker's commitment to, and membership in, the Calvinist community, before detailing the interplay among the four concepts.

Madame Necker and the Display of Calvinism

Evidence of Suzanne Necker's adherence to Calvinist principles and of her desire to display her fidelity through public gestures is readily available. Madame Necker's commitment to her faith expressed itself in two ways: in material terms, through her charitable projects, and in spiritual terms, through her published writings. From the practical, domestic concerns of family to the provision of public charity and philosophical reflections on the meaning of religion in daily life, her activities speak to a conscious awareness of the importance of her reformed belief and her deep desire not only to ensure her adherence to its tenets, but also to display her faith publicly. Most obvious, perhaps, are the personal choices she made as an adult in Paris: she was married in the Reformed chapel of the Dutch embassy in Paris and she baptized and later married her daughter there. In addition, she consciously chose to educate her daughter within the Calvinist tradition, requesting Calvinist educational materials and advice from her friend Sophie Réverdil:

> My angel, I would like it if you could send me my Bible, if you can find one among my books (or, if not, if you can buy me one along with a New Testament, all in the newest version); to this you will add a prose translation of the psalms … it's a large, thin, cardboard-covered volume in *quarto* that should be in the chest. I would also like the Osterwald catechism … in short, all the books of piety that could be necessary for the instruction of my daughter, who has begun to speak and to understand.[39]

Necker's approach was highly characteristic of the reformed faith, which envisioned moral reform in both spiritual and civic spheres. When Calvin, together with Guillaume Farel, implemented reformist principles in Geneva, he concentrated not only on the workings of the church and the faith of his parishioners, but also on the development of strong civic institutions – like the Consistory – that could publicly support the moral foundation of the reformed polity. Similar ideals underpin the writings of eighteenth-century Genevan Calvinist leaders. In response to the precepts and teachings of Geneva's spiritual leaders, Madame Necker sought to use her wealth for good by cultivating an active role in the provision of public charity. If the world was indeed a mirror reflecting the purpose and ideals of divine grace, as she suggested, then that world had an obligation to aspire to grace. For Madame Necker, a wealthy woman who enjoyed the economic benefits of a successful and politically powerful husband, *bienfaisance* – or charity – was a natural avenue for expressing the civic aspects of her Calvinism.

Madame Necker's extended financial and moral support of impoverished family members and colleagues in Switzerland offers one striking example of her commitment to addressing the needs of the poor and suffering in her community. A newly wealthy woman, she was still clearly able to recall her own family's financial struggles, a social positioning that clearly marked her outsider status within the French elite. As she observed in a letter to an unidentified correspondent: 'I, myself, was born without wealth'.[40] Necker was also disturbed by the immensity of her fortune and by the large expenditures required for the successful realization of an elite existence in Paris. Expressing her discomfort in numerous letters to Madame Réverdil, she touched on topics such as her ineptitude in Parisian high society, the cost of maintaining a home in Paris and her obvious unease at bringing an ailing and suffering aunt to Paris, a woman whose dress, manners and way of speaking would be entirely at odds with the expectations of the world around her.

Necker's charitable programme, initiated with the assistance of Henriette Réverdil and enacted in response to her mother's final wishes, enabled her to respond to the financial needs of a wide array of beleaguered family members, most of them women and children. Among her beneficiaries were the children of the Albert family, two sons and three daughters whom she supported throughout their education and into professional – but socially appropriate – placements in Lausanne. Using connections established during her youth, she sought out appropriate tutors for young M. Albert and morally sound domestic work for the girls. In addition to the Albert children, she supported two aunts: Tante Bellami, who lived in relative isolation and extreme poverty,[41] and Madame Puthod, a devout woman with numerous children and a feckless husband.[42] Finally, she made provision for her family's old and trusted servant, Marion Pellet.[43] In each of these cases, she was concerned not only with economic viability, but also with moral development and she ensured that her funds would be directed with those ends in mind. In 1774, for example, she wrote Madame Réverdil to express concern over the behaviour of Lisette Albert, asking if it might be possible to correct 'the effects of the bad blood she has received'.[44] Madame Necker supported these individuals and families for many years and received regular reports on their progress.

In addition to practising her Calvinist faith on a material level, Madame Necker also reflected on it in a philosophical and moral sense, using the medium of print as a podium for the public display of her Calvinist belief. Particularly relevant are the ideas underpinning her treatise against divorce, the *Réflexions sur le divorce*, written in the last year of her life and published within a few months of her death. The main purpose of the *Réflexions* was to argue against the 1792 French revolutionary law legalizing divorce:

> This dangerous law that authorizes and promotes divorce has just been published. Divisions along party lines were not enough; it was deemed necessary to separate spouses further, isolate children and fight against all natural affections; it is, however, their union that lies at the heart of the nation and protects it; these are the branches of a sacred tree that we cannot continue to separate without leaving its trunk bare and disgraced.[45]

Drawing in particular on republican values that emphasized the role of the family in the construction of society, Madame Necker echoed the sentiments put forward by Burlamaqui, who had also insisted that the family was the basis of national identity. For Suzanne Necker, divorce threatened the stability of society as a whole and, as such, undermined the concept of communal identity so central to Calvinist belief and practice.

On the surface, however, this deeply conservative work appears to align itself with Catholic interdictions against divorce and seems directly to contradict the teachings of Jean Calvin, which specifically allowed for the possibility of divorce. A more probing look at Calvinist practices reveals a very different perspective. Illuminating, in this case, are the dissonances between the basic beliefs underpinning Catholic and reformed understandings of marriage. In the Catholic faith, marriage was understood as a sacrament and the ritual of marriage, as a result, as transformative. The act of marriage was a benediction that removed sin, in the process initiating the couple into the understandings of the Catholic Church as a whole. Like baptism, marriage in the Catholic Church was seen as a confirmation of acceptance into the Catholic faith, with all the benefits and responsibilities this entailed.[46] From this perspective, indissolubility is self-evident: the contract of marriage between man and woman was akin to the union between Christ and the Church. Marriage symbolized not only the commitment of each spouse to the other, but also a parallel commitment of the spouses to the Church and, further, of the Church to Christ.

Calvinist understandings of marriage were very different. First and foremost was Calvin's assertion that marriage was not a sacrament: 'For it is required that a sacrament be not only a word of God but an outward ceremony appointed by God to confirm a promise. Even children will discern that there is no such thing in matrimony.'[47] Calvinist marriage still reflected the union of Christ and the Church, but did not bestow grace. Rather, the Calvinist institution of marriage was more engaged with practical matters: it existed to promote fidelity, to create children and to encourage love between husband and wife. Madame Necker's reasoning thus followed the more concrete understandings of the Calvinist tradition. As Charmarie Jenkins Blaisdell points out, Calvinist marriage served four purposes: it fulfilled social requirements for procreation and child rearing, controlled unruly sexual drives and satisfied human needs for companionship.[48] Accordingly, Madame Necker argued that marriage had to be upheld for the sake of spousal happiness, the happiness of children of the marriage and the maintenance of social conventions.[49]

But there are also other apparent contradictions. The stated purpose of the *Réflexions* – to argue for the indissolubility of marriage – would appear to contravene directly Calvinist civil approaches to the institution of marriage and, in particular, the much-vaunted right to divorce that so clearly delineated the boundaries between Catholic and Calvinist practice. But a closer look at Calvin's practical approach to the dissolution of marriage suggests not only a far more conservative ethos than one might expect, but also a distinctly gendered approach to family values. The 1546 Marriage Ordinance, for example, offers the following directives for the dissolution of marriage: men were able to petition for divorce after one year of desertion; women, meanwhile, had to wait ten, a model that effectively rendered woman-initiated divorce almost impossible to obtain.[50] Calvin also regularly counselled his female adherents *against* divorce, instructing them that the emotional trials and sufferings caused by the actions of an unfaithful spouse could be seen as God's tests of faith and fidelity:

> I easily conceive what sorrows you endure, when you see your yoke-fellow continuing unfaithful to you, and that even after having given you some hope of his amendment, he again returns to his debaucheries of former times. But the consolations which the

Scriptures hold out to us should needs have so much the more power over your heart to alleviate your sadness.[51]

Instead of divorce, Calvin urged patience, devotion and prayer. Ultimately, as Jeffrey Watt observes, Calvin '[believed] that a permanent separation was a travesty of marriage which was unfair to the innocent spouse'.[52]

Given this context, Necker's conservative stance with regard to divorce is not at all surprising, nor does it undermine the essentially Calvinist nature of her work. In view of these conceptual theological differences, Necker's critiques of divorce can be clearly linked to the principles of her Calvinist upbringing, even as they were, ironically, more frequently deployed in favour of Catholic arguments against divorce during the subsequent century.[53]

Necker's charity work and published treatise, both public testaments to her commitment to demonstrate her faith in action, combine to offer a broad picture of her understanding of Calvinist practice and her role as a member of the reformed polity. As public projects, they lent credence and authority to her autobiographical presentations as a woman of faith and piety. At the same time, this position on divorce also had the effect of further distancing her from elite Parisian social conventions and practices. While opinions were shifting, marriage was generally seen as a way of cementing fortunes and building allegiances. The elite approach wholly undermined the sanctity of marriage and subverted the principles of companionship and care that underpinned Calvinist beliefs.

The Consistory Within: Madame Necker's Intimate Theology

Madame Necker's public activities are not, however, the only sources of insight into her moral stance and belief. The thoughts expressed in her *Mélanges* and *Nouveaux mélanges*, together with those shared in letters to Henriette Réverdil, offer an intimate portrait of her personal theology and, as private musings, provide a fascinating counterpoint to the civic manifestations of her belief. This is not to suggest that the two realms of her faith – spiritual and civic – never overlapped. This duality was, in fact, symbiotic. Her civic duties enabled her to recognize her spiritual duties and to envision the possibility of paradise. Her acknowledgement of human suffering, for example, allowed her to practise her virtue, thus bringing her closer to an ideal spiritual relationship with God. 'How religion changes the tableau of life!' she exclaimed, 'Sorrows, even those of the body, are the prediction of a new existence: our shortcomings and those of others offer us two ways to exercise our virtues; thus paradise is already in our thoughts'.[54]

Most remarkable, in this regard, are the intimate, reflective epistles she wrote directly to God. These letters, of which only a few remain, suggest that Necker developed a highly personal relationship with God, a relationship characterized by supreme introspection. They reveal an intense desire to attain a position of deep spiritual communion, and the conviction that such communion was possible only after death. These letters are characterized by loss, longing and desperate isolation. While Madame Necker recognized the power of divine grace, she was intimately aware of the immense chasm that separated her from God: 'I adore you and raise myself up to you. My love will dissolve the distance that separates us; it is as immense as [the distance between us].'[55] Taking a position of submissive abjection, she fully acknowledged the depth and magnitude of her moral failings, recognizing herself as a weak being corporeally marked by her suffering and wholly undeserving of divine grace and intervention:

> What, then, will I leave behind ... a half-worn machine that seems to remind me daily of its impending departure, that rejects all of my feelings, offering suggestions that run contrary to my reason. If this is your will; oh! My God, end without pain a life that you have filled with your most special favours, but which is poisoned by remorse, memories, disdain and ingratitude ... My God, please bestow upon your creature a look of benevolence and forgive the rashness of her prayer.[56]

More significant is the undercurrent of isolation and alienation that characterized her devotional relationship. In her letters, Necker evoked the paradoxical loneliness of moral struggle: only God could help her recover, but she was unworthy of his grace. 'I am at the source of happiness, but it escapes far away from me like a rapidly running river, and will soon be lost in an unknown canyon.'[57]

This was, without a doubt, a confessional relationship: Madame Necker was deeply aware of her personal transgressions and longed to overcome them. However, it differed significantly from a Catholic penitential relationship. Necker did not confess her sins to an anonymous church leader in the quiet isolation and security of the confessional, but rather carried her moral weaknesses within her own body. Her confessional acts, as autobiographical gestures, were corporeally imprinted in such a way that the sufferings of her body reflected the moral anguish to which she subjected herself. Necker's close friend Thomas linked her illnesses with her desire to fulfil her various duties: 'I fear, madame, that you are not doing all that is necessary to restore your health. I fear, for you, this activity which you perform out of duty, which consumes you, and makes you constantly sacrifice yourself to those you love.'[58] One could argue that Madame Necker, acting as judge and jury, internalized the juridical power of the Consistory. In this sense, she was her own confessor, a stance that curiously mirrors the intense self-scrutiny that accompanied the actualization of the elite social ideal. Witness to her personal transgressions, Necker was also the author of her own self-inflicted exile.

Madame Necker's intimate theology, a relationship with God founded on her experience of loss and read through the memory of her beloved mother, exemplifies what Calvin defined as the continuous internal struggle of the reformed believer. Calvin perceived a paradoxical relationship between the individual and God. While this relationship was oppositional, it was also, at the same time, symbiotic. On the one hand, God was perceived as the author of good, and the individual, filled with sin, as necessarily the author of evil.[59] On the other, the reformed individual was a part of God, and therefore, enveloped in his grace. Indeed, as Calvin observed:

> We are not our own: in so far as we can, let us therefore forget ourselves and all that is ours. Conversely, we are God's: let us therefore live for him and die for him. We are God's: let his wisdom and will therefore rule all our actions. We are God's: let all the part of our life accordingly strive toward him as our only lawful goal.[60]

These thoughts are echoed in Suzanne Necker's private writings: 'Our soul is one; it has been made to follow a single idea, just as our heart has been designed to love only one person'.[61]

Calvin's approach suggests a tension between two parallel realms: the unfortunate reality of a fallible and inevitably flawed earthly realm, the site of human suffering in which the reformed believer sought grace through the enactment of civic and religious duties, and the inherent purity of the spiritual realm, the longed-for site of divine grace and communion with God. As Calvin pointed out: 'There are in man, so to speak, two worlds, over which different kings and different laws have authority'.[62]

This split was perhaps most evident in the human body itself, which Calvin's theology posited as the site of the essential and irrevocable rupture between the spiritual and earthly realms.[63] This body, created in the image of God as proof of God's grace and evidence of his power, was a sacred space, referred to by Madame Necker as 'a mirror that reflects the idea and the views of the Divinity'.[64] It was, at the same time, permanently sullied by the inevitable human weakness which resulted from the Fall. In Calvin's words:

> The unfortunate [believer], wanting to be something in himself, incontinent, begins to forget and ignore from whence the source of good in his life comes, and through outrageous ingratitude, begins to raise and elevate himself and take pride in himself against his maker and author of all of his graces.[65]

The lived-in body, positioned at the intersection between divine grace and the Fall, was, therefore, an inherently troubled space. The nature of this encounter could be mediated through the believer's dedicated participation in the religious and civic duties deemed essential to the realization of the faith, but these activities failed to reconcile the fundamental contradiction of the human condition as defined by Calvinism. The human individual, conceived in Calvinist theology as an essentially communitarian being responsible not only for her own salvation but also for the redemption of her community as a whole, thus sought to achieve grace through the very relationships that corrupted her.

What this conflict suggests is a subtle and complex interplay between the forces of exile, longing and communion. By postulating a rupture between the spiritual and earthly worlds, Calvin put religious believers in a position of misery, a space of exile from which they sought a deliverance that they were never fully able to achieve. The forced exile of the Calvinist believer, as exemplified in the moral abjection of the human body, can be likened to a form of spiritual purgatory. In this ill-defined space between heaven and hell, the believer was tortured by the irreconcilable split between believer and creator, and so experienced an intense – if ultimately futile – desire for communion, or wholeness. The believer's material existence, mandated by God, was simultaneously that which denied her full communion with God and that which enabled the relationship to exist at all. Divine grace remained out of reach until death and even then was uncertain.

Exile, Longing and the Desire for Communion

At a concrete level, the exile and longing of French Calvinists appear to have manifested themselves in the form of diasporic wanderings. Forcibly exiled from the legal and juridical rights accorded to Catholics, French Calvinists were wholly denied the rights of citizenship and many were forced to seek safety elsewhere. Such was the case of the hundreds of thousands of adherents of the reformed faith who fled France during the late seventeenth and early eighteenth centuries. A closer look at Madame Necker's maternal heritage, in particular the experiences of her mother and grandfather, is illustrative in this regard. The Albert family hailed from the Dauphiné region, a well-recognized Protestant stronghold.[66] By the late seventeenth century, the family was well established in Montélimar. Jean Albert worked as a lawyer and his wife, Magdeleine Répara, brought a dowry of 6,300 *livres* to her marriage.[67] Their two daughters – Magdeleine and Anne – were born within a few years of their marriage. The family might well have stayed in Montélimar had it not been for the ever-increasing persecutions related to the Revocation of the Edict of Nantes.

The Edict of Fontainebleau, more commonly referred to as the Revocation of the Edict of Nantes, was handed down in October 1685 by Louis XIV. It overturned the premise of toleration enshrined in the 1598 Edict of Nantes and introduced a series of stringent measures designed to suppress the spread of the Protestant faith in France. Protestants were no longer permitted to practise their religion or baptize or educate their children in a Protestant manner and Protestant ministers were banished from the kingdom. Punishments were severe, ranging from fines for refusing to baptize children as Catholics, to imprisonment and death for practising the faith. Those who chose to leave France incurred significant financial losses, since, under the Revocation, all abandoned properties were to be confiscated after four months. This ordinance was subsequently followed by even more stringent proclamations. One of Louis XIV's final acts, an ordinance delivered in March 1715, was a severe blow to adherents of the reformed faith. In it, he declared that only Catholics could be buried in consecrated ground and further, that only children born to baptized Catholics were legitimate children.[68] Finally, in 1724, an even more repressive decree declared Protestant marriage rites invalid, defined Protestant wives as concubines of questionable morals and reaffirmed the status of Protestant children as bastards.[69]

Magdeleine Albert and her father left France sometime between 1720 and 1723 in the face of mounting persecutions. Magdeleine's sister, Anne, meanwhile, remained in Montélimar in an attempt to retain control of the family property. The family continued to suffer difficulties as a result of the persecutions. After Anne's death, the family property and inheritance were sequestered, became only partially accessible in 1732, and were finally recovered in 1758 by a family member who was able to produce a 'Certificate of Catholicity'.[70] Magdeleine Curchod was, however, unable to recover these funds – and so benefit from them after the death of her husband – before her own death. Instead, after extensive negotiations that involved diplomatic interventions on the part of close family friends, Suzanne Curchod travelled to Montélimar to claim this inheritance in 1763, just a few months after her mother died.[71] The inheritance, which consisted of property and material goods that Curchod's relative finally received permission to sell in November 1764, amounted to 9,200 *livres* payable in annual instalments to 'Mademoiselle Suzanne Curchod, bourgeoise of Echalens and Lausanne, formerly living in Crassy, Vaud, as the sole daughter and heir of Louis-Antoine Curchod'.[72]

The Revocation had far-reaching implications. In 1685, there were between 730,000 and 850,000 adherents of the reformed church living in France.[73] Together they made up just under 5 per cent of the population. Of this group, around 200,000 decided to leave France, seeking exile in such countries as Switzerland, The Netherlands, Great Britain, Germany and Ireland. This mass emigration, which reached its peak in 1687, was to continue until well into the eighteenth century. The immensity of this migration – over 45,000 Huguenot refugees travelled through Switzerland between 1680 and 1700 alone – had a deep effect on the Calvinist identity and profoundly influenced Calvinist understandings of community. While Switzerland was perhaps perceived as a haven by Huguenots fleeing the restrictions and persecutions that followed the Revocation, it was not a safe or secure haven. A somewhat ill-balanced group of thirteen independent states, Switzerland was divided by religion. The Huguenot refugee crisis exacerbated pre-existing tensions and, in addition to this, the sheer num-

bers of asylum seekers placed an enormous strain on the small communities that
bordered Lake Geneva. As a result, the Protestant Swiss cantons did not entirely
welcome the refugees. Conceding to the concerns of their Catholic compatriots
and faced with an influx of thousands of impoverished migrants, most of whom
required charitable assistance in some form or another, the reformed cantons
did not encourage settlement. Not only did they limit the number of refugees
allowed to enter the territories, they also insisted that the migrants' stay in Switzerland was temporary only and redirected them to other countries, particularly
Germany and The Netherlands.[74]

The Revocation of the Edict of Nantes offers one powerful example of the
material effects of religious persecution. The mass exodus that resulted coloured
Protestant experience in France, where remaining reformed believers were forced
underground, and it fundamentally transformed the city of Geneva and the
neighbouring *pays de Vaud*. Protestant families, like the Alberts, were divided,
their lives uprooted, fortunes appropriated and cultural traditions often lost.

Involuntary exile and the diasporic existence have generally been equated
with the experience of forcible loss. The *Oxford English Dictionary* associates
exile with such terms as 'enforced removal' and 'banishment',[75] words which res-
onate strongly with French eighteenth-century understandings of the term. But
exile can also be self-imposed, a chosen space for the performance of alterity; in
effect an internalization of exile, whereby suffering, incurred through the experience of exile and loss, becomes intrinsic to an exile's identity.

As Madame Necker's writing demonstrates, this state of mind was tempting
for the Calvinist believer. Madame Necker argued that suffering was integral to
her religious belief:

> In a mind subject to divine will, the habit of suffering still produces certain moral
> changes, and fools witnesses, who assume the lessening of pain; but they do not see
> that we learn to shoulder the persecution of pain, like those of a stranger from whom
> we will very soon be separated.[76]

According to this view, loss and suffering were essential to Madame Necker's
experience of Calvinism, but are also temporary conditions that preceded the
spiritual union and 'homecoming' only realized after death.

In this sense, exile must be re-evaluated. In Madame Necker's case, exile
transformed into acceptance might be productively understood as a process
of abjection whereby loss became synonymous with desire and was manifest
through longing, something that Belden C. Lane considers an essential part of
the reformed believer's journey of faith.[77] The Calvinist believer who fled France
in order to practise her faith was not only fleeing externally imposed religious
prosecution, but also consciously seeking exile, a mechanism whereby alterity
was actively courted as a way of acknowledging and performing difference. Situated at the intersection between loss and longing, expulsion and desire, the

Calvinist believer took on a posture of spiritual abjection. Because alterity was chosen, this diasporic existence of the persecuted Calvinist became integral to her experience and autobiographical identity. Exile, consciously chosen, paved the way for a radical reconceptualization of identity, and, in the case of Calvinism, of community and nation as well.

Madame Necker regularly invoked the idea of a spiritual *patrie* in her letters. Using this 'imagined community' as a way of distancing herself from French associates and the nation she once identified as 'this ungrateful country',[78] she also deployed the term in relation to her Calvinist belief.[79] But while she invoked the idea of national boundaries, the Calvinist communion was, for her, defined not by physical boundaries, but rather by a religious belief that informed both civic and spiritual spheres. As Calvin observed:

> Let us first consider that there is a twofold government in man: one aspect is spiritual, whereby the conscience is instructed in piety and in reverencing god; the second is political, whereby man is educated for the duties of humanity and citizenship that must be maintained among men ... The former resides in the inner mind, while the latter regulates only outward behavior.[80]

In other words, the nation of Calvinism, while conceptualized on an abstract level by Calvinists as a single spiritual community of believers under God, was 'another country'. But at the same time, this spiritual community was physically realized in the form of the nation, with Geneva as its capital. As a result, the Calvinist identity could potentially pose a powerful threat to Catholic French national identity, stability and coherence. The continuing persecution of French Huguenots well into the eighteenth century suggests that the French state was aware of this threat.

This became important during the eighteenth century, a period during which the rigorous understandings of sixteenth-century Genevan Calvinism gave way to largely aristocratic understandings of social relationships and customs. While Genevan religious and civic leaders continued to espouse Calvin's perspectives on issues of divine grace, they moved from an understanding of the individual as proof of divine grace to a broader understanding of society as a whole as evidence of providence. Society, suggested the jurist Jean-Jacques Burlamaqui, was created not by man, but by an act of God, which, 'by the assistance that men draw from one another, provides for them all of their knowledge, all of their comforts and pleasures that form the security, happiness and the charm of life!'[81] Burlamaqui, like Rousseau, regarded the family as the fundamental unit of society and further, of the nation itself, observing that this basic unit was 'the most natural and the most time-honoured of all, and it serves as the foundation for the national society: because a people or a nation is nothing but a combination of many families'.[82]

In Madame Necker's letters, the idea of nation or homeland was associated mainly with the physical space of Switzerland, in particular the Vaud region (including her hometown of Crassier and Lausanne) and Geneva. For Madame

Necker, situated in cosmopolitan Paris, this exile resulted in a sense of physical dislocation that brought on illness. Indeed, she identified homesickness as one cause for her ill health, noting that 'I need the air of my homeland'.[83] As will be demonstrated in subsequent chapters, Madame Necker's illnesses came to embody her social, cultural and religious alienation from the Parisian social sphere, functioning as a barometer of her spiritual dislocation and a conscious marker of her difference.

Patrie was also linked with the idea of spiritual belonging, however, in the sense that civic and religious duties were seen as necessary – and indistinguishable – from one another. Paris provided the laboratory in which Madame Necker could test her own beliefs against those of her French neighbours:

> The system of certain philosophers tends to extinguish all interests by cooling all emotions: religion, piety, filial respect, conjugal love, love of the homeland; in their books, all of the important things in life, except for cold drinks and warm meals and so forth, are destroyed, a situation which cannot produce many great men.[84]

Since religious duty was inextricably tied to patriotic duty, the obligations of the physical world could never be separated from the parallel obligations to the spiritual world. As Necker confirmed, 'For those who can think, this world is [everywhere] a mirror that reflects the idea and the views of the Divinity'.[85] What this statement demonstrates is that the experience of exile was paradoxical, in that it embodied not only rupture, but also desire.

The idea of the nation, or communion, became extremely important in the development of Calvinism, particularly in the relationship between Calvinist practice and religious persecution: for many believers, their only 'home' was the spiritual home of the reformed faith. This consideration, combined with Calvin's strong assertion of the contradictory relationships – antagonistic and symbiotic – between spiritual and civic spheres, enabled the idea of Calvinist doctrine and spiritual practice as a form of nation, one nation, indeed, under God. In this sense, 'nation' became inextricably linked with ideas of faith, duty and reform.

The physical state of the nation, while necessarily important in terms of one's geographic location and grounding, was nonetheless of less relevance than the spiritual communion shared by reformers of the Protestant diaspora. Nevertheless, the experiences of Madame Necker demonstrate that display, exile, longing and communion – characteristics intrinsic to the Calvinist refugee experience and to the practice of spiritual abjection – continued to mark and otherwise influence Calvinist understandings of the relationship between God, self and nation throughout the eighteenth century. They also shaped Madame Necker's filial and maternal experiences, as the next chapter demonstrates.

3 FILIAL DUTY AND THE MATERNAL BODY

[T]he daughter is for her mother at once her double and another person, the mother is at once overweeningly affectionate and hostile toward her daughter; she saddles her child with her own destiny: a way of proudly laying claim to her own femininity and also a way of revenging herself for it.[1]

Madame, permit me to finish [this letter] by assuring you of my most tender affection; this will be the last letter that I will have the honour of writing you before I have doubled my being, or, in other words, before I have brought forth a new heart to love you; I feel that my child must share the sentiments of her mother.[2]

The Calvinist reform had profound implications for women's lives, many of which were appealing. In certain respects, the source of this appeal can easily be discerned. Women were central to the reformed polity. Calvin's theological approach offered them equal opportunity for spiritual communion with God and, on an earthly level, expanded their role in the family. Under Calvin's leadership, marriage and family became central elements of the reformed faith. The moral transformation initiated by the Calvinist reformation resulted in women's access to more extensive legal rights, including greater access to public education and the right to petition for divorce on the grounds of adultery or desertion.

There were also significant inconsistencies in the Calvinist approach. The increased focus on marriage, combined with the dissolution of convents and the move away from Marian worship, left women less able to realize themselves outside the conventional marriage framework.[3] In addition to this, while women enjoyed increased presence and power within domestic relationships, they were not allowed a public voice in Calvinist theology; rather, their roles were almost entirely circumscribed by the domestic concerns of the private sphere. As a result, the reformed church became strongly identified as a paternalistic institution from which women, at an official level, were virtually excised.[4] As John Lee Thompson explains:

As a consequence of both creation and fall ... woman is subjected to man and is restricted to the private sphere: she is not to teach, preach, or lead – a lesson taught not only by scripture, Calvin says, but by nature and custom as well ... On the other

hand, Calvin also teaches woman's equality with man, an equality which is manifested in their common humanity, their equality in sin and grace.[5]

These fundamental contradictions translated into legal double standards and
theologically-based interdictions for women. The established institutions of the
Calvinist religion continued to propagate the idea of women's infidelity and
inherent untrustworthiness, thus cultivating and nourishing generally held beliefs
about women's apparently deserved exclusion from the institutions of power.[6]

The contradictions and tensions between spiritual equality and earthly sub-
ordination were most clearly manifest in the reproductive female body. On the
one hand, the maternal ideal was one of the prime sites of Calvinist potential.
Richard Greaves points out that the virgin birth allowed for the possibility of
moral and corporeal purity, thus '[exalting] the status of motherhood'.[7] Furthermore, the mother encapsulated both spiritual and civic ideals. Her reproductive
body, the space in which the abstract notions of God, self and nation converged
in the form of the child, represented a concrete manifestation of devotion and
offered the promise of everlasting life.

As the natural guardians of the domestic sphere, women assumed prominence within the family of God as a whole: they were the mothers who, as
guardians and teachers of morality, ensured the propagation and dissemination of the faith from generation to generation and acted as guarantors of their
husbands' fidelity.[8] On the other hand, the maternal body was a fundamentally
troubled entity whose earthly presence confirmed the abjection of the Fall.[9] As
the concrete symbol of original sin, the female body represented the impossibil-
ity of divine grace and the futility of human efforts to guarantee salvation. The
pregnant body evoked dangerous moral afflictions such as lust and seduction
and, if the woman was not married, manifested concrete proof of illicit sexual
activity. Raymond A. Mentzer observes that: 'among the surest and plainest evidence of sexual misconduct was an unwed woman who was pregnant or who
had recently given birth'.[10] Each act of divine creation, in other words, implied
a concomitant sexual act associated with sin. The mother, positioned abjectly
between the divine and the diabolical, was, therefore, the site of Calvinist exile.

From this perspective of contradiction and ambiguity, then, I want to continue where the previous chapter left off: from externally imposed exile, I turn
now to internally experienced exile. More specifically, this chapter explores the
nature and function of Suzanne Necker's performance of maternal abjection.
Key to this analysis is the troubled relationship between the elite social body,
which fostered Madame Necker's literary desires and ambitions, and the Calvinist body, imprinted with the legacy of original sin. The principles of social display,
described in the first chapter, were deployed by Madame Necker in the service
of the domestic, maternal body, a process whereby the public presentation of the

Calvinist maternal self in the space of the salon was also simultaneously an act of pious devotion through which she attempted to display her fidelity to God's will. I argue that Madame Necker's salon, as the site of the abject, takes on a dual role in this analysis. Emerging as a space in which virtue could be displayed, it served also as a stage for the evocation of moral failure. Calvinist exile, longing and communion, introduced in the previous chapter, are thus, in this chapter, reassessed through the maternal body and then explored through the lens of French eighteenth-century understandings of motherhood.

In this chapter, I focus in particular on the intersection between Madame Necker's understanding of herself as a dutiful daughter and her expectations and experiences of the maternal relationship she later crafted with her own daughter, Anne-Louise-Germaine Necker, later Madame de Staël. Locating Madame Necker in the tenuous space between mother and daughter, I argue that her perceived filial neglect of her mother is critical to understanding her subsequent maternal relationship with her daughter. As she tried to reconcile her familial duties towards her mother and daughter with her human ambitions and desires, she struggled to maintain her relationship with God and to cultivate the virtuous existence she understood as essential to the attainment of true happiness. Fully aware of her personal failings, however, she recognized that this struggle was ultimately futile, thus condemning herself to a position of eternal abjection, a hellish purgatory where duty and desire became indistinguishable from one another and from which she felt she could never escape. Central to this discussion are eighteenth-century understandings of virtue and, more specifically, the complex relationships between filial duty and maternal desire that played themselves out on the virtuous reproductive body.

Introducing Virtue

Madame Necker's name was regularly associated with virtue. She was recognized for her charitable acts, her public devotion to her husband and her commitment and dedication to her daughter's upbringing. Jacques Necker painted his wife wholly in terms of domestic virtue, linking his life companion to the sensibilities of the private sphere: succour, support and understanding.[11] Her virtue consisted of her inherent selflessness and generosity, qualities he attributed to her strict moral code and her intense and indomitable reformed religious belief.[12]

The comments of Madame Necker's friends and contemporaries were similarly effusive. The philosopher and academician Antoine Léonard Thomas lauded her virtuous behaviour and celebrated her moral character, describing her as a uniquely virtuous individual in a sea of moral decrepitude and excess,[13] while the philosopher and *encyclopédiste* Denis Diderot reflected on what he perceived to be her innate capacity for responding to the needs of others. Comparing Madame Necker's first annual report from the Hospice de charité with her husband's *Compte rendu*, Diderot identified Madame Necker's tenderness and generosity as perfect foils to Jacques Necker's heroic public dignity:

> I wanted a copy of *The Hospice* in order to combine it with the *Compte Rendu*, so as to encompass in one volume the two most interesting works I have ever and that I could ever read. In one I saw justice, truth, courage, dignity, reason and genius using all of their forces to restrict the tyranny of powerful men; while in the other benevolence and pity extend their helpful hands on behalf of some of mankind's most pitiful, the sick and destitute.[14]

Virtue was a central tenet of Enlightenment thought. Theorized by intellectuals as diverse as Rousseau, Diderot and Bernardin de St Pierre, it was nevertheless a nebulous concept that remained notoriously difficult to define. While the accolades accorded to Madame Necker, with their celebrations of morality, piety, generosity and sensibility, offer some pertinent insights into the matter, they do not tell the whole story.

Traditionally, virtue was a masculine ideal, a construct which drew on a Latin and Roman heritage.[15] The republican virtue in antiquity was also an inherently political concept, linked to ideas of national identity and civic responsibility. During the eighteenth century, new understandings emerged. In a general sense, the eighteenth-century thinker understood virtue as an innate human capacity for goodness which manifested itself in the fulfilment of duties and obligations. As Romilly, author of the article 'Vertu (*Ord. encyclop. Mor. Polit.*)', in the *Encyclopédie*, wrote: 'but ultimately, what is virtue? briefly, it is *the constant observation of the laws which are imposed upon us, for whatever respect a man applies to himself*.'[16] For Romilly, the idea of virtue described a state of constant attention and awareness, in which one focused one's gaze entirely on the needs of others. To Romilly's extended discussion, Louis de Jaucourt introduced religious, mythological and gendered elements.[17] Observing the word's association with the celestial, the supernatural and the miraculous, as well as with such qualities as chastity and modesty, Jaucourt's definitions suggest direct links to gendered religious practice, moral duty and, ultimately, spiritual communion.

Read in conjunction with the republican ideals of antiquity, the eighteenth-century model manifested itself in the so-called 'man of virtue', who possessed integrity, independence, fidelity, sensibility and civic responsibility and who, as Marisa Linton observes, 'took his familial obligations with the utmost seriousness and was an exemplary father, son and husband'.[18] Eighteenth-century virtue thus involved both a civic and a domestic component, each integral to the realization of the other.

This interlocking relationship between political and domestic virtue echoes what eighteenth-century thinkers began to perceive as the complementary relationship between the sexes. Just as men were perceived to be naturally designed to lead public lives and women naturally formed for domestic existences dedicated to the care and raising of children and the maintenance of the family, the sexes were destined to embody similarly complementary understandings of virtue. This complementarity takes on immense importance in the work of Rousseau, who made virtue a central tenet of his political thought. For Rousseau, virtue was an all-encompassing endeavour in which the heroic masculine dignity of political virtue, paired with the modest generosity and demure feminine humility of domestic virtue, was realized in the innate moral goodness of the child, who represented the hope and potential of the virtuous republican society.[19]

While the success of Rousseau's tripartite system of virtue was wholly dependent upon the fortuitous alignment of the individual parts, Rousseau's virtuous polity placed considerable power in women's hands. As corporeal entities, they were at once the linchpin of social reform and its weakest link. As the physical incubators of the republic of virtue they assumed full moral responsibility for human creation. Their bodies became public property, subject to the gaze of the patriarchal state. In the process, the female body was entirely reconceived: gendered Rousseauist virtue entailed, in Carol Blum's words: 'the reabsorption of the sexually active woman into the lactating mother, [and] the substitution of a nutritive for a genital function'.[20] The reproductive female body, appropriated to civic ends, enabled the practice of domestic feminine virtue. The message was clear: virtue, appropriately channelled, could transform society. This model of domestic virtue – presented in the form of the reproductive body and commandeered in the service of the state – is perhaps most convincingly portrayed in Rousseau's evocation of Julie d'Etanges, the heroine of his eponymous novel *Julie, ou la Nouvelle Héloïse*. In *Julie*, Rousseau painted a picture of reclaimed virtue, presenting Julie as a woman whose renunciation of illicit and passionate love in favour of a relatively bland life of domestic duty reduced her liberty but increased her virtue. As Marisa Linton has observed: '[Julie] is transfigured: as wife, mother, friend, mistress of the household and benefactress of the villagers, she generates sublime virtue all around her and becomes the emotional heart of the idyllic little community at Clarens'.[21]

Because virtue resided at the intersection between the public and domestic spheres, it was a difficult concept to categorize. Thinkers such as Rousseau imagined a direct correlation between the family and the state, thus imbuing the private sphere with political import and the public with domestic sensibility, even as, paradoxically, the two realms became ever more separate and distinct from one another. This public/private divide highlights the contradictions inherent in the gendering of virtue. The performance of manly virtue, an essentially narcissistic endeavour, required the theatricality of the public stage and the concentrated gaze of the enlightened spectator. Womanly virtue, however, called for humility, modesty, sacrifice and domesticity. It was, therefore, performed in the shadows, by which I mean to suggest that the successful practice of femininity entailed not only a woman's complete dedication to the domestic concerns of home and family, and, as a result, her virtual absence from the public sphere, but also a modesty that required the veiling of her successful accomplishment of her duties. The successful performance of womanly virtue thus depended on a careful negotiation of social and cultural conventions that otherwise limited and controlled women's experiences and behaviours.

Gendered understandings of virtue, therefore, reinforced the social and cultural realities of the female condition during this period and, on a philosophical level, complemented pre-existing theories of sexual difference. Feminine virtue encouraged piety, devotion, humility and chastity and promised women, as domestic moral guides, a leading role in social and cultural reform. Just as the family was the foundation of the virtuous society, so too were women – as wives and mothers – the nucleus of the virtuous family.

This split between masculine public and feminine private virtue is key to understanding Madame Necker's psychic malaise.[22] On the one hand, she fully adhered to the tenets of feminine virtue. All evidence suggests that she was committed to her home, fully faithful to her husband and completely dedicated to her daughter. Virtue is a common theme in her *Mélanges* and *Nouveaux mélanges* and central to her correspondence with intimate friends. In addition, her piety and its concrete manifestation in the form of numerous charitable initiatives provide substantial proof of her concern for the moral and physical well-being of others in her community. From this perspective then, Necker emerges as an innately virtuous being who fully merited the enthusiastic accolades of her contemporaries and subsequent biographers.

From another perspective, however, she did not at all comply with the requirements of feminine virtue. On a public level, her role as *salonnière*, while integral to elite sociability, was viewed by some as a fundamental transgression of the virtuous ideal and, as such, a subversion of the virtuous social order. Rousseau, for example, famously imagined the salon woman as an indolent creature whose very presence in the public sphere threatened heroic republican masculinity.[23] Madame Necker's role in the area of hospital reform was similarly viewed with some suspicion. The virulent commentary of Joseph Weber accused Madame Necker of political conspiracy designed with the sole purpose of agitating the lower classes against the supposed intransigence of the government, even as the virtues she espoused fully conformed to normative gender conventions.[24]

Gendered eighteenth-century understandings of virtue left little room for feminine ambition or desire and the transgressive woman, the object of public criticism, was disparaged by women and men alike.[25] The case of the Marquise du Châtelet offers one pertinent example of this process. The Marquise's decision to devote her life to intellectual accomplishment was met with unease. Madame du Deffand's satirical portrait of her colleague is revealing:

> she had worked so hard to appear to be what she was not that we no longer know what she actually is. Her faults themselves are perhaps not natural to her, but could arise from her pretentions; her rudeness and lack of consideration are like those of a princess; her coldness and inattentiveness those of a bluestocking; her shrill laughter, her grimaces and contortions are those of a beautiful woman.[26]

Just as Rousseau's salon woman threatened to undermine the fundamental principles of natural sexual difference, so too did the Marquise du Châtelet's intellectual ambitions subvert gendered understandings of social relations.

The tension between Madame Necker's apparent domestic virtue and her literary and social ambitions was equally controversial. The commentary of Madame de Genlis is particularly incisive:

> A woman so Christian, with such high principles, should naturally have modesty and sincerity; but the disproportionate ambition of a brilliant celebrity cannot but alter in large measure one's taste and character in this respect. How much has she poured into projects she did not like at all and lavished upon people whom she could not respect in order to be praised?[27]

More telling than the critiques of her contemporaries, however, were Madame Necker's internal struggles. She did not consider herself to be a virtuous being and her various writings attest to a strong sense of Calvinist culpability. She perceived her filial neglect and her desire for literary success as moral failures, instances of personal weakness which undermined her virtue. Continually chastising herself for activities left unfinished and obligations left incomplete, she initiated an elaborate programme of personal reform and dedicated herself to balance and control.[28] Among her various activities in this regard was her *Journal de la dépense de mon temps* – a time-management journal – in which she outlined, in detail, each of her obligations and the amount of time she could accord to them.[29] She also engaged in an extensive process of critical self-reflection, crafting a rational life that accorded with the Calvinist principles of her youth. To judge from her various writings, however, these activities were to no avail, for she remained wholly unconvinced of her inherent worthiness or right to salvation.[30]

Much of Madame Necker's moral discouragement had to do with her definition of virtue and her understanding of its implications in society. Like her contemporaries, Madame Necker espoused an all-encompassing perspective which included both the heroic qualities of masculine virtue and the gentleness, purity and grace of feminine virtue. She observed, for example, that her husband's public virtue derived from a balance between his civic commitments as a leading actor in the French administration and the simple values of his childhood.[31] At the same time, she adhered to conventional understandings of feminine virtue, imagining womanly virtue as a hidden jewel carefully swathed in feminine humility:

> Happy are the women who have long understood the necessity of masking their merit with simplicity and modesty and who have taught this secret to others before knowing it themselves! Happy are those who have known how to make themselves loved, before being tempted and who have learned early on that the quiet example is the most useful of all![32]

Like Rousseau, she stressed the inherently practical nature of virtue: 'We are more fond of virtue when we practice it than when we paint it; this continual practice of virtue seems to call the divine presence into being more often and also gives a grandeur and breadth to the small things in life.'[33] But she also took these ideals further. Virtue, Necker believed, was intrinsic to spiritual salvation,[34] and, therefore, directly linked to human happiness.[35] In this framework, virtue emerged from the dedicated practice of one's duties, a process through which one attained the pure happiness of spiritual communion. 'It is impossible to exaggerate the pleasures that one receives from the accomplishment of one's duties', she explained.[36] As a gift of the Supreme Being, virtue was analogous to divine grace and required a posture of humble obeisance and active sacrifice, acts of devotion which demonstrated one's selfless commitment to a greater good. 'We do not at all cool towards these duties by multiplying them', she argued, 'This continual exercise of virtue seems most often to beckon the divine presence and thus gives both a grand character and semblance of scope to small things.'[37]

Madame Necker believed that the individual's journey towards virtue could be monitored through the practice of one's duties and the cultivation of an ordered inner environment. Self-control, which can be understood as the careful management of one's otherwise unruly passions and unseemly ambitions and desires, was fundamental to a life of virtue, enabling a constant and continual self-surveillance that challenged the individual to live up to the highest moral standards: 'We must focus our attention on this secret work within ourselves, and teach ourselves to understand better the agent that presides therein'.[38] Necker believed that self-control enabled resistance to vice and a concentrated focus on duty, both of which would lead naturally to a life of moral purity. While suffering and struggle were integral to the quest for virtue, the honouring of one's duties was, for Necker, a blessing that offered transformative potential in the form of a true happiness that she equated with the experience of unencumbered spiritual communion. Indeed, for Madame Necker, virtue was the 'secret of happiness'.[39] She observed that:

> Virtue depends on our efforts, which the Supreme Being always favours. It gives us hope of returning to those who are no longer with us: each day the fulfilment of all of

our duties increases the affection and esteem of those whom we love; a healthy mind and a strict diet fortify the constitution; and as we are endowed with youth, beauty and talents, so must we always lose them to old age and death. Only virtue grants us all the gifts linked to immortality.[40]

Necker's reflections offer an abstract conceptualization of virtue's place within the spiritual framework. However, the reality of the human condition – the misery-laden experience of unchecked moral vice brought about by original sin – rendered Necker's theoretical formulations fundamentally unattainable at a practical level. Calvinist doctrine, to recall the previous chapter, envisaged all believers as sinners who actively participated in their own downfall through their indiscriminate actions. While the Lutheran tradition held such a rupture to be recuperable, since Luther preached salvation by faith alone, for Calvinism, such a project was essentially impossible to realize. The five principles of the Calvinist faith outlined the believer's position of absolute and irrevocable sin and confirmed that God alone had the power to bestow salvation on select members of his flock.[41]

The dictates of Calvinist theology suggest that in this system, Madame Necker's moral struggle was fundamentally unwinnable. Unlike Rousseau, who argued for the innate goodness of the individual and thus set the stage for redemption, Madame Necker did not believe that virtue, once lost, could be recovered. While she fully acknowledged Rousseau as a leading proponent of virtue,[42] she remained, nevertheless, entirely unconvinced by his vision of virtue as embodied in the character of Julie d'Etanges. Necker argued that Julie was not a moral being, because she established her virtue on a foundation of vice.[43] Julie's only virtue emerged from her recognition of her moral weaknesses, but even this was partial and could never lead to true happiness. As Necker observed: 'I don't think that I can repeat this point too often: this mixture of vice and virtue is extremely dangerous as it only embellishes vice and diminishes the charms of virtue'.[44]

Necker's belief in the absolute purity of virtue, as a quality that could not be recovered after an initial instance of moral weakness or failure, recalls the punitive consequences of Calvinist understandings of original sin. I would argue that the doomed wanderings and eternal quests of the Calvinist believer are essential to understanding her life. This commitment to absolute moral purity governed Necker's relationship with her mother, directly informed the one she later developed with her daughter and underpinned her performance of maternal abjection. It also sheds more light on the conflicted relationship between her literary ambitions and her maternal duty and suggests how she may have perceived the troubling slippage between her roles as *salonnière* and mother. While such an internal struggle might be considered characteristic of the Calvinist condition broadly speaking, I would argue that the case of Suzanne Necker offers an extreme example, particularly as it played itself out within the maternal body, the intimate corporeal space in which divine potential – through the act of creation –

encountered human fallibility and desire. As noted previously, the maternal body symbolized the irrevocability of original sin in that each act of divine creation engendered a concomitant act of sin. Divine grace, once lost, was irredeemable.

Virtue and the Good Mother

On the evening of 18 April 1766, Suzanne finished a letter to her close friend Etienette Clavel de Brenles:

> Madame, permit me to finish [this letter] by assuring you of my most tender affection; this will be the last letter that I will have the honour of writing you before I have doubled my being, or, in other words, before I've brought forth a new heart to love you; I feel that my child must share the sentiments of her mother.[45]

Madame Necker was right. Her daughter, Anne-Louise-Germaine, was born just four days later, on 22 April 1766.

Madame Necker described her long and gruelling labour in her next letter to Madame de Brenles. Drawing on religious and mythological imagery, she evoked a hellish experience which exceeded even the tormented visions conjured up by her imagination. Over a period of three days and two nights, she suffered 'the torments of the damned'.[46] Watched over by her *accoucheurs*, or male-midwives, 'a type of being much more terrible than the furies, expressly invented both to make one's sense of modesty shiver and to revolt nature',[47] she suffered in near mortal agony until the arrival of a woman midwife.

Madame Necker's direct corporeal encounter with abjection – her sense of fear and revulsion during her birth experience – offers a concrete example of Calvinist beliefs about the maternal body. While on a symbolic level, as outlined previously, the mother embodied the social and civic ideals of the Calvinist faith through her role as the propagator of social and moral values, her corporeal existence was far more complex. Within Calvinist belief, the human body, by its physical presence, was inherently defiled; in Calvin's words, it represented 'the sorry spectacle of our foulness and dishonor' which stood in marked contrast to the act of creation itself.[48] Calvin reminded his faithful that while they were born blessed by grace, they had, as a result of original sin, descended into corruption: 'We confess and acknowledge without pretence, before your sacred majesty, that we are poor sinners, conceived and born in iniquity and corruption: predisposed to bad deeds, in all things considered, useless'.[49]

The slippage between creation and defilement is particularly clear in the relationship between two very distinct Calvinist understandings of the verb *naître*, or to be born. Early Calvinist theology associated *naître* with defilement, that is, with the physical entry of the individual into a human world of pain and suffering. But it could also be seen as the opportunity for spiritual rebirth; in other words, as a precondition for entry into communion with God. This dual relationship is exemplified in the Calvinist baptismal liturgy dating from 1542. Here, the believer acknowledged that human birth was both an entry into sin and a site of redemptive potential: 'Our Lord shows us in what poverty and misery we are all born, by telling us that we must be reborn'.[50] The 1724 baptismal liturgy clarified this second point further by observing the direct relationship between spiritual rebirth and membership in God's kingdom: 'We must be born anew if we wish to enter into the Kingdom of God'.[51]

These doctrines had profound implications for women, whose reproductive bodies and obligations were located at the intersection between oppositional and competing understandings of birth. Suzanne Necker's filial – and, later, maternal – experiences epitomized this paradox. Madame Necker was tied to the duties she owed to the memory of her dead mother, obligations which required her to extend her maternal inheritance through her own mothering practices. Caught between the roles of mother and daughter and fully cognizant of the complex and contradictory nature of the reproductive body, Madame Necker experienced the exile of the wretched, a space which was at once deeply desired and greatly feared.

The relationship between mothers and daughters, often troubled, has been the subject of numerous contemporary theoretical studies. Most hard-hitting, perhaps, are the ruminations of Simone de Beauvoir. In *The Second Sex*, Beauvoir conceives the mother as an essentially antagonistic and competitive being who perceives her daughter as a blank canvas upon which she imprints both her narcissistic desire and her innate resentment.[52] The daughter, as maternal double, realizes her mother's aspirations even as she confirms her mother's abjection, a cycle reiterated through each passing generation. Beauvoir founds her analysis upon a perspective of female corporeality as limiting; in other words, she understands the reproductive body as a prison that denies women's possibilities for self-realization. Alternately figured by Beauvoir as the cave, abyss or hell, the female body represents the antithesis of the creative, intellectual endeavours that have shaped culture and society.[53]

Other work on the relationship between women and the reproductive body, however, has posited a more felicitous encounter. Theorists such as Luce Irigaray, Julia Kristeva, Hélène Cixous and Iris Marion Young posit a subversive corporeal alterity, suggesting that women's 'other-ness' might actually be conducive to new and radical forms of conceptualization.[54] Cixousian 'white ink', when read together with Irigaray's 'corps-à-corps avec la mère' and Young's 'pregnant embodiment', offers insights into the seductive and transformative nature of the abject reproductive body. Within such a formulation, the inherent defilement of birth is re-inscribed, so that the essential fluidity of birth is always, necessarily, a creative, communitarian act. As Kristeva has observed: 'By giving birth, the woman enters into contact with her mother; she becomes, she is her own mother; they are the same continuity differentiating itself'.[55]

Madame Necker's experiences of mother- and daughter-hood suggest an interplay between defilement and creation. While she was deeply aware of her maternal inheritance and conscious of her responsibilities to the furtherance of her filial obligations, Necker was also drawn to the intimacy and fluidity – the sensual promise – of the mother/daughter relationship. The relationships she imagined and cultivated with her mother on the one hand and her daughter on the other present opportunities to examine more closely the tensions and inter-actions within the mother/daughter bond as they manifested themselves in an eighteenth-century maternal life.

Mon Ange Tutélaire: Refracting the Maternal Mirror

Very little physical evidence remains of Suzanne Necker's relationship with her mother, Magdeleine Curchod, née Albert. As a result, Magdeleine's direct influence on her daughter is difficult to discern. Biographers such as Hausson-ville have pointed to Madame Curchod's physical attributes as the source of her daughter's beauty, but offer little insight into her further influence and impact on Madame Necker's life.[56] Madame Curchod's correspondence, of which only a small amount remains, suggests limited exposure to formal education and would therefore appear to confirm the generally held view that Suzanne's father was almost entirely responsible for his daughter's intellectual development. The following is clear: Magdeleine Curchod was almost forty years old when she gave birth to her only child, Louise Suzanne, on 2 June 1737. She died after an extended illness in 1763, at the age of sixty-five, leaving a distraught daughter who was seemingly never able to recover from her loss. As we know, Suzanne Curchod, twenty-six years old at the time, entered into an extended period of profound corporeal suffering which was to affect the rest of her life.

There is strong evidence to support this statement. According to Madame Necker's doctor, Théodore Tronchin, her maladies developed as a direct result of the extended period of near-hysterical mourning that followed the death of Magdeleine Curchod.[57] In addition to this, Madame Necker herself attributed her various sufferings to the death of her mother, observing that 'the death of my mother irreparably altered my health'.[58] Necker's close friend Thomas, mean-while, linked his friend's illnesses to her desire to save the world.[59] This desire, Madame Necker confessed in letters to Madame Réverdil, was directly tied to the duties she owed to the memory of her dead mother.[60]

Necker's corporeal manifestation of maternal loss offers one tangible instance of her mother's influence on her life. Her correspondence with Swiss friends, in particular Henriette Réverdil, offers further insights. Here, Magdeleine Curchod emerges as her daughter's moral conscience, a woman who educated her daughter into the forms and conventions of the Calvinist tradition, instilling in her an understanding of the obligations and duties required of a woman of faith and piety. Unfortunately, Magdeleine Curchod's death interrupted this process, leaving her daughter's moral education incomplete and her maternal legacy unfulfilled. This rupture was to haunt Suzanne. Not only did she find herself without the maternal support so integral to the furtherance of the Calvinist maternal tradition, but she also felt morally adrift, orphaned by the one person whose moral goodness defined her existence.

I would suggest, however, that Magdeleine Curchod's death had an even more devastating impact on her daughter's life and thought processes. In later years, as we know, Madame Necker was to express a sense of deep guilt with regard to her mother's final illness and subsequent death.[61] In particular, she believed that her personal ambitions and desires were the cause of her mother's death and lamented the moral weakness that caused her to neglect her filial duties towards her mother. This neglect was a serious – and to Madame Necker's mind irredeemable – breach of virtue.

Necker expressed her profound sense of culpability in numerous letters, among them an extended soliloquy addressed to her mother seventeen years after her death:

> In vain I would like to confide my troubles: who will hear me? I try to remember you during the illusions of sleep, I think I see you, I speak to you: my soul pours out its feelings in your bosom, the bosom of a mother, where is it? ... oh! My mother, do not reject your child; she has sinned against you, but so little time and so many tears and so much tenderness, so much emotion and so many outbursts have redeemed these moods ... and once again, during these three years where my character was so disturbed, I did not for one instant stop adoring you, so pardon [me], have mercy on me; the Supreme Being pardons those who have offended him. Have seventeen years of all-encompassing remorse not atoned for my faults? See this flood of tears, receive your child, do not push her away, she begs for your pity.[62]

Necker's moral desolation is palpable. In this letter, she is acutely aware of her mother's absence and desperate to bridge the chasm that separates them. In addition to this, she is deeply conscious of her personal failures and of their impact on her mother's final years.

Necker expressed similar thoughts in letters to her close childhood friend Elie-Salomon-François Réverdil, then working as a tutor in the Danish court. Writing in 1770, she commented:

> You must take such happiness, sir, in ornamenting, as you do, the life of a respectable mother. I adored mine; and during her old age, I was unable to give her anything but tears and regrets; without this ever poignant memory my fate would have been so

sweet that not a day would have gone by without leaving me with regret for her loss and the hope for tomorrow.[63]

The situation had not changed by 1779, as is evidenced in another letter to her friend: 'May you, Sir, enjoy all the blessings that the heavens grant to children who have assured the happiness of their mother'.[64] So it was, then, that from the moment of her mother's death, Necker dedicated herself fully to the ultimately futile task of recovering her lost virtue. Cultivating an active relationship with her mother's memory, thus ensuring Magdeleine Curchod's continuing moral presence in her life, she transformed filial duties into spiritual duties: 'May she see, from the heavens above, my heart still burning with the desire to please her'.[65] Madame Necker's commitment to the principles of her faith was, in this sense, as much a demonstration of her devotion to her mother's memory as it was to the Calvinist tradition in the abstract. 'God wishes to bless our cares', she wrote to a close friend, 'It seems to me that my dear mother approves them from the heavens; and that I will dare to present myself before her at the moment when I will rejoin her'.[66] The memory of her dead mother, representing all that Madame Necker had lost – her virtue, her moral support and, finally, her nation – thus embodied the Calvinist experiences of abjection, exile, longing and *patrie*.

Magdeleine Curchod's close friend Henriette Réverdil played a key role in this process. As the mirror upon which Suzanne Necker projected her maternal longing, Réverdil functioned as a maternal surrogate, becoming Necker's moral guide, spiritual confessor, advisor and counsellor – the woman best suited to the role vacated by Magdeleine Curchod. She acted as a maternal presence with whom Madame Necker was able to share her personal experiences and her deep and intense desire for maternal communion. As she wrote to Elie-Salomon-François Réverdil: 'You forget, perhaps, everything that I owe to Madame your mother and to Madame your sister; they sought me out during my periods of greatest misery and have never abandoned me in my prosperity'.[67] Necker's letters to Henriette Réverdil, seventy-nine of which are housed in the Bibliothèque publique de Genève, reveal the extent of her filial guilt towards her mother. In them, Necker writes with a candour that is otherwise rare in her correspondence, sharing with Réverdil her deepest desires and fears. These are personal letters in which the events and personalities of elite Parisian social life make very little appearance. Indeed, since these letters are, at times, almost painfully intimate, they offer revealing insights into the nature of the mother/daughter relationship as Suzanne Necker imagined it.

Henriette Réverdil, the wife of Urbain Réverdil, a public official in the Vaudois village of Nyon, was the mother of seven children, two of whom – Elizabeth Sophie Salomé (1737–1806) and Elie-Salomon-François (1732–1808) – remained close friends with Madame Necker throughout her life. Réverdil had known Necker since childhood and was, as Necker points out, the model mother and friend: 'mother of the family in all senses of the term, mother of all the unfortunate, constant example of the most respectable of virtues; incomparable friend'.[68] In addition to this, she possessed consistent moral fortitude, keen discernment and astute powers of observation, skills eminently useful in judging not only the moral aptitude of Necker's needy relatives and friends, but also Necker's own fidelity and rectitude. Réverdil had high moral expectations for her best friend's daughter and it is clear that Suzanne wanted to live up to them.[69]

Necker welcomed this transformation from family friend to maternal surrogate and regularly invoked the filial nature of her relationship with Réverdil. Most striking, in this regard, is a letter dated 3 November 1765, in which Madame Necker, suffering from one of her long illnesses, employed the assistance of a scribe, in this instance, none other than Madame Réverdil's son, Marc-Louis Réverdil.[70] By 'writing' a letter ultimately penned by a biological child, Necker superimposed the hereditary power of a friend's biological relationship on the emotional pull of her adoptive connection, thus further strengthening the filial bond between herself and the Réverdil family.

As the embodiment of Ami Lullin's Calvinist maternal ideal, Réverdil offered a concrete example for Suzanne to follow. She was not only a model of grace, piety, nobility and eloquent truth, but also a woman whose generosity, moral clarity and active *bienfaisance* coalesced in the form of a maternal ideal without parallel.[71] Réverdil's presence in Suzanne Necker's life served as a moral anchor to which Necker could cling during periods of inner tempest and her example functioned as a beacon of hope in an otherwise morally corrupt society:

> Your letter affected my sensibilities greatly. In it, I see a soul still painfully affected, but which the most sublime virtues have elevated beyond its pain; in my opinion, I see an inestimable and untiring goodness; all of your expressions and all of your feelings remind me of those angelic qualities which I no longer witness here, neither in model nor in image.[72]

Indeed, Réverdil acted as Necker's counsellor and Necker regularly sought her advice on a variety of issues and deferred to her opinions. During her pregnancy, for example, Madame Necker expressed her desire to breastfeed her child and linked this with advice proffered by Madame Réverdil: 'I will follow your advice, Madame, and will no longer persist against nature; however, though I may sound self-serving, in breastfeeding I seek only to carry out my work; it would be counterproductive to harm my child'.[73] In addition, Réverdil acted as Necker's confessor, a woman to whom she turned when she needed to share the most intimate aspects of her being. As Necker stressed, 'You are, Madame, the [sole] confidante of my situation and my secret duties'.[74] It was to Réverdil that Necker confided her fundamental unhappiness, even in the face of great wealth, and Réverdil, too, who acted as witness to her continuing feelings of sorrow and failure with regard to her mother.

But Réverdil also played another, more profound role in Necker's life: her presence enabled Madame Necker to keep her mother's memory alive. 'It is in your letter alone that I am able to rediscover the memory of a beloved mother and the image of her virtue', she asserted in a 1771 letter to Madame Réverdil.[75] As the guardian of the memory of Magdeleine Curchod, Réverdil acted as the mirror through which Necker recalled her aborted relationship with her own mother and upon which she could re-inscribe her filial duty. Taking a submissive posture, Necker inhabited the position of the dutiful daughter, using the reflected glory of the maternal surrogate to illuminate her own filial performance. Necker's filial claim to Madame Réverdil, which imposed a series of obligations and duties to which Necker, as surrogate 'daughter', was obliged to submit, can be read as a rewriting of filial negligence in the language of daughterly virtue. In this sense, Réverdil can be seen as a conduit who enabled Necker to fulfil her responsibilities to the memory of her mother: 'Permit me to tell you, therefore, Madame, that with your help, I think I have exceeded the desires of my blessed mother; and as a result of this, all of my duties'.[76]

Madame Necker's relationship with Réverdil strengthened her bonds to her religion, culture and national identity, so that the maternal act, imagined through the memory of Magdeleine Curchod and embodied in the physical and epistolary presence of Henriette Réverdil, took on transformative power. Indeed, Necker's intimate correspondence with Henriette Réverdil anchored her to her Swiss Calvinist heritage, even as she felt herself seduced by the delights of Parisian cultural and intellectual life.

The Réverdil mirror also performed a darker function. While it made it possible for Madame Necker to begin to re-imagine her relationship with her mother, it also forced her to confront the horror and pain of her loss. Through Madame Réverdil, she continually replayed that moment of separation, the point of absolute abjection that changed the course of her life. 'I have the same respect for the memory of my father as for that of my mother; and I confuse the two in my heart, although with a different sentiment', she observed, 'One is a sweet memory that retraces unequalled virtues for me and consoles me during life's sufferings; the other reminds me of an irreparable loss and presents itself to me only that I might experience the heartbreak once again'.[77] Madame Réverdil's presence recalled Necker's failed filial responsibility. Even as she attempted to re-inscribe her filial identity, she was faced with a heightened awareness of her negligence and the reality of fundamental and irredeemable loss. No matter how hard she tried to recover her mother's grace, the project was ultimately futile. In a blunt assessment of her situation, she noted that: 'when I do not do enough, I think I hear the soul of my dear mother complaining of my negligence'.[78]

But what was 'enough'? Necker's correspondence with Réverdil provides substantial evidence of her commitment to her mother's final wishes and her ardent desire to reclaim the essential virtue of her filial inheritance. Her inability to resolve the profound break that accompanied her mother's death seems, however, to point to a self-imposed awareness of failure, a belief in her inherent unworthiness to claim the maternal legacy. This futile quest for virtue played itself out in the context of the relationship that Madame Necker developed with her daughter, Germaine. The long shadow of maternal memory loomed over this relationship, even as it represented Necker's only opportunity to recover a connection with her mother and, from there, to recuperate her filial virtue. A discussion of the maternal ideal as it was understood in France during the eighteenth century is necessary in order to comprehend more fully the nature of Necker's understanding of motherhood.

Eighteenth-century feminine virtue was realized in the form of the mother, as an idealized construct that embodied the promise and potential of the virtuous society. Elisabeth Badinter suggests that a sea change in philosophical, medical and public opinion took place sometime during the last third of the eighteenth century. In particular, she notes the emergence of a naturalized maternal instinct, what she refers to as 'the spontaneous love of all mothers for their children'.[79] This new approach, propagated through myriad conduct books, philosophical essays, novels and medical treatises, inculcated into mothers a language and culture of obligation, duty and guilt.[80] Writers and commentators naturalized duty and obligation by introducing the language of instinct, thus suggesting that maternity and motherhood – the realization of women's duties to the family, the nation and the species – conformed to the laws of nature and were, therefore, intrinsic to the female condition.[81] These writers suggested further that this natural instinct manifested itself in love. Together, these three ideas – nature, instinct and love – formed the basis for a revolutionary understanding of the maternal imperative and laid the groundwork for a radical reconceptualization of French social relations.[82]

Motherhood and maternal practice were among the central preoccupations of Enlightenment philosophers, moralists and thinkers. French society was in crisis. The excessive behaviours of the aristocratic class, combined with fears of depopulation and dwindling political power on the international front, set the stage for a significant reformulation of the maternal ideal. Rousseau's radical domesticity defined women as the prime nurturers of the family and ultimately of society as a whole. Where society had once depended on the powerful father figure embodied in the form of the king and church, it now turned to a less visible figure, the mother and in particular the good mother, as its hope for the future.

Within the new Rousseauist maternal polity, women-as-mothers took on central roles. Responsible for care, nurturing and moral education, they were the cornerstones of a new society founded on the principles of virtue. *La bonne mère* emerged as a vanquishing heroine, an ideological construct poised at once to reverse the worrying trend in depopulation and, at the same time, to transform social mores. Within her body resided the promise and potential of the French nation. The *Encyclopédie* article on the mother offers a revealing portrait and identifies two distinct, but directly related, facets of the maternal ideal.[83] The ideal mother existed both as a moral construct and, more importantly, as a physical being. Her primary duty, contended Boucher d'Argis, was to nurse her children. These two ideas interrogated and intersected with one another, collapsing into the meta-construct that loomed large over eighteenth-century thought and practice. They also actively informed Madame Necker's maternal practices and performances. A pious and erudite woman, Madame Necker was fully implicated in the maternal debates of her day. Her experiences as both daughter and mother reflected the tensions inherent in eighteenth-century understandings of maternal virtue and powerfully shaped her autobiographical understandings and presentations.

Necker was impatient to have children after her marriage. Pregnancy did not, however, come easily. After eight months of marriage she was still not pregnant, a situation which caused her some distress.[84] She worried she would be unable to provide her husband with an heir and that, as a consequence, she would find herself incapable of fulfilling a fundamental tenet of Christian marriage. Within a few months, however, she became pregnant with her first and only child, a daughter, Anne-Louise-Germaine Necker, nicknamed Minette.

Both Necker's writings and actions demonstrate that she was determined to be a good mother to her child. Central to the fulfilment of her maternal duty was breastfeeding, a responsibility that she had already acknowledged during her pregnancy, and to which she wholeheartedly dedicated herself upon her daughter's birth: 'I am breastfeeding her myself and with great success despite your concerns'.[85] The decision to nurse her child fully conformed to medical and moral prescriptions and directives. The reproductive body came under intense scrutiny during the eighteenth century. Women, while natural nurturers and caregivers, were equally conceived as dangerous entities, whose moral weakness and emotional instability threatened the physical existence and moral development of foetus, infant and child.[86] These conflicts played themselves out most notably in the space of the female breast, which came to embody the idealized concerns of the nation. At once the site of woman's sensual appeal (and thus, the location of dangerous, threatening and potentially all-consuming desire), women's breasts also symbolized the potential for human life and growth. Good mothering practice resided in the breasts. Milk, as the source of national, religious and cultural identity, flowed through them, thus linking mother to infant and infant to nation. Indeed, breasts were the conduits of the maternal legacy and from them the infant imbibed a cultural inheritance. As the French Revolution's Marianne would later demonstrate, the mother who nursed her own child also nursed the nation.[87]

Maternal nursing was a physical symbol providing concrete evidence of good mothering in action. From a public health standpoint, this was a valid, indeed important, consideration. Mother's milk was deemed essential to the survival of the child. An initiative by the Société pour encourager les mères peu fortunées in Lyon, for example, which offered indigent women a monthly 'wage' to nurse their children for one year, resulted in a dramatic decrease in the mortality rate, which fell to 16 per cent from an average of over 60 per cent for wet-nursed children.[88] But public health motivations were eclipsed by moral motivators. Nursing was interpreted as tangible and demonstrable proof of a mother's *moral* goodness. Maternal nursing became a powerful symbol, not only for the survival of the child, but more significantly, for the physical embodiment of Rousseau's overarching desire: the moral regeneration of society. 'When mothers deign to nurse their children', he counselled his readers, 'then will be a reform in morals'.[89]

The equation of breastfeeding with morality was not new. Mother's milk, in early modern Western thought, carried symbolic and psychological meanings that went far beyond mere health concerns. First and foremost among these was the belief that breast milk carried the temperament and passions of the mother or nurse.[90] The implications of this are clear. As Roze de l'Epinoy observed, a wet nurse, or mercenary mother, would pass on greed, avarice and selfishness, while the birth mother, selflessly nurturing her young child, would pass on only generosity and goodness.[91] But these beliefs went still deeper. Maternal milk carried not only beneficent moral qualities, but also transmitted qualities relating to social status and cultural heritage. Mother's milk, passed from generation to generation through the generosity of the maternal body, thus became synonymous with the maintenance of the patriarchal bloodline. Madame Necker's metaphor of cultural assimilation through the breast is entirely *à propos*: 'In order to have perfect taste is it necessary to have been born in a country or in a society – in Paris, for example – where one receives the principles of taste through the milk and by authority?'[92] This question also offers further proof of her feelings of cultural and religious isolation. Madame Necker, unlike her colleagues, had not suckled at a French breast; rather, her maternal inheritance – a legacy of Calvinist belief, cultural dislocation and forced exile which she sought to pass to her daughter through her own breastfeeding – was decidedly different.

The deeper implications of the eighteenth century's fascination with the maternal breast were many. Not only did the practice of wet-nursing break a vital cultural link, thus divorcing the family from its traditional heritage, but it also, more insidiously, subverted the traditional social hierarchy, mixing the milk of the lower-class individual with the blood of the upper-class family.[93] Rousseau's words were written atop a virtual minefield of received ideas and superstition: 'contamination by the nurturing female body', wet nurse or otherwise, was a very real concern.[94] Only the milk of the mother could guarantee the lineage of the family, but only the milk of the *good* mother could carry within it such incorruptible values as purity, innocence and virtue. Rousseau was not just looking for a mother, he was searching for a good mother and it is clear that the two were not synonymous.

At the same time, the eighteenth-century maternal ideal offered women significant potential for self-realization in a role that hitherto had been accorded little cultural importance or attention. Maternal goodness permeated all aspects of a woman's life, from her conscious decision to nurse her own child, to issues of personal hygiene (such as nutritional concerns) and the cultivation of the highest standards of morality. Women's public lives were equally transformed. Rousseauist mothers, as their children's primary caregivers and teachers, spent far more time with their children than mothers of the past. Badinter observes that, 'The new generation lived constantly at their children's side. They nursed them, watched over them, bathed them, dressed them, walked them and cared for their sicknesses.'[95] As the many portraits of mothers by Elizabeth Vigée-Lebrun suggest, mother and child were an inseparable unit, the one incomprehensible without the other. Many women welcomed these developments and fully embraced their new-found roles. Among them were both Marie-Jeanne Roland, the radical revolutionary who recounted to her husband the concerted efforts she undertook to nurse her own children, and Madame Necker.[96]

That Madame Necker understood the symbolic role of breastfeeding as proof of maternal goodness is evident from the following commentary, found in a later letter to her husband:

> I was obliged to work hard on my delicate machine in order to make myself suitable to nurse, and I will not include here the details that demanded all of the courage of maternal tenderness, traumatic ordeals whose marks I still bear and which continued during four months of painful breastfeeding, but during which time maternal instinct compensated me for all of this suffering.[97]

Unfortunately, Madame Necker's virtuous choice to breastfeed her daughter proved ultimately unsuccessful. Less than four months after her daughter's birth, she was forced to hand this responsibility over to a wet nurse. 'I had … the bitter grief of being obligated to stop my nursing activities after having overcome all the pains and sufferings of this condition for nearly four months', she confessed. 'My little girl was becoming visibly weaker, as was I'.[98]

Madelyn Gutwirth reads Madame Necker's aborted attempt to breastfeed as evidence of her inability to come to terms with the essential corporeality of her maternal body. She further argues that this rupture might be seen as emblematic of the 'mutual disappointment' experienced by both mother and daughter.[99] From this perspective Madame Necker's professed allegiance to – but failed actualization of – the dictates of corporeal maternity, highlights not only the fraught nature of Madame Necker's maternal performance, but also the tensions in her daughter's filial response.

Conventional wisdom has constructed a strained relationship between Suzanne Necker and her daughter. Ascribing a rigid, stern and somewhat imperious character to Madame Necker and an impetuous, liberated and fun-loving personality to young Germaine, scholars and biographers have succeeded in crafting an oppositional relationship marked by somewhat crudely drawn individual portraits. The comments of Béatrice d'Andlau are particularly revealing in this regard: 'A perpetual constraint, that is what this mother probably represented for this happy and spontaneous child', she writes, confirming the generally held impression that Suzanne Necker's understanding of maternal tenderness as 'a chore, like the poor or grooming', amounted to nothing more than a rigid severity that compromised young Germaine's natural genius and talents.[100] Other biographical works confirm Andlau's perceptions, painting Madame Necker as a woman so concerned with moral fortitude and severity that she neglected her daughter's need for freedom and movement.[101] From such a characterization, Germaine emerges as a heroine who succeeds – and indeed ultimately triumphs – in spite of tremendous adversity. Madame Necker, on the other hand, fares poorly. 'Few women seem less suited for procreation than Madame Necker', notes Ghislain de Diesbach.[102] In the hands of many Staël biographers, Necker was an 'abusive' mother whose 'impossibly high standards' resulted in a relationship that lacked warmth and stifled Minette's natural precocity and all of her creative impulses.[103]

This dichotomous characterization supports the Freudian argument for a fraught and tension-filled filial relationship in which both women vied for the attention of a beloved husband and father, in this case, Jacques Necker. In this narrative, Madame Necker viewed her daughter as a failure and, in addition to this, 'as an unwelcome rival'.[104] Dena Goodman uses this approach to highlight gendered social inequity, arguing that competition among women family members resulted from their oppressed position within patriarchal French society.[105] Staël biographers, however, take a different perspective, viewing the conflicts between mother and daughter as evidence of a deep schism that laid the groundwork for what they see as Germaine's eventual usurpation of her mother's role, both on the salon stage and within her father's heart. Béatrice d'Andlau argues that Germaine shifted allegiance from mother to father during her teenage years, developing what Andlau terms variously as 'a sort of complicity', a 'secret accord' and an alliance from which Suzanne Necker was wholly excluded.[106] Maria Fairweather suggests that Germaine's success derived in large part from her personal qualities, claiming that Jacques Necker was drawn to the very qualities in her that Suzanne did not possess. Germaine, she contends, was 'warm, generous, vivacious, spontaneous, effortlessly brilliant yet never pedantic'.[107]

The approach taken by Staël scholars is perhaps unsurprising given their desire to paint their subject's life in a positive light. However, it does little justice to Madame Necker. Instead, it positions her as a rigid, authoritarian and self-centred Beauvoir-esque maternal figure determined to mould her daughter in her own image: as a model of controlled sensibility and rational piety. Seen from this perspective, Madame Necker appears little concerned with her daughter's emotional needs and emerging intellect. Some of this may well be valid; certainly, there is enough evidence to suggest that Madame Necker was so consumed with her own psychic suffering that this directly impacted her maternal practice. But their relationship was far more nuanced than most of Staël's biographers have been willing to accept. While it definitely turned on Madame Necker's desire for narcissistic display, it also reflected her fundamental belief in her personal unworthiness; in other words, her essential understanding of herself as a moral failure incapable of recovering lost virtue.

Moral Modelling and Maternal Dissonance

From the outset, Madame Necker was determined to raise her young daughter in a morally rigorous fashion. Minette was baptized into the Protestant faith during an intimate ceremony in the chapel of the Dutch embassy and raised under the watchful eyes of her mother and a series of Protestant caregivers: from her wet nurse – 'a large Flemish woman'[108] – to her governesses and finally, her single childhood friend, the carefully chosen and vetted Catherine Rilliet Huber. Minette's education was deeply informed by Calvinist moral principles. Madame Necker supervised her daughter's active initiation into the Calvinist faith by ordering books on the Catechism from Swiss friends before her second birthday.[109] Within a few years, Minette was reciting catechismal texts and discussing religious principles. Madame Necker thus sheltered her daughter within a Calvinist cocoon, laying the foundation for her subsequent intellectual development.

Minette's academic education was equally rigorous. Attentive to her role as maternal teacher and spiritual guide, Madame Necker designed an educational programme which in many respects mirrored her own. Minette learned a variety of languages, was immersed in scientific studies and undertook the various activities suitable to a young woman of gentility: not only did she paint, but she also learned to play a number of musical instruments and took lessons in elocution and acting from the great Clairon, the leading actress on the French stage during this period. Minette's education, like that of her mother before her, was remarkable for its time and a testament to Madame Necker's belief that the social disparity between men and women was the result of educational inequity.[110] With her daughter, she was determined to take a different path. She would not raise her daughter in ignorance, like Rousseau's Sophie, but would instead model her child on Emile.[111] While contemporary commentators have correctly suggested that her approach differed markedly from that proposed by Rousseau,[112] the goals and ends were the same: the crafting of a critical and sensitive mind capable of independent thought and fully prepared for roles of moral and civic leadership in a new society of equals. From her writings, it is clear that Madame Necker's pedagogical approach was the result of careful and thorough deliberation. She encouraged her daughter to think critically, challenged her to cultivate a morally rigorous stance that would prepare her for a pious adult life dedicated to serving God and society, and revelled in her daughter's precocity and intellectual prowess.[113]

One aspect of Madame Necker's educational approach, however, rings dissonantly. Minette's early childhood was spent in relative isolation, carefully protected from the dangers of the Parisian social sphere, with only her mother, governess and her mother's close friends for company. All of this changed when Madame Necker, following the model introduced by her mentor, Madame Geoffrin, initiated her daughter into her salon at the age of eleven. For the next seven years, Minette was an active presence in her mother's intellectual world. Seated on a wicker stool at her mother's feet, she conversed with her mother's close friends, in particular Raynal, Thomas, Marmontel and the Marquis de Pezay, and followed the conversations with great interest. As Catherine Rilliet Huber recalled:

> It was understood that during dinner we would say nothing; we listened; but you should have seen how Miss Necker listened! Her gaze followed the movements of those who spoke and seemed almost to anticipate their ideas. She never opened her mouth and yet appeared to speak when it was her turn; such was the mobility of her expressions. She was aware of everything, knew everything, understood everything, even politics, which was already one of the great topics of conversation at this time.[114]

For Minette, this must have been a remarkable experience. The salon became her classroom, a space in which she thrived. Here, she first encountered and then cultivated the seductive delights of conversation and intellectual exchange that would later become so central to her identity.

While Madame Necker apparently fully approved of her daughter's presence, viewing her daughter's conversations and discussions as a form of intellectual 'exercise',[115] this salon education was nonetheless a curious pedagogical choice, particularly given her penchant for moral rectitude and pious devotion. It is worth recalling Madame Necker's own ambiguous relationship with salon culture, as outlined in the first chapter. Indeed, Necker's marked antipathy towards the artifice and dissimulation of Parisian social life must be considered in relation to her pedagogical choices. From this perspective, the salon was a space that threatened to undermine her carefully laid moral foundation, replacing it with the secular worldliness and excessive opulence of the Parisian philosophical and aristocratic communities.

This maternal salon approach also troubled the French elite. After all, the example set by Madame Geoffrin, who also raised her daughter in the salon, had not proven particularly successful. Geoffrin and her daughter, Marie-Thérèse d'Estampes, Marquise de La Ferté-Imbault, had a particularly acrimonious relationship punctuated by violent outbursts and lengthy periods of silence.[116] The Marquise completely disavowed the philosophical principles propagated by her mother's salon guests and close friends. Denouncing all contemporary philosophers as moral vagrants, she clung to the ideals of seventeenth-century moral philosophers such as Nicolas Malebranche. In a century that viewed the child as the 'ouvrage', or 'work', of the mother, Geoffrin's maternal success was questionable at best.

Necker's decision to model the approach taken by her mentor aroused the suspicions and doubts of her contemporaries. Among the most enduring and most articulate of these critical responses are the reminiscences of Madame de Genlis, whose multi-volume *Mémoires* includes numerous vignettes featuring various members of the Necker family. After outlining what she perceived to be curiously excessive behaviour on the part of young Germaine Necker, Genlis continued:

> Madame Necker raised her very poorly, letting her spend three quarters of her days in the salon, with that crowd of intellectuals of the time, all of whom surrounded mademoiselle Necker; and while her mother occupied herself with others and especially the women who came to see her, the intellectuals spoke with mademoiselle Necker about feelings and love. The solitude of her room and some good books would have done her more good.[117]

In this short tableau, Genlis, a prolific writer and astute commentator on aristocratic social and cultural life, outlined the main points of contention. She suggested that the salon was an inappropriate place for children and, more particularly, for young girls. With its emphasis on *galanteries* and the sensuous and suggestive interplay of themes such as love and passion, it was a space dedicated to the cultivation of adult conversation and the discussion of mature subject matter. As proof of the inherent impropriety of Madame Necker's pedagogical approach, Genlis cited the later published work of Germaine de Staël, in particular her 1796 publication *De l'influence des passions sur les nations et sur les individus*. 'The goal [of the book] is to prove the usefulness of the passions', she observed. 'This was the doctrine of encyclopedists, who surrounded the childhood and youth of Madame de Staël. We must forgive her memory such pernicious principles: they were inspired in her from the cradle.'[118] Madame Genlis spoke from a position of public authority. As the author of *Adèle et Théodore*, a two-volume work on aristocratic pedagogy which was a finalist for the 1783 Prix d'utilité, she was an acknowledged expert in the field of children's education.[119] In addition to this, she was a celebrated playwright and novelist who considered all of her creative work to be moral in nature.

The question of Madame Necker's salon education continues to baffle scholars and biographers, most of whom observe that between Madame Necker's religious belief and spiritual stance and the views propagated by her largely irreligious guests there was a chasm. Her decision appears even more unusual when viewed in the light of her own discomfort in – and indeed, aversion to – the salon and its practices. It is at this point of apparent dissonance, however, that we can learn the most about Suzanne Necker's Calvinist beliefs and their relationship to her maternal practice. In many ways, the salon functioned as the site of Madame Necker's maternal abjection. In order to examine this more fully, it might be useful to consider the following questions. Why did Suzanne Necker choose to raise her daughter in the salon? What purpose did such an education serve? Finally, what role did Minette play within the salon?

Mothering in the Salon

According to the recollections of Germaine Necker's only childhood friend, Catherine Rilliet Huber, Germaine joined her mother's salon at the age of eleven and was a regular presence until the age of eighteen.[120] She was an attentive, obedient and much-loved member of her mother's salon community and developed friendships with some of her mother's most intimate guests, among them Marmontel and Thomas. With these men, she extended the conversation of the salon through epistolary exchanges, sharing humorous verses and correspondence.[121] As she grew older, she herself became remarkably adept in salon sociability and thrived in the space of the salon, ultimately eclipsing her mother in skill and brilliance.[122]

This aspect of the story is well known. What is open to further speculation is the purpose behind Necker's decision to raise her child in her salon and Minette's function within the context of Madame Necker's self-presentation. While Rilliet Huber offers one possible rationale for Madame Necker's decision, arguing that Necker perceived Minette's salon education as a form of mental and intellectual athleticism,[123] this reasoning proves unsatisfactory, particularly in light of Madame Necker's professed moral fear of the Parisian social sphere and her concomitant determination, until that point, to raise her child in obscure privacy, nestled within a protective cocoon of Calvinist religious belief. Why, indeed, would Madame Necker, so very cautious about her daughter's moral upbringing, suddenly release her into the tumultuous and, as Genlis points out, socially inappropriate, environment of the salon? In order to answer this question, I turn to the complicated relationships between maternity, virtue and display as they played themselves out in the salon.

Madame Necker was fully aware of the performative power of virtuous practice.[124] But maternal virtue, as noted previously, depended on women's seclusion
within the domestic sphere: the mother's first duty was to her child and family,
to the cultivation of the virtuous family unit that would function as the foundation for a reformed, virtuous society. In a society that viewed the daughter as the
'work' of the mother, however, public recognition of successful maternal practice was essential. The daughter embodied the results of maternal care, physically
displaying the commitment and devotion of virtuous motherhood.

Germaine Necker, at eleven, was a prime reflection of dedicated and con-
scientious maternal care. Intellectually precocious and vivacious by nature, she
functioned as an ideal foil to her more reserved mother. Her position, seated
demurely on a stool at her mother's feet, reinforced both the familial and the
hierarchical bonds. There were also political implications to this positioning,
implications that suggest Minette's salon role as an integral element in the construction of a constellation of Calvinist virtue. Jacques Necker assumed the
position of Directeur général du Trésor royal in 1776 and, in 1777, became
Directeur général des finances. While these nominations effectively ensured
Necker's control over the largest political portfolio in the French nation, they
were not without controversy. As the director of French finance, industry, agri-
culture and commerce, Necker should rightfully have been given the post of
Contrôleur général. Instead, as a foreigner and a Protestant, Necker was forced
to practise subterfuge. Aligning himself with a series of puppet finance ministers,
he served king and state from a lesser position.

Read in this light, Germaine's salon presence, which dates from about 1777,
was critical to the Neckers' self-fashioning as a family of virtue and integrity,
united in Calvinist belief against what Madame Necker perceived as the preju-
dice and intolerance of the French state. Germaine, as the product of the virtuous
Protestant marriage, embodied the profession of faith, a public act of Calvinist
witness in a political environment still somewhat hostile to the Protestant religion. Jacques Necker was a regular, if mostly silent, presence in his wife's salon.
The inclusion of his daughter, a conscious choice given the conventions of the
period, suggests that even in the face of politically inspired religious persecution,
Necker and his family would, nonetheless, persevere. Together, they embodied Rousseau's virtuous trio, with Madame Necker – mother and wife – at its
moral core and Germaine – the dutiful daughter – as its mascot. In this instance,
Germaine emerged as an emblem designed both to demonstrate publicly the
religious fidelity of her parents and to promote religious toleration, which would
not be officially enacted for another ten years.[125]

Such a move, I suggest, dramatically reconceived the nature of the salon. No
longer a space dedicated to the cultivation of the French aristocratic identity, it
was instead re-imagined for the display of religious and cultural alterity through

the active display of maternal virtue. By inserting Germaine into the salon at this critical juncture in Jacques Necker's political career, Madame Necker gestured towards her husband's innate moral virtue, as represented in the form of his only child, Germaine.[126]

But there exists also a further possibility, which derives from the previous two. In this scenario, Madame Necker's personal anguish takes centre stage. By raising her daughter in the salon, Necker acknowledged the salon as the site of her moral downfall, accepting and claiming the dangerous threats posed by unchecked feminine ambition and desire. She also demonstrated her renewed commitment to the memory of her mother by claiming the space for the performance of domestic virtue. From there, she exerted the importance of the obligations imposed on her by her faith. Necker's approach fundamentally challenged the social and intellectual nature of the salon by imprinting on it a domestic model more properly suited to her religious beliefs. The salon, in this instance, became a performative space in which Madame Necker, rather than her elite guests, took centre stage. In this reading, Germaine takes on a supporting role in order to bolster the self-fashioning of her parents. Positioned to reflect the success of her mother's teachings, she provided confirmation of Madame Necker's inherent maternal goodness.

This positioning served a dual function. First of all, it enabled Necker to mark herself as 'other' to the Parisian elite. By performing domesticity before a limited public, she reconceived the sociable sphere, not by emphasizing its publicity, but by stressing its intimacy. She also went further. By demonstrating her difference – by physically asserting her alterity from the people around her – she sought to reconcile herself with the internal exile that had haunted her since her mother's death. In other words, her public maternal practice can be seen as a demonstration of her pious devotion to both God and her mother and her allegiance to their teachings. Indeed, through her salon performances, Madame Necker expressed her devotion, faith and fidelity in much the same way as the Protestants of Calvin's day had maintained their religious fidelity in the face of extreme opposition. Seeming to gesture towards the martyrdom of persecuted Huguenot women in centuries past, Madame Necker publicly professed her allegiance to Calvinism in a space otherwise culturally marked as both Catholic and French. In so doing, she laid claim to a maternal religious inheritance that transcended the severed relationship with her own mother and reached back to heroic actions of the first generations of French Calvinists. In the process, she re-imagined not only the religious and geographic exile imposed on her mother and grandmother before her, but also the cultural and moral exile that marked her own life experiences.

By figuratively rewriting the space of the salon, Madame Necker also rewrote her own culpability. The decision to locate her maternal practice at the very site of her moral downfall thus emerges as a forced confrontation between literary ambition, maternal desire and filial duty. This combination set the stage for the corporeal suffering that marked her adult life. In the process, the salon, previously understood as an instance of Parisian aristocratic identity, was subsumed into a domestic performance of Calvinist maternal virtue.

As discussed earlier, the salon was an inherently performative space in which each actor, in the words of Jolanta Pekacz, 'was expected to incarnate characteristics considered appropriate for his or her social position, gender, age, marital status and circumstances'.[127] In this hierarchy, the guests starred in leading roles, while the *salonnière*, guiding and directing the action on the salon stage, took a necessarily supporting role. Necker transformed this relationship entirely. Even as she maintained the superficial accoutrements of her role as *salonnière*, projecting selflessness, generosity and concern for her guests, her appropriation of the salon as a projection screen for her public performance of conflicted maternal desire, filial obligation and conjugal bliss, effectively subverted the unwritten law of the salon itself by sidelining its leading actors.

Instead, the salon became the stage upon which Necker colonized and realized her maternal role and through which she attempted to come to terms with her filial responsibilities. By presenting her family – an enchanted constellation of virtue which included a benevolent father, a loving, generous and affectionate mother and a charming and precocious child – as the embodiment of the enlightened domestic utopia, Madame Necker laid claim to membership in the republic of virtue and forced her guests into positions of captive and somewhat uncomfortable spectators. As voyeurs into the intimate and personal relationships of the Necker family, they were no longer able to gaze adoringly upon pleasing reflections of themselves through the mediation of the *salonnière*'s mirror, but were instead faced with the risky and potentially unpleasant task of self-reflection. Madame Necker, by refusing the social mirror, powerfully destabilized the perceived coherence of the elite identity.

Such a reading posits a heroic gesture on Madame Necker's part, paving the way for the recuperation of her sullied virtue and for the cultivation of a praiseworthy life lived in the warm light of divine grace. Necker's actions speak to a deep desire to recover her filial loss, an intense longing to retrieve that from which she had been separated. In rewriting the salon, she was also rewriting the maternal story, projecting her filial responsibility though her maternal desire. In other words, by being seen to be actively mothering her daughter, she sought to rewrite the narrative of original sin, imprinting on it a different story with an altogether happier ending.

Unfortunately, this was not to be. Germaine blossomed in the salon, developing there the formidable conversational skill that she would take into adulthood. As Germaine grew older, her relationship with her mother grew increasingly acrimonious and maternal dominance on Suzanne's part came into conflict with filial rebellion. The dutiful daughter, so lovingly constructed and so proudly displayed by the devoted mother, came into her own as a prodigiously talented, wilful woman whose thirst for passionate displays mirrored her mother's equally intense need for strict balance and moral equilibrium. The adult Madame de Staël would neither require nor desire her mother's involvement in her life. As Madame Necker observed: 'My daughter does not need me in order to be happy; our tastes differ and soon she will cease even to miss me'.[128]

Germaine, as her mother's only child, represented Necker's only opportunity to recover her virtue. In a telling observation Suzanne Necker noted that: 'There is a certain degree of virtue that renders us indifferent to all glories, except that of having children who resemble us'.[129] Her daughter, a symbol of successful maternal practice proudly displayed in the salon, offered the possibility of filial redemption. However, Germaine's repudiation of her maternal inheritance through, among other things, ill-advised romantic attachments, subverted Necker's recuperative project.

In giving birth, Madame Necker did not, as she so fervently wished, double herself. Instead, she saw her daughter take a consciously different path. Challenging her mother's authority and ultimately far surpassing her in conversational prowess, intellectual abandon and ill-advised passionate excess and display, Germaine left her mother with the realization that her quest for virtue was ultimately futile. Indeed, Germaine's refusal to conform to Suzanne's expectations only reinforced the consequences of her mother's own youthful negligence. By superimposing her own sin upon that of her daughter, Madame Necker gestured towards a troubling truth: the sins of the daughter were, in a sense, the sins of the mother, so that Madame Necker's own filial culpability became, to her mind, the source of her daughter's moral downfall. History, for Madame Necker, had repeated itself. Just as Suzanne had failed her mother, so too, Germaine now failed hers. Madame Necker, already marked by personal moral weakness with regard to her own mother, was, she believed, now doubly marked by what she perceived to be the moral disarray of her daughter.[130]

4 PERFORMING PATHOLOGY: STAGING THE SICK BODY

It is certain that the exercise and enthusiasm of virtue kindles the soul and I believe that every honest action undoes a link of the chains that tie the soul to the weakness of the body; I sense, I confess, that the self depends absolutely on my health and my heart alone is not a slave to this.[1]

It has been said that medicine is the theology of the body.[2]

Madame Necker's moral stigma and suffering were physically imprinted on her body. Her husband and first biographer, Jacques Necker, cited her extensive physical debilitation, noting that:

from a very early period, she was subjected to such painful nervous anxieties that she gradually lost sleep; and during the day, obliged to succumb to restlessness, she held herself up, even in company, and received only a bit of rest in the bath.[3]

This theme of continual suffering is later taken up in the portrait penned by Laure Junot, Duchesse d'Abrantès, in the six-volume *Histoire des salons de Paris*, her monumental paean to aristocratic sociability and sensibility. In the first chapter, entitled, 'Salon de Madame Necker. 1787', Madame Necker emerges, perhaps unsurprisingly, as a somewhat stiff woman little prone to outward displays of affection.[4] Most of all, however, she appears pale and weak, a woman consumed by suffering, who was 'beautiful nevertheless, as much as one could be with that deathly pallor that covered her face, and in which the eternal look in her eyes confirmed the sad truth'.[5]

In 1787, the date of Abrantès's literary portrait, Madame Necker was fifty years old. In many ways, she was in her prime. The director of an experimental charity hospital, she enjoyed an active presence on the public and political stage. On a personal level, she was soon to become a grandmother. In addition to this, the Edict of Toleration, signed in late November 1787, finally allowed her to practise her Calvinist faith publicly. But all was not smooth sailing. The political situation in Paris was tense: France was on the verge of bankruptcy and Jacques Necker's actions and 1781 *Compte rendu* were publicly called into question by his successor, Calonne. After Necker illegally published his rebuttal, he was officially exiled for a period of four months. Madame Necker's closest French friend, Antoine Léonard Thomas, had died in 1785 and the Comte de Buffon, another intimate ally, would die in 1788. Meanwhile, the actions of her daughter were cause for concern. Newly married to Eric Magnus, Baron de Staël-Holstein, in 1786, Germaine was reputedly amorously linked to the rakish Jacques-Antoine-Hippolyte, Comte de Guibert.[6] Further worries ensued: in 1788, Germaine's daughter Gustavine fell ill. She died in April 1789 after months of suffering.

Madame Necker herself was very sick. In preceding years, she had sought the advice of numerous medical professionals, among them the celebrated Swiss doctor Théodore Tronchin, and had travelled to Spa (1765), Mont d'Or (1768), London (1776), Montpellier (1784), Marolles (1785) and, most recently, in September 1786, Plombières, in search of respite.[7] But respite was difficult to come by. An unsent letter to Louis XVI, penned in 1787, reveals that she was still experiencing significant physical distress.[8]

Illness was a recurring theme in Suzanne Necker's life. From the abject torment during the period immediately following the death of her mother through to the intense sufferings that marked the two years prior to her own death in 1794, her body was consumed by malady. Her correspondence details a litany of physical complaints, from easily definable symptoms such as coughs, fevers and vertigo, to more amorphous generalized feelings of suffering, languishing and weakness. To date, these illnesses have received little attention. Instead, biographical interpretations, consigning Madame Necker's sufferings to the realm of narcissistic hypochondria, have either quickly dispensed with them or treated them as evidence of her inherent morbidity and emotional excess. Maria Fairweather, for example, identifies Necker's obsessive compulsions regarding death as a 'tiresome' characteristic, while J. Christopher Herold pokes fun at Madame Necker's elaborate burial plans.[9] Understood within the context of a pious, Calvinist existence and read through her experiences of filial and maternal torment, however, they point to another perspective.

This chapter considers Madame Necker's experience of illness. I seek to understand its purpose and function in her life by reading her sufferings through a double lens. Situating her experiences in the context of eighteenth-century conceptions of public health, hygiene, morality, gender and embodied understandings of the self, I further develop the theme of spiritual and maternal abjection by linking her corporeal distress to a variety of factors, including the profound spiritual malaise which emerged after her mother's death, her moral struggles between literary ambition and maternal desire and her need to cultivate a position of cultural alterity. I assert that the rupture of the maternal body resulted in the sick body, a process whereby filial and maternal anguish, enacted on the salon stage, came to reside in a new performative entity: the suffering body. I argue further that Madame Necker's staging of malady can be seen as central to her Calvinist belief and, therefore, integral to her conception of self. The principles of display, exile, longing and communion – concepts so central to her understanding and practice of her Calvinist faith – were expressed on the corporeal stage, which was conceived as a site for the abject veneration of God and a memorial to maternal loss.

It is worth noting that Madame Necker was undoubtedly prone to the myriad nervous maladies that characterized the women of her social class at the time. In many respects, her experiences mirrored those of her salon colleagues, Madame d'Épinay, who spent time under the care of Tronchin in Geneva, and Mademoiselle de Lespinasse, whose tortured letters to the Comte de Guibert provide clear evidence of the links between psychic trauma and somatic suffering.[10] In stating this, I also want to argue that to dismiss entirely Necker's corporeal experiences on these grounds is problematic. While her illnesses can be seen as unremarkable or unexceptional, the overwhelming presence of illness in her life experience, particularly when read together with her public commitment to French hospital reform, her deep interests in medical literature and her concern for the dying body, demands not only acknowledgement, but also further examination. Such a reading, while concerned only with the activities of one particular woman, can nonetheless also provide a framework for a better understanding of eighteenth-century women's experiences of illnesses in general.

Illness as Everyday Experience in Eighteenth-Century France

Illness was a fact of Suzanne Necker's life from her childhood on. In the early 1760s, Magdeleine Curchod detailed her daughter's slow recovery from a bout of smallpox.[11] Béatrice d'Andlau cites Madame Necker's comments about her deafness in one ear, the result of a childhood malady.[12] Throughout her adult years, too, Necker enumerated recognizable medical symptoms such as fevers, coughs and chills that waxed and waned with the seasons. In this, she was not alone, since illness was a central facet of eighteenth-century lived experience. David Vess paints a picture of a society marked by recurring seasonal ailments, vicious epidemics and contagious diseases that affected all social and economic classes:

> Diseases bred freely in polluted streams and in refuse-clogged roads and narrow, puddled streets. Diphtheria, measles, smallpox, and scarlet fever were killers known in every town ... Every winter and spring, epidemic pneumonias and *la grippe* appeared. Typhoid fever, dysentery, and malaria repeatedly ravaged France during the eighteenth century ... Lice and the itch were endemic, affecting practically everyone ... venereal disease was prevalent.[13]

In this environment, physical suffering was an inescapable fact, relief almost impossible to find and early death an all too common occurrence. Medical care was sporadic, largely inaccessible and perceived to be not only ineffectual, but also dangerous. While there was a diverse range of options available to would-be patients, the medical profession was, in general, only locally organized and largely unregulated.[14] Only the wealthy had unrestricted access to medical opinion.[15]

Among the lower classes, mistrust of the medical profession was high, and not without reason. Overcrowded hospitals were not known to heal people, but rather contributed to ever worsening symptoms and, all too frequently, death. The Hôtel-Dieu in Paris, for example, was a space of unimaginable suffering where contagion ran rampant, infecting helpless and otherwise innocent individuals who were desperate to be healed. In the words of Diderot, it was:

> the most sprawling, most populous, wealthiest and most frightening of all of our hospitals ... Imagine a long row of adjoining rooms where patients of all kinds are put together, often three, four, five and six in the same bed; the living next to the dying and the dead; the air infected by the odors of this multitude of unhealthy bodies, carrying the foul germs of their sicknesses amongst themselves; the spectacle of grief and pain offered and received from all sides. This is the *Hôtel Dieu*.[16]

Diderot paints a picture of unrelenting horror, evoking extremes of physical suffering and dangerous contagion that threatened not only the life of the individual, but also the French populace as a whole.

Diderot's observations were not isolated. Jacques Tenon's report on the state of Paris hospitals, the *Mémoires sur les hôpitaux de Paris* (1788), both confirmed and extended Diderot's critique. Citing mortality rates that were the highest in Europe, far outpacing those in Edinburgh or Vienna, Tenon penned a damning indictment of Parisian medical practice, fully revealing the extent to which the profession and the state had failed society's weakest members.[17] In response, Tenon proposed a series of minimum standards to ensure improved patient care. Tenon's work represented the culmination of a public health movement that had emerged early in the second half of the eighteenth century and in which Madame Necker played an active role.

The publication of Samuel-Auguste-André-David Tissot's *Avis au peuple sur sa santé* in 1761 paved the way for a profound reconceptualization of social responsibility for the health and well-being of the citizenry as a whole.[18] Tissot's work was immensely influential and widely available. Appearing in sixteen translations, among them German, Dutch, Swedish, Hungarian, Russian and Greek, it was constantly in print until 1830.[19] The *Avis* was written in plain language in the vernacular and emerged as a direct result of Tissot's work with rural Swiss peasants and was designed specifically to enable community leaders – such as parish ministers – to take a more active role in fostering the well-being of their parishioners.

It also allowed suffering individuals themselves to take a more direct role in their care by offering them concrete ways to shape their experiences in words in order to make them comprehensible for medical professionals. As Tissot observed:

> It requires much attention and experience to judge properly the [physical] state of a patient that one cannot see, even when one is as educated in this as well as one can possibly be from a distance, but this difficulty is greatly increased – and even becomes impossible – when the information is not accurate ... It is in order to prevent this risk that I have attached a list of questions to which one should be able to respond.[20]

By outlining the barriers to societal well-being and proposing concrete solutions to endemic problems, Tissot introduced the idea of public health as a relevant issue of civic concern. Such a stance would no doubt have resonated with Madame Necker. Just as Tissot developed his ideas from his experiences as a doctor to the poor in the areas around Lausanne, so too would Necker, the daughter of a village pastor, have witnessed at first hand the sufferings of impoverished parishioners.

In Paris, discussions about public health took on even greater urgency in 1773, as the city came to terms with the extensive damage wrought by a devastating week-long fire at the Hôtel-Dieu.[21] The effects of the fire brought the conditions in the hospital into high relief. As Dora B. Weiner observes: 'The murderous overcrowding at the Hôtel-Dieu and the neglect of safety in its layout and storage of inflammable materials became topics of daily discussion'.[22] The founding, in 1776, of the Société royale de médecine, for the express purpose of coordinating an organized effort towards the prevention of human and animal disease, offered further opportunities for critical reflection.[23] A surge in small-scale hospital projects in the 1770s and 1780s included not only Madame Necker's experimental Hospice de charité, founded by royal edict in 1778, but also the Vaugirard Hospital, which offered a revolutionary treatment for infants born with venereal disease, and the tiny six-bed Protestant Hospital run by the Swedish embassy. All of these projects represented concrete movement towards improving the situation.[24]

Madame Necker was a committed participant in the public health movement. Not only was she subject as a patient to the travails of corporeal fallibility, but she was also an influential philanthropist in the area of hospital reform and an avid reader and consumer of medical texts and treatises. A friend of Tissot's from the period immediately preceding her marriage, she maintained a close relationship with him and received copies of his latest publications, which she read with great interest. In Tissot's work, Madame Necker perceived the beneficent union of faith and public duty on behalf of 'l'humanité souffrante' – suffering humanity – and she was singularly impressed with its moral implications: 'One believes and feels oneself to be almost like a Doctor and philosopher after having read your work, and fortunately, at the same time one becomes more virtuous and yet better'.[25]

Madame Necker's involvement in Parisian hospital reform offers one striking example of her commitment to addressing the medical and moral needs of the poor and suffering in her community. She was horrified by the squalid conditions of Parisian hospitals,[26] in particular the Hôtel Dieu, noting that 'These monuments to humanity have become, in many places, monuments to indifference and almost, to barbarism'.[27] In addition, the Hôtel Dieu was, from Madame Necker's perspective, inefficiently managed. In response, she proposed an experimental charity hospital governed by the dual principles of hygiene and economy.[28] The 120-bed Hospice de charité, located in the parishes of Saint-Sulpice and Gros-Caillou, opened in 1778. Directed by Madame Necker and a local parish curate, Jean Joseph Faydit de Terssac, and managed by Soeur Cassegrain, one of twelve Sisters of Charity employed by the hospital, it offered medical care to the suffering but morally sound poor of the community. Admission to the hospital was carefully scrutinized and potential patients were screened in order to weed out possible thieves who sought to evade justice – 'fainéans', or lazy, good-for-nothings who used illness as a pretext for not working – and miserly individuals who were able to pay for medical care, but chose instead to seek medical attention at the expense of the poor.[29] Patients, one to a bed, recuperated in well-aired rooms, cared for by a staff that included a resident doctor and surgeon.[30] Madame Necker directed the project for more than ten years, from its inception in 1778 until her departure from France in 1790. Throughout this period, she oversaw its activities and produced annual published reports which included detailed financial accounts and medical statistics.[31]

These annual reports, four of which remain, are prefaced by lengthy introductions which gave Madame Necker a prime opportunity to display the principles of her Calvinist faith. As such, they appear to function as testaments to the broader ideas that underpinned her reformed belief. Particularly evident is Necker's understanding of herself as part of a larger community of individuals and her responsibility, as a wealthy woman of faith, to respond to the needs and concerns of the less fortunate. Necker's self-enactment can be understood as a mobilization of her spiritual sensibility, an active engagement with the physical sufferings of others in order to fulfil the requirements of Calvinist duty and to achieve spiritual communion. Indeed, it is worth noting in this regard that Louis de Jaucourt, author of the article 'Sensibilité (morale)' in the *Encyclopédie*, defined sensibility as that 'tender and delicate disposition of the spirit which makes it open to being moved, to being touched ... sensibility is the mother of humanity, of generosity'; it praises, helps the mind and encourages persuasion, each in their turn'.[32]

While the project was conceived under the rational principles of economic efficiency and hygiene, it was governed by a sensibility deeply informed by religious belief. By suggesting that the poor and indigent of her community were 'a living altar, destined by a kind god to receive the only offerings and the only homage that can reach all the way to him,'[33] and further, that individuals of wealth and learning had a duty to respond to their sufferings,[34] Madame Necker drew upon a number of Calvinist assumptions: among them, that suffering was intrinsic to the human condition; that Calvinist practices required active commitment and involvement in one's own salvation through the provision of good to others; that wealth and learning could – and should – be mobilized in the service of divine grace and that, at a fundamental level, humanity was not made up of a series of disconnected individuals, but constituted an inherently interrelated and interdependent community. These ideas are echoed in Jacques Necker's 1781 *Compte rendu*, a work which, though mainly an account of the fiscal state of the French nation, also included a personal tribute to Madame Necker, in which Jacques Necker emphasized the gendered attributes of 'charity' and highlighted the social importance of the married unit.[35]

Madame Necker's decision to become directly involved with the provision of public charity differed markedly from the precepts promoted in Catholic conduct books of the period. In the 1730 publication *Conduite d'une dame chrétienne pour vivre saintement dans le monde*, a conduct book designed specifically for French Catholic women, the author, Duguet, counselled strict adherence to the womanly virtues of modesty and humility and argued for moderation in the practice of one's civic obligations. While he did not doubt his readers' commitment to the needs of the poor, he nevertheless recommended a cautious approach:

> You will sometimes visit the Hôtel-Dieu where you will feed the suffering and the downtrodden; and this you will ordinarily do during the major holidays. I would like it to be a little more often, but do not worry about it. When I say 'more often', I mean something like once a month.[36]

Necker's 'hands-on' approach, deeply informed by Calvinist values, represented a completely different kind of intervention. The twinned aspirations of economic security and moral fortitude, which blossomed on the very public stage of French politics, were honed through her many years of quiet, private sponsorship of impoverished Swiss family members and friends. Her support and direction of the Hospice de charité represented a large-scale act of benevolence enacted on the stage of French pre-revolutionary politics and in the full gaze of Parisian public opinion.

Necker's role in the area of public health should not be underestimated. Her work in hospital reform laid the groundwork for the development by others of further hospitals founded on the same model, among them a tiny six-bed project bearing her name and designed for the care of indigent Protestants in Montpellier.[37] In addition to this, her work set in motion the development of a large variety of charitable initiatives led by the French moneyed elite.[38]

Madame Necker was also active on other fronts. Sickness, postulated in the *Encyclopédie* as the intermediary space between life and death,[39] was an area that required public commitment. Not only did society have a responsibility to respond to the desperate plight of its ailing members, but it also needed closely to consider its collective purpose as 'the protector of the dying'.[40] 'Can we look upon men stacked in the same bed, abandoned to a filthiness that revolts even the coarsest senses, and forced to breathe a rotting air that destroys the effect of all remedies, without being moved by compassion?' she asked.[41] In 1790, in addition to her work with the Hospice de charité, Madame Necker published a treatise and policy proposal on premature burial. She was also a member of the Société de la charité maternelle, a Parisian philanthropic organization founded in 1788. In each of these cases, Madame Necker positioned herself on the side of the suffering populace, entreating society as a whole to make the plight of the less fortunate a central focus of social and civic concern.

Central to the improvement efforts initiated by Tissot and carried forward by individuals such as Madame Necker, Tenon and others, was the idea of hygiene. Defined in the *Encyclopédie* as a medical method that enabled the conservation of health and well-being, hygiene encompassed not only physical gestures, but also moral behaviours.[42] Thus doctors and other medical professionals took a multilayered approach which focused on such issues as air quality, nutrition, rest and movement, sleep, fluxes and secretions, and finally 'the passions of the soul'.[43] Madame Necker stressed the healthy environment of the Hospice de charité by outlining the project's commitment to caring for patients in single beds placed in well-aired rooms.[44] She also reflected on the moral nature of the project itself, putting the focus directly on what she perceived as society's lack of concern for the poor and indigent members of society.[45]

The language of medicine was deeply implicated in social and cultural reforms of the period. The eighteenth-century emphasis on medical and moral hygiene was fully deployed in the service of public health and well-being, forming the basis of a discourse on social responsibility and cultural obligation in which each individual had a moral duty to ensure not only his or her personal well-being, but the fitness of society as a whole.[46] Building on ideas put forward by medical practitioners trained in the Montpellier vitalist school, doctors and civic leaders advocated an approach that defined health as a position of felicitous equilibrium; in other words, a state of being in which all aspects of lived experience – moral, intellectual and physical – were in balance. Equilibrium offered optimal efficiency, providing a smooth, well-oiled psychic and corporeal frame that was ideally capable of supporting all of the healthy individual's activities and undertakings. The state of equilibrium could, however, be compromised by any number of events. The cultivation and maintenance of the healthy body and mind therefore required the individual's complete and undivided attention.

Tissot, by presenting the simple peasant as the model of health, suggested that individual well-being was the result of a balanced life lived in simplicity rather than excess. He recommended regular exercise together with a healthy diet low in fats, sugars and spices. In addition to this, he cautioned against the dangers of alcohol, coffee and hot chocolate.[47] Accordingly, Madame Necker's Hospice de charité presented a sterling example of efficiency and hygiene. Its annual reports, produced by the medical and nursing staff and prefaced by Madame Necker herself, are models of statistical clarity which outline in detail not only patient statistics, illnesses and mortality rates, but also the consumption cost and rates of food and wine.[48]

Integral to the discourse of hygiene and social fitness was the relationship between the idea of public health, which, as Ludmilla Jordanova points out, referred to the philanthropic efforts undertaken by the elite classes on behalf of the impoverished and disenfranchised labouring classes,[49] and individual embodied experience and responsibility. In other words, the process of public reflection on the nature of civic responsibility and national well-being engendered a parallel process of individual reflection and an intimate awareness of the subjective experience of the lived-in body. The letters exchanged between Madame Necker and her close friend Thomas offer one example of the ways in which subjective embodied experience was understood and displayed. In this correspondence, the shared subjective experience of illness is constructed as a performative gesture. By sharing their maladies, Thomas and Necker transformed the letter into a stage upon which they engaged in a performance of corporeality. In 1781, Thomas thanked Necker for her concern for and interest in his sister's health and outlined her medical progress. This recitation subsequently functioned as a springboard for his own interest in Necker's well-being: 'It is with your health that both brother and sister are concerned at this moment, much more so than with their own', he argued, turning the focus back onto Madame Necker. 'You will have to make up for five years of pain and work, which have drained as much strength as they have brought you glory'.[50] In these letters, illness was understood as a shared experience and as a way of bringing individuals together, and can therefore be seen to take on the characteristics of *politesse*, or social refinement and polish, as introduced in the first chapter. It was through this *communal* experience of human suffering that Suzanne and her friends were able to access their sensibility and, from this sensibility, to recognize and respond to their duties.

This subjective experience initiated dialogue on a completely different level. Where the prime negotiations had formerly taken place between the doctor and the ailing body, new relationships came to the fore: the first between the patient and the lived-in body and the second between the patient and the spectators, whether doctors, friends, colleagues or others. This process of self-reflection enabled a sentimental culture of narcissistic display in which the subjective experience of illness, related in texts by patients and sufferers, became a central element of autobiographical presentation. Indeed, Jean-Pierre Peter posits the ailing body as a theatre for the display of illness and suffering, a perspective which offers intriguing insights into eighteenth-century medical culture.[51] Such an interpretation suggests a direct collusion between the patient and the medical establishment and accords authority over the body not only to the medical professional but also, significantly, to the patient.[52] In this culture of display, the patient's body performed a dual function: the displayed body was also, at once, the displaying body, thus recalling the mirroring imperative of elite social behaviour. The corporeal structure manifested its illnesses, which patients catalogued and codified in detailed letters to medical professionals, revealing previously hidden interior experiences of malady and inviting the onlooker to participate in and engage with the signs and messages of the ailing corporeal shell. Necker's writing demonstrates that elite patients were fully aware of the performative power of their illnesses and of their potential in the context of interpersonal relationships. By invoking corporeal distress, Necker anticipated a response which conformed to the principles of a dialogic relationship: in other words, her narrative of illness stimulated her correspondents' sense of their duties and imposed a concomitant response. As Madame Necker observed: 'My illness has become dear to me through the interest which you have deigned to take in it'.[53]

In a culture where much medical consultation took place by correspondence, the performative body took centre stage. One prime example of this process can be found in the correspondence between Jean-Jacques Rousseau and Tissot. In a long letter to the famous doctor, Rousseau described a variety of physical ailments in great detail.[54] However, Rousseau's recitation had a doubly performative function: in textually displaying his body and the sufferings to which it was subject, he invited the participation of a broader audience, one which extended even beyond the gaze of his doctor. 'Sir, please note this sickness in your registers if you feel that it might be worth your trouble', he wrote, 'and may it supply you with a few instructive reflections either for the conservation of this short and miserable human life, or to teach men more and more to value it only for what it is worth'.[55] In a social and cultural framework in which the workings of the internal body were only just beginning to open themselves to the medical gaze, Rousseau's gesture rendered the opacity of the lived-in body completely transparent. The suffering body was put on open display: on view to the public gaze, it was offered to the scrutiny of medical science, a specimen of corporeal suffering eagerly laid out for the spectator.

While only the medical consultation letters offer the kind of detail contained in Rousseau's letter, personal correspondence of the period nonetheless included frequent references to a variety of ailments. The individual's intimate and subjective experience of illness operated within a larger cultural and social matrix of doctor/patient relations in which suffering conferred not only social acceptance, but further, social attractiveness. The elite body, posited by Tissot as an inherently sick body, was also a treated body. Subject to the gaze of the celebrity doctor, it revelled in illness and basked in reflected social glory. In this environment, medical tourism, which saw patients travel around Europe in search of the ideal doctor, flourished. As Séverine Pilloud points out: '[medical tourism] generates... a veritable court or salon culture, where it is in good taste to be seen in the company of people of power'.[56] Illness came to define the elite body in much the same way as the art of conversation defined the elite *esprit*. Illness, thus performed and displayed through discourse, became an essential aspect of elite identity, a mark of acculturation that conferred membership in a select – and clearly identifiable – social category. So it was that Rousseau sought the advice of Tissot and that elite women such as Madame d'Épinay and Madame de Vermenoux travelled to Geneva to spend months and even years under the care of Tronchin. To this extent, Madame Necker's myriad illnesses can be understood as integral to the culture of which she was a part. A closer examination, however, discloses undercurrents that suggest new possibilities for understanding the intimate experience of illness during the eighteenth century.

Séverine Pilloud and Micheline Louis-Courvoisier provide a compelling framework for understanding doctor/patient relationships during this period.[57] Focusing directly on the 1,200 extant consultation letters written to Tissot during his lifetime, they posit a complex relationship between what they perceive as exterior and interior medical experiences; in other words, between that which can be grasped by observers – the element of corporeal experience subject to and codified by the external gaze – and that which exists only in the domain of the patient; that is, those experiences that remain invisible to the external gaze and need to be formally articulated either orally or in writing.[58] They argue that this formal process of exteriorization, undertaken either by the patient or by a close family member, local physician or religious leader, was integral to the doctor/patient relationship and accorded significant authority to the ailing patient. As Pilloud and Louis-Courvoisier demonstrate, exteriorization was a conscious gesture specifically enacted in order to assert the authority of subjective understandings and to claim ownership of personal suffering and lived experience. Each of Tissot's patients, well aware of the cultural dominance of the medical gaze and its implicit authority to diagnose and define the experience of illness, chose to lay claim to his or her own telling of the story. In so doing, the patient took authorship away from the medical profession, otherwise entrusted with the narratives of sickness and health. The words of one Monsieur Thomassin are particularly revealing in this regard. 'My sickness is internal, there is no one but me who feels it', he insisted,

> I also believed that there is no one but me who could describe it; this is why I have chosen not to use a university [trained] doctor as my interpreter, [a man] who, in using the terms of his art, would perhaps explain my case less effectively than would my poor jargon.[59]

But the subjective experience of illness – that dialogue between the suffering individual and the lived-in body that extended out to the enlightened gaze of the medical spectator – could also be taken further. From this perspective, illness was not debilitating, but could also be perceived as nourishing, in that the ownership of illness functioned as the impetus for heightened emotional and intellectual awareness. The various corporeal sufferings of François-Marie Arouet de Voltaire offer perhaps the most notable example of the performative potential of illness. Indeed, the self-styled 'old sick man of Ferney' spent many years under the care of Tronchin.[60] Voltaire is best known, however, for his particular ability to use the performance of illness as a conduit in the service of artistic and romantic creativity. In a 1773 letter to Madame Necker, he explored the implications of the blindness of her associate, Madame du Deffand, observing that, 'Her loss of eyesight takes away nothing from the character of her society; [rather] it makes the spirit more attentive and even increases the imagination.'[61] It is clear from Voltaire's words that illness was not perceived as entirely disabling; in fact, the sick body could function as a site in which other senses were heightened, so that the sick individual could enjoy better access to deeper states of being.

This belief also appeared in the context of his own life. Deidre Dawson, looking closely at the epistolary relationship between Voltaire and his lover and niece, Madame Denis, observes a relationship characterized by and understood through the writing of illness. In this epistolary exchange, physical trauma enhanced the nature of Voltaire's desire, so that 'the passion [was] metaphorised into an illness'.[62] Corporeal suffering was in this sense not disabling, but enabling, providing a stimulus for the performance of amorous passion. In this scenario, illness was deployed as an erotic gesture, a way of linking Voltaire to his beloved Madame Denis. Thus, while it remains important to examine critically the nature of the power relationships that informed doctor/patient relationships during this period, relationships which gave credence to the construction of women's bodies as naturally ill, for example, it is equally important to look at the ways in which individuals negotiated these prescriptions on a subjective level. The lived-in body, located at the meeting point between the authority and institutional power of the medical establishment and imagined, personal experience, must be envisioned as a fundamentally troubled entity that acted on its own behalf even as it was acted upon.

Philippe Rieder and Vincent Barras postulate an active and dynamic patient who was fully immersed in her physical experience and directly involved in her medical care. In an almost seductive move, this patient courted medical opinion through the act of sharing physical infirmities, actively drawing the medical gaze into her internal bodily experience. Such a patient, Rieder and Barras suggest, was hardly the mute, passive, gazed-upon entity theorized by Foucault. Rather, 'The patient must be thought of otherwise: a character who constitutes a dynamic figure, interacting all at once with his own past, with his surroundings, with the health professionals and with the medical know-how of his times'.[63] This patient negotiated the exterior and interior gaze with aplomb, crafting an autobiographical experience of illness which meshed with medical and cultural understandings of the day.

This, almost certainly, was the framework in which Madame Necker experienced her illnesses. As a patient of both Tissot and Tronchin, an avid reader of medical literature and a committed philanthropist in the area of hospital reform, she was thoroughly embedded in the principles of the external gaze. She was also, at the same time, through her correspondence and private writings, the author of her own illnesses. In full command of the discursive evocation of her suffering, she both acquiesced to and revelled in the emotional and sentimental power of disease over her life experiences. In order to appreciate more fully the slippage between subjective embodied knowledge and the institutional authority of the medical gaze, I turn to a discussion of Madame Necker's understanding of the relationship between illness and performance. More specifically, I examine the link between malady and sensibility as they played themselves out on the female body and subsequently, in Madame Necker's case, on her Calvinist body.

Pathologizing Women: Vitalism, Illness and Gender

On 6 April 1773, Suzanne Necker remarked to a friend: 'I am losing track of my time and my health; my sensibility alone is unlimited'.[64] In this statement Necker acknowledged not only the frantic pace required by her public roles as *salonnière* and political wife, but also the deep relationships between illness, sensibility and female experience. For Madame Necker, illness functioned as a channel for her sensibility, a way to engage with the most personal aspects of her being and, from there, to engage more fully and more deeply with the physical and moral sufferings of others. Illness was, finally, a vehicle through which she could express the full extent of her psychic distress and feelings of filial culpability. Madame Necker defined cultural, religious and filial alterity through malady. In so doing, she demonstrated that the interplay between psychic and somatic markers of illness functioned as an integral aspect of her conception of self.

Madame Necker's experiences were directly informed by the emergence of medical vitalism. A medical movement which appears to have originated some-time around the middle of the century, vitalism moved away from anatomical and humoral understandings of the body by positing the body as a vital entity – living, moving and dynamic. This body was created of multiple parts, all intimately linked together through the property of sensibility.[65] The vitalist perspective fundamen-tally transformed medical and moral understandings of the body. By positing an interconnected psychic and corporeal system, vitalists theorized sensibility as an active agent and argued for a holistic understanding of the individual. In con-trast to the work of anatomists, which relied on static understandings of the body, vitalist philosophy posited a dynamic body that was continually in process and organized through a series of constantly mobile inter-relationships. Physical and mental disease were intrinsically connected, the vitalists argued, the health of one dependent wholly upon the health and fitness of the other.

Vitalist *médecins philosophes* understood the body as an entity constructed of multiple individual parts, impulses and ideas, each of which was intimately linked to the other by a sensitive and nuanced nervous system. Integral to vitalist thought was the desire to bridge the gap between the Cartesian mind and body, a move beyond the purely mechanist understanding of the body as a system apart from the mind. In the vitalist framework, the mind acted upon the body as much as the body acted upon the mind, thus laying the groundwork for psychic trauma to become manifest in the form of physical distress.

The inter-relationships central to the vitalist model were made possible by the idea of sensibility, which was seen as a mediating or bridging dynamic facilitating the interaction between psyche and soma. As Elizabeth A. Williams suggests, vitalists 'luxuriated in the passional origins of disease, which functioned as the most persuasive proof available of the soul's direct action on the body'.[66] While such a fluid interplay was generally perceived as beneficent, it was equally perceived as threatening: left unchecked, sensibility metamorphosed into dan-gerous instability. Diderot's controversial *D'Alembert's Dream* makes this point. In this work, Diderot posited a dynamic body, envisaging the nervous system as a network or bundle comprising an infinite number of strands that: 'vibrate [and] transmit to the common centre a multitude of sensations often discordant, disconnected and muddled'.[67] While sensibility animated the threads and ena-bled the networks, it was understood by thinkers like Diderot as a volatile power whose potential had to be mediated by the logical operations of the rational control centre. To invert this relationship, Diderot warned, was to invite chaos: the system as a whole was threatened with confusion if the individual threads attempted to control the centre. The frightening imagery he chose, of a network in complete disarray, suggests the social dangers inherent in the vitalist model of indeterminacy. Indeed, if the coherence of the individual body could be threatened by excessive sensibility, how much more damaging might be the impact of rampant sensibility on society as a whole?

This fraught relationship between beneficence and volatility was central to vitalist medical thought, particularly as it concerned women. Regularly evoked by vitalist *médecins philosophes* such as Pierre Pomme and Théodore Raulin, the perception of a direct link between women and emotional instability reached its apogee in Pierre Roussel's immensely influential 1775 work, the *Système physique et moral de la femme ou Tableau philosophique de la constitution, des moeurs et des fonctions propres au sexe*.[68] According to these practitioners, women were, as Jean-Pierre Peter has suggested: 'ill because they were women'.[69] Indeed, contemporaneous thinkers regularly associated women with pathology. Within such a system of belief, Madame Necker's hyper-sensibility – her ability to experience intimately the emotional and physical states of those around her – manifested itself in the form of continual illness.[70]

A discussion of the relationship between vitalist medicine, sensibility and the female body is necessary in order to understand the impact of this way of thinking on Madame Necker's experience and understanding of illness. At a basic level, vitalist understandings of sensibility were not explicitly gendered. Indeed, while women suffered from *hystérie* – hysteria – men suffered from *hypochondrie*, or hypochondria. Both 'vaporous' ailments appeared to manifest themselves in a series of bizarre and erratic behaviours and both disorders were seen as the product of immoderate lives of luxury and excess. In this respect class, not gender, would seem to have been a precondition for nervous ailments, for the *vapeurs* appeared to emerge largely within the elite classes who lived in the nation's capital, Paris. Since physical excess could directly influence the nervous system, nervous disorders were imputed to lives of idleness, debauchery and over-consumption.[71] The sensible body could not be divorced from its surroundings, since it was both a product of and a catalyst for the workings of the individual mind and those of society at large. As Necker observed of her own sufferings, 'my weakness is, I think, a woman's illness, which is common enough in this country and unknown in our own'.[72]

Nevertheless, most vitalist physicians seeking to understand and define the nature and scope of the volatility of the female body identified gender and not class as inherently problematic for individual well-being. More specifically, vitalists believed that sensibility served to highlight the already fraught relationship between the concepts of 'woman' and 'body'. Women's 'natural' emotional capacity for sensibility, when viewed in the light of emergent understandings regarding the radical potential of a delicate and sensitive body, was assumed to render the female body particularly unstable. Most vitalists agreed that women were prone to nervous disorders. Raulin, for example, pointed out that women had been particularly susceptible to nervous disorders since the time of Hippocrates, but that these diseases had become ever more serious and complex, so that by the middle of the eighteenth century 'the illnesses of women exceed by more than two hundred those specific to men'.[73] Women's inherent sensibility, he suggested, was a prime source for the health problems they experienced:

> The sensibility associated with the essence of women, or with particular constitutions which are more susceptible than others, means that their feelings, sometimes brought to extreme delicacy, are affected by the slightest accident; this is the source of an infinite number of vaporous symptoms & often of the most violent vapours.[74]

What this description suggests is that because sensibility inhered in their sex, women were required to take greater pains to moderate their behaviour than men. The existence of a specifically female sensibility made them more prone to vapours, precisely because of their inner delicacy and refinement.

Unlike Raulin, Tissot connected gender and class. Linking female sensibility and illness with the practices of elite sociability, he suggested that nervous maladies, particularly those of elite women, stemmed from psychic causes: they could be directly attributed to excessive imaginations over-stimulated by the almost infinite proliferation of novels:

> From birth to the most advanced old age, they read them with such zeal that they fear being distracted for even a moment, remain immobile and often stay up quite late to satisfy this feeling, [a fact] which most certainly ruins their health; not to mention that of those who are themselves authors, and this number is growing daily.[75]

The consequences of such emotional imbalance were profound and devastating: 'A ten-year-old girl who spends her time reading rather than running will become, by the age of twenty, a vaporous woman and will not be able to breast-feed well'.[76] The sufferings of elite women, Tissot argued, were a natural outcome of their lives of gluttony, inactivity and, more importantly, excessive passion. Their sufferings were culturally induced, the products of over-civilization.

Tissot's comments suggest that because of its sensitive frame, the female body assumed monstrous properties. Not only could women, through the idea of corporeal sensitivity, infect and influence the bodies and minds of those around them, but they could also infect themselves and, more worryingly, the fetuses that developed within them. Indeed, the medical establishment defined women as the epitome of dangerous pathology, seeing in them corrupt entities that threatened and undermined social cohesion. While women possessed the 'principle of all life', as François Azouvi has observed, this principle was subject to the threatening environment of the womb.[77] 'This womb can create everything – the best and the worst', notes Jean-Pierre Peter, 'Monsters flourish here almost as commonly as the lives of innocents are tragically crushed'.[78] Doctors argued that women, morally corrupt through the actions of the first woman, Eve, functioned as the repository for human weakness and as a result were condemned to the dangers of a reproductive life as punishment for their sin.[79] Defined in these terms by their reproductive pathology, women, in turn, pathologized society. The medical model of sensibility thus conspired with cultural understandings about gender to posit the sensitive woman as a menace whose volatile and capricious passions – aided and abetted by the instability of her organs and the essential vulnerability of her physical form – upset the stability of the social system.

It is exactly at this moment that beneficent moral sensibility, initially perceived as a social good, was transformed into pathology. Nowhere was this more incisively articulated than in Roussel's *Système moral et physique de la femme*. Roussel observed that while young boys and girls shared very similar physiological features, men and women were markedly different. Young men gained strength and solidity at puberty, while young women retained strong ties – both physically and emotionally – to their child-like selves. Not only were they less robust, but their organic instability and weakness created a state of emotional frailty. 'More sensitive than sturdy', women were governed by their essential 'mollesse', or softness, a diagnosis that rendered them overly sensitive to the impulses of the world around them.[80] Though education could alter this tendency, softness and sweetness were – and should continue to be – women's natural destiny.[81] Indeed, Jean-André Venel observed that the very differences that defined women as women were the qualities which ultimately made them attractive to the men they would marry.[82] For Roussel, sexual difference was not a matter of medical theory; rather, it inhered in the state of nature itself. Roussel's woman was radically other – weak, vulnerable, unstable – precisely because nature made her this way. Furthermore, because nature made her this way, woman-as-other was fulfilling her natural and inescapable destiny. This approach was also evident in the work of other vitalists. Raulin, for example, while quick to position himself against the claims of the ancients, who argued that the womb alone was the source of female hysteria, nonetheless devoted a large portion of his book to the intricate details of female reproductive organs, thus emphasizing sexual difference as the cause and source of women's emotional and nervous weakness.

Here, then, we come to a curious self-fulfilling prophecy: not only were women, by their natures sensitive, a fact which rendered their physical bodies weaker, but these bodies, by their very weakness, served to confirm women's innate sensibility. By locating sexual difference in the body, asserting it through the lens of sensibility and, finally, arguing from the perspective of natural law, the vitalists rendered sexual incommensurability not only as fact but also as utterly irrevocable. In this framework, women could not possibly escape their biological destiny.[83] One could argue that such an interpretation was not necessarily limiting. After all, according to philosophers such as Thomas, women held exalted social positions precisely because of their innate sensibility, and, as we have seen in earlier chapters, many an etiquette treatise and moral essay waxed poetic on women's essential role in the civilizing process. Thomas's famous essay on the qualities of women, for example, builds on the framework proposed by the Genevan Ami Lullin, presenting the women of virtue as those who, 'link a well-cultivated reason with a strong spirit, and uplift their feelings of courage and honour through virtue'.[84] In this light, the sensitive female body could appear as a natural extension of such benevolent and almost universally lauded character traits. Unfortunately, no such benign relationship existed between psychic and corporeal sensibility. Instead, the gendered bodily encounter with sensibility was inevitably fraught. For if sensibility relied on the indeterminacy of the individual and if, at the same time, the idea of woman relied on the over-determinacy of the individual, then the combination of woman and sensibility was profoundly threatening to the social order. Ironically, while the very fluid, undefined, flexible nature of the female body would appear to offer the greatest potential for the realization of the vitalist framework, the opposite appears to have been the case: women's predisposition to sensibility, as determined by the weakness of their organs, rendered their sensibility contaminated, impure and poisonous. As Azouvi explains:

> if life is defined by capacity for feeling ... we must accept that, of all living beings, woman is the one who embodies, to a notable degree, all the essential properties of life ... In effect, to live is to feel; now, this is the definition of woman but it is also the origin of her illnesses and of the inevitable weakness which leads her to final exhaustion.[85]

Women's bodies transformed the beneficent qualities of sensibility into monstrous qualities, with the result that women themselves – defined and understood through their bodies – became the monsters.

Health, Sensibility and Duty: The Illnesses of Madame Necker

Madame Necker was deeply aware of the medical currents of her time. Indeed, this naturalized relationship which connected women, sensibility, illness and, ultimately, contagion or contamination directly influenced Necker's experience and understanding of illness. In her writings, she conceived of her illnesses, at both psychic and somatic levels, as sufferings which played themselves out on an ever-present ailing body. For Necker, illness was disabling, in that it prevented her from writing, caused her family stress and hardship and further geographically isolated her – through her inability to travel – from her Swiss homeland. At the same time, however, her illnesses took on a deeply performative cast, in that they enabled her to plumb more fully the depths of her sensibility and, further, to enact in physical ways her filial neglect and Calvinist guilt. From this perspective, Madame Necker's body became the site for the performance of Calvinist abjection, a way of claiming the suffering of society as a means of recovering from her own moral failure. The section that follows explores her maladies in greater detail and demonstrates the ways in which each of these ideas played itself out within her ailing body.

While Madame Necker made regular mention of her illnesses throughout her correspondence, her understandings were most clearly and thoroughly developed in her extended correspondence with her two Swiss friends, Etienette Clavel de Brenles and Henriette Réverdil. The observations of her colleagues and family – in particular the letters written by her friends Antoine Léonard Thomas and the Comte de Buffon, and her daughter Germaine – provide further context. The correspondence indicates that Suzanne Necker's illnesses can be broadly divided into two categories. While at times these two categories can be considered as wholly distinct from one another, at other times they overlap, so that the effects of one aggravated or heightened the impact of the other.

The first category includes those illnesses which she described in great detail. These had relatively clear beginnings and endings and recognizable and definable symptoms including fevers, chills, coughs, tooth problems and so forth. In a 1767 letter to Madame de Brenles, for example, Necker recounted a perilous journey that was further exacerbated by her ill health: 'I caught the fever en route and I have had the infection for two days'.[86] Similarly, in 1790, she warned the pastor David Levade that she was not fit to welcome visitors, noting that, 'Last night, Sir, I had a coughing fit that has thrown me into great despondency; I am in no condition to receive anyone'.[87] In each of these cases, Necker described her symptoms and the duration of her illness was clearly recorded: it had a beginning and a projected end. In addition to this, the ailments appear to have been purely physical. Writing of this category of illness, Madame Necker did not refer to psychic or emotional distress, but described only physical weakness.

The second category of illness is markedly different. In this case, the symptoms were not clearly defined, nor were they chronologically delineated. Rather Necker's sufferings remain vague and somewhat amorphous. Described variously by terms such as 'foiblesse', 'incommodité', 'infirmité' or 'langueur', among others – terms which relate to such conditions as fainting or swooning, illness, indisposition, chronic illness and what we would understand today as psychosomatic distress or depression – these maladies appear at least superficially to resemble the nervous ailments so widespread during this period.[88] This resemblance is more profound if one considers that Madame Necker's illnesses seem to be directly related to emotional turmoil or disturbance. For example, in 1765 she suggested that her health might not allow her to travel. 'I still carry the mark of my old suffering', she confided to Madame de Brenles, marking herself physically with the psychic experience of emotional loss.[89]

While the intensity of Madame Necker's psychosomatic suffering fluctuated, the experience of illness dominated her physical landscape. At some points, the situation was terrifyingly desperate and she felt very close to death;[90] at other

times, she sensed improvement. In April 1768, she reported to Madame de Brenles that she was getting better, but still maintaining a special diet even as she
had returned to her normal daily schedule; just two months later, however, she
apologized for not writing as she had been suffering from six weeks of fever and
was only just beginning to pick up her pen with difficulty.[91] Even though her
health was improving, it was still precarious, for she noted that she remained at
her country home at St Ouen and was not yet up to the intensity of the Parisian
social scene. By September 1768, she was suffering yet again, but this time from
'a new accident [that] made me fear that my languor was becoming very dangerous', a situation which caused both her husband and Thomas to urge her to
journey to Mont d'Or to take the waters.[92] The trip was perilous, but the waters
did appear to have some positive effect. By December 1768, she was coughing
again, though she was quick to mention that she felt healthier than normal, particularly during a season that was the source of much illness for many people.[93]

This situation, in which Madame Necker described periods of grave illness
followed by periods of recuperation, appears to typify her life experience and
continues throughout her correspondence. To a certain extent, as mentioned
earlier, these sufferings resembled the numerous indefinable nervous disorders
to which women of her class were regularly subject. But while it might be tempting to suggest that her careful codification of illness amounted to nothing more
than narcissistic hypochondria, it is important to note that both family members
and friends confirmed her assessments. In 1786, Germaine de Staël reported that
her mother, while suffering, endured a health-related trip to Plombières reasona-
bly well.[94] Thomas's letters to Madame Necker are even more revealing. Between
1781 and 1785, he referred constantly to the state of Necker's health, suggesting
her role as a martyr for the good of society: 'I fear, madame, that you are not
doing everything that needs to be done to restore your health', he admonished
her in 1781, adding, 'For you, I fear this business of duty, which consumes you
and which makes you endlessly sacrifice yourself for those whom you love'.[95]

How might we understand the nature of Madame Necker's illnesses? How
might we distinguish her suffering from that of contemporaneous society
women who also sought out the medical opinions of specialists and whose indefinable and seemingly interminable maladies severely inhibited their public and
private lives? The answer, I believe, lies in her profound faith, her deep guilt and
her intimate awareness of her own mortality.

Madame Necker's illnesses came and went, but she herself used a very different barometer to assess her psychic and somatic well-being, citing the death
of her mother as a turning point in her life: 'I am very convinced that the death
of my mother altered my health irreparably because in this moment, when everything turns according to my desires, I have barely two hours of well-being'.[96]
Madame Necker's doctor, Tronchin, confirmed this diagnosis, observing that

the profound distress that Necker experienced as a result of her mother's death occasioned severe bouts of weeping and many sleepless nights that fundamentally undermined her health and constitution.[97] From this point onward, she experienced relentless psychic and physical suffering in the form of ailments and maladies that bore little resemblance to the seasonal colds and influenzas that otherwise marked her life. For Madame Necker, the primary cause was obvious: her illnesses emanated directly from her experience of loss, not only of her mother and father, but also of her homeland.[98]

As noted previously, loss was a central theme in Suzanne Necker's life and figured prominently in her correspondence. She used her letters to relive the losses of her past, most notably the deaths of her parents (particularly her mother), but also to acknowledge the other losses that marked her adult existence. Her experience of parental loss, which she wrote and rewrote through her extensive correspondence with her Swiss friends, informed and influenced all of the experiences that followed. Significantly, for Necker, loss was not just an emotional state, but also a physical reality. In Paris, for example, she experienced not only cultural and emotional dislocation, but also geographical dislocation, since some of her closest friends lived at great distances from the capital. From this perspective, Madame Necker's illnesses can be seen as the physical embodiment of cartographic distance, an attempt to register, in an embodied way, the physical reality in which she found herself and also to bridge the space between the home of her birth and her life in Paris. Today, we would perhaps classify such suffering under the rubric of homesickness. Eighteenth-century nostalgia – or *hemvé*,[99] as it was called in France – differs significantly from its contemporary counterpart. Understood as a medical disorder, it was a respiratory malady that manifested itself in a violent desire to return to one's home country. Jaucourt observes that homesickness 'only becomes a pain of the spirit because it is truly a pain of the body. Water and air different from those to which we are accustomed, produce changes in a weak machine.'[100]

Madame Necker's homesickness, which manifested itself in various maladies, became an indispensable autobiographical instrument, a way of bringing people closer to her through sensibility and a way of attaining a heightened sensibility. In this sense, her performance of illness can be seen as supremely narcissistic. Through her words and actions, she ensured her active presence in the minds of others, in the process becoming the direct focus of their social duty. This approach can be seen in a 1767 letter to Madame de Brenles, in which Madame Necker lamented the fact that she had not heard from her friend in a long while. In order to elicit a quicker response, she wrote:

> There were moments where I would have wished for a frightful accident to overcome me just so that I could enjoy the concern that you take in my life even more; but I

suppressed this bizarre hope for the fear of losing my life right at the very moment when you brought it so much happiness.[101]

At the same time, Necker's actions were not entirely self-indulgent. Just as her illnesses provoked her friend's sensibility and, from there, her duty, so too did the illnesses of Madame de Brenles (and those of her family members) similarly torment Necker's body in a sympathetic performance of illness and obligation. As a woman of acute sensibility, Necker was physically assailed by her friend's attacks of vapours, suffered on her behalf during her son's illness, and trembled 'for [this] health so precious to my heart, the certainty of which is the sweetness of my life'.[102]

Ironically, Madame Necker's physical weakness undermined her attempts to maintain connections in the face of profound and debilitating loss. Her poor health, as read through the physical instability of her body, rendered her own existence eternally precarious, a fact that made the physical separation between Necker and her friends even greater and consequently widened the psychic distance between Paris and the country of her birth. Letters were often delayed because of her illness and she regularly resorted to dictating them to a secretary or friend.[103] Her frequent maladies also inhibited and interrupted her ability to travel, particularly to Switzerland. Thus disease, while it enabled the exchange of shared sensibility, actually further distanced her from her native land and deepened her experience of exile. As she wrote to Etienette Clavel de Brenles:

> Please excuse me, Madam, for employing the services of a secretary. An inconvenience, less dangerous but more unwelcome than the previous one, does not allow me to hold a pen. To me, it seems to be a new separation that I have put between the two of us; all of the hardships that I experience make me all too aware that distance, like death, only adds to friendship.[104]

Illness, in this sense, functioned as a physical barrier between Madame Necker and that which her heart desired: her homeland and the values of her people.

But her illnesses also functioned as a barrier on another level altogether. While her extended suffering may have allowed her to lay claim to the sick aristocratic body and to subscribe to the cult of the celebrity doctor, a process which would appear to offer her the opportunity to transcend her otherwise culturally stigmatized state, I want to suggest an alternative reading. I believe that Madame Necker's illness actually served as a way of defiantly marking herself as morally 'other' to the social conventions and cultural mores of elite Parisian society. This process of self-stigmatization occurred on two distinct levels: not only did Necker claim her illness in order to take on the stigmata of the impoverished masses that surrounded her (a process which might be seen as the ultimate expansion of her charitable duties), but she also claimed the stigmata of original sin, professed and decreed by the moral philosophers of her homeland. In this sense, the performance of corporeal weakness allowed her to embody the social and moral ills of elite French society. Through this act of double abjection, Madame Necker was able to claim and perform both physical and moral scars with and on her own body and, from there, to use these performances to stimulate and further develop her already pronounced sensibility.

Madame Necker's abjection, staged in the space of the salon, ultimately functioned both as an act of penance for her filial neglect and, on a broader level, as a powerful public profession of her Calvinist faith in a country otherwise hostile to its tenets. Her thoughts are particularly revealing:

> How religion changes the picture of life! Even the pains of the body are an omen of a new existence: our faults and those of others offer us a twofold means to exercise our virtues; thus paradise is already in our thoughts – unfortunate is he who torments himself in order to foresee its pleasures and whose piety has not let him enjoy them in advance.[105]

How might such a performance have operated? If Madame Necker's actions seemed, at least superficially, to conform to those of her contemporaries – if, in other words, she appeared to acquiesce fully to the state of suffering and malady which defined the female body during this period – a reading of cultural and religious alterity becomes difficult, if not impossible, to sustain. Indeed, it could very easily be argued that her performances of illness were, as Maria Fairweather has suggested, merely 'tiresome': thoroughly narcissistic gestures designed solely to claim the undivided attention of family and friends.[106]

But what happens if we change the nature of the performer/spectator relationship? As mentioned previously, eighteenth-century understandings of illness relied on the staging of illness through the body and its subsequent enactment in the presence of a spectator. This framework allowed for the agency of both body and patient as they engaged the gaze of the audience. Throughout this chapter, the audience has been understood as the eighteenth-century public; in other words, the friends, family and guests who were witness to Madame Necker's continued and often debilitating struggles with weakness and illness.

In a Calvinist framework that relationship can be differently conceived; no longer a relationship between private individual and larger public, it is repositioned on an intimate level in the form of a spiritual dialogue between the believer and her creator. Such a performance might be considered from a penitential perspective, as the believer engaged in activities and behaviours designed to demonstrate her commitment and fidelity to the tenets of her faith. For while the body may only have been the 'temporary home' of the soul,[107] it was nevertheless intrinsic to one's humanity and evoked humanity's relationship with the Supreme Being. As Jean Calvin himself observed, in a 1563 letter to one of his French followers, Madame de Coligny:

It is certain that all diseases ought not only to humble us in setting before our eyes
our frailty, but also cause us to look into ourselves, that having recognized our own
poverty we may place all our trust in [God's] mercy ... since they are to us the mes-
sengers of death, we ought to learn to have one foot raised to take our departure when
it shall please God.[108]

Calvin's comments suggest that Madame Necker's illnesses formed part of an
intricate, intimate theological practice founded not only upon the principle of
total depravity preached at the Synod of Dort, but also on the model of civic
duty introduced by eighteenth-century theologians such as Ami Lullin. On the
one hand, Necker's philanthropic activities and corporeal suffering functioned
as proof of her spiritual fidelity and paved her path to heaven. On the other,
they served as a continual reminder of the essential uncertainty, frailty and failure of human existence, thus alluding to the transformative promise of divine
grace, the possibility of everlasting life and the seemingly arbitrary nature of
divine will. 'Everything is temporary on earth', she noted. 'In our weakness we
can barely make out the terms; and if it has been said that they are all present
to the Supreme Being in his immensity, it can also be said of us in our small-
ness.'[109] Indeed, while her beneficent acts and religious fervour would no doubt
strengthen her relationship with God, redemption was not assured. Divine grace
was a gift bestowed by the Supreme Being alone.

Thus Madame Necker's body, the stage upon which she performed her
spiritual fidelity, incarnated not only her own culpability, but also that of eighteenth-century French aristocratic culture and society as a whole. In transforming
the secular stage of elite sociability into a religious one, she enabled her own communion with God, in such a way that her body functioned as the link between
her spiritual aspirations and innate human suffering and weakness. Significantly,
this human suffering was both physical, as manifest in the patients of her hospice
and in the dying bodies evoked in her 1790 treatise; and psychic, as understood
through the myriad sufferings of the French elite.

Thomas reflected on the toll that philanthropy had taken on his friend's life.
Her tireless labour on behalf of the poor and indigent had depleted her own
already weak resources; he noted that Madame Necker had sacrificed her health to
the good of the nation. 'Be that as it may and whichever path you take', he wrote:

I will learn with great emotion that you are leaving Paris, if you *can* leave, if the new
circumstances do not restrain you yet again, if your life is not destined to be a perpetual sacrifice of yourself to the good you want to do and to the well-being of others.[110]

Read in this light, Madame Necker's suffering can be seen as part and parcel of a
selfless gesture of virtue and generosity.

Her appropriation of her adopted culture's psychic disarray is more difficult
to discern, but no less relevant to her understanding of her role as a Calvinist

believer within the French state. As explored in the first chapter, throughout her adult life, Madame Necker felt both seduced and repelled by French aristocratic manners and behaviour. Elite social practices were foreign and mysterious and the superficiality that passed for intimate conversation exhausted her. On a personal level, she yearned for her homeland, her religion and her society.

On a broader level, French society, too, was becoming aware of the inherent dangers of city life, social artifice and over-civilization. The works of Rousseau and Tissot contributed to the romanticizing of a simple, balanced peasant existence in the idyllic rusticity of the Swiss countryside, presenting the image of a 'noble' rural labourer who enjoyed physical health and moral well-being because he drew his inspiration from a beneficent natural environment. The 'homme du monde', or person of society, meanwhile, suffered deeply, his physical health undermined by moral weakness. Tissot warned that ambition, avarice, gluttony, luxury and immoderation kept the elite body in a state of perpetual agitation and fundamentally undermined the individual's state of health.[111]

Tissot's portrait could easily have been based on Madame Necker, whose experiences exactly mirrored those he presented. Indeed, agitation, torment and languishing marked her Parisian existence. In one key respect, however, she did not conform to Tissot's model. Unlike her Parisian colleagues, Madame Necker feared the social whirl and the intricacies of elite social practice. But, as Thomas observed, duty – to her husband, to her social commitments, to her philanthropy – kept drawing her back to the French capital:

> I thought of your weak health, of this Paris which keeps calling you back, and where you will lead a life that is so very different from that which is suited to you. Ah! Your stay in the country was so necessary to your recovery! You are going to seek out new troubles ... you had [the glory] of putting [virtue] into action in a country and during a century when almost everyone else just talks about it.[112]

From this perspective, Necker's illnesses might be understood as corporeal manifestations of French elite society's moral weaknesses. Imprinted on Madame Necker's already suffering body, they extended and expanded the nature of her physical suffering, providing ample proof of humanity's need for divine grace and salvation.

Physical suffering can further be understood as evidence of moral fortitude; in particular, of Madame Necker's commitment to maintaining her spiritual fidelity in the face of profound difficulty and distress. As the Comte de Buffon observed:

> I see you in the middle of the whirlwind of a troubled world, surrounded by tumultuous crowds, pressed by tedious importunities, preserving your unfailing nature of kindness and dignity and maintaining that wonderful peace, an inner peace so rare that it can only be part of firm, pure souls whose clear consciences and noble intentions render them invulnerable [to moral corruption].[113]

Buffon imagined his friend as a moral beacon of conscience and goodwill, a unique figure of goodness and charity in an otherwise troubled aristocratic society. Paris and Parisian mores were dangerous to Madame Necker; not only did they add to her psychic distress, but they also exacerbated her corporeal suffering. In the city, she quite literally became the sick elite body imagined and evoked by Tissot and Rousseau. Indeed, Madame Necker's close friend Thomas frequently referred to what he perceived as a direct link between Paris and Madame Necker's illnesses, contrasting the city's frenetic pace with the quiet rest he deemed necessary to her health.[114]

At the same time, Necker's interminable illnesses enabled her to envisage a closer relationship with God. It was through her corporeal suffering that Necker was able to approach her creator. As she confessed to her old friend, the Genevan pastor Paul Moultou: 'Never have I had greater need of courage to support the weight of my existence; it seems that my long anxieties have already allowed me to know eternity'.[115] Thomas concurred. Noting that Madame Necker was called by 'the feeling and the need for the infinite',[116] he chided her gently, writing: 'you anticipate eternal life a little too much and you forget that you are on earth, just as you make others forget, by your thoughts and ideas'.[117] Bodily suffering, the conduit that enabled shared experience between Madame Necker and her distant friends, also, in this case, enabled spiritual communion. By claiming the sufferings of others, Madame Necker could try to absolve herself of her own moral transgressions.

During her final years Madame Necker imputed her illnesses to her daughter's moral failings.[118] Such an understanding suggests a desire to bridge the maternal chasm by imprinting her daughter's moral infirmity on her own frail body. This process of self-mortification, in which the sins of the daughter were superimposed on the sins of the mother and the memory of her deceased parents, enabled Madame Necker to approach God, death and redemption. Her nostalgic desire to recover her past takes on new significance when read in this light. 'I have always loved melancholy thoughts', she wrote in 1776.

> This taste was sharper when I was younger; therefore, I often walked in the sanctuaries of the dead; I felt, without admitting it to myself, that they would soon hold what was dearest to me and that it would be a long time before I could meet up again with those precious remains.[119]

Near the end of her life, Madame Necker experienced almost no periods of good health. Her daughter commented that she was always ill,[120] an observation confirmed by one of the Neckers' guests, Maria Josepha Holroyd, who noted in 1791 that while Madame Necker was 'rather a fine woman', she was 'much painted and, when she is not painted, very yellow'.[121] By 1794, the situation was grave. In early February, Germaine reported to her lover, Narbonne, that her mother was dangerously sick.[122] Just a few days later, Suzanne's physician, the celebrated Tissot, corroborated this diagnosis.[123] Suzanne Curchod Necker finally died, in the arms of her husband, on 14 May 1794.[124] She was fifty-seven years old.

5 SPECULAR DEATH: STAGING THE VIRTUOUS BODY

One day, the flies gathered on a mushroom. One of them, weighed down by age, had this to say to the younger ones: 'Listen to me for I have much experience; I have seen day break and I can see the end of the world.' Night was approaching.[1]

Death is certain and it is not.[2]

I am no longer surprised by the courage of the martyr. It seems very clear to me at the moment that a good conscience is man's only power.[3]

The revolutionary journal *Le Sans Culotte* reported the details surrounding Madame Necker's death and burial on 2 August 1794: 'Madame Necker, recently deceased, requested that she be placed in a lead coffin with a glass cover, and in alcohol'.[4] Necker's grieving husband, the article further noted, had followed her requests almost to the letter, with a single exception: he chose not to cover her casket with glass. Jacques Necker's reasoning was simple. Illness had disfigured his wife's features, leaving only a memory of her youthful beauty.

Madame Necker had prepared meticulously for her death. Deeply concerned with maintaining the sanctity of her body, she consulted with numerous doctors in order to gain a thorough understanding of the best and most efficient approaches to embalming.[5] She crafted elaborate plans for her tomb and spelled out her final wishes in minute detail. Her precise directives, developed over a period of ten years, stipulated that her body would be embalmed, positioned in a casket as described in the newspaper account and placed in a tomb for which her husband alone would have the key:

> You will have an iron door, for which you alone have the key, made in the wall. Your body will pass through this door when you exist no longer and it will be placed on the same resting place [as mine], so that your remains might be united with mine and you will follow the same procedures, except one: one month after your death, you will order the iron door permanently locked so that we can remain alone together ... remember that we should be united both on earth and in heaven and follow my final wishes. This heart, which has been dedicated to you and which continues to beat for

you, deserves your respect for its two weaknesses: the fear of being buried alive and that of being separated from you.[6]

Madame Necker decreed that her husband was to visit this tomb weekly and that he was to retrieve, one by one, a series of letters which she had specifically designated to be opened after her death.[7] Finally, she insisted that he would follow the same embalming procedures upon his death, so that the two could be reunited. When death finally came, during the night of 14 May 1794, she was ready: every detail was accounted for. Her body was prepared according to her careful instructions and laid out in a lead casket. Three months later, upon the completion of her tomb, her body was laid to rest in a vat of alcohol. In control of her corporeal autobiography to the very end, Madame Necker put her infirmity on permanent display, embalmed and preserved for eternity.

Even in an era concerned about the finality of death and preoccupied with fears of premature burial, the reasons governing Madame Necker's detailed plans lay well beyond the range of society's comprehension. Indeed, to her contemporaries, Necker's death and burial were objects of morbid fascination. Philippe Ariès recounts that the spy assigned to the Necker family 'reported that Mme Necker had "ordered her body to be preserved in alcohol, like an embryo"'.[8] An anonymous quatrain, apparently popular in the immediate aftermath of Suzanne Necker's death, caricatured her plan:

> Here lies one who, in her dying,
> Imagined nothing more beautiful
> Than to be placed in a tomb
> Like a peach in brandy.[9]

Discerning or assigning meaning to her instructions at two centuries' remove is even more difficult. How might we understand these rituals? What purpose did they serve? Finally, how can these practices elucidate our understanding, not only of Suzanne Curchod Necker, but also of her culture?

In this final chapter, I explore the relationships between dying, death, burial and spectacle. I argue that Madame Necker's complex and detailed burial rituals function as part of an elaborate process of memorialization in which she linked her frail corporeality, lived out through three decades of physical suffering, to the moral disease of elite French society. Hers was, in this sense, a specular death, a process whereby the tormented corporeal relic became a mirror though which humanity could gaze on its moral weakness and reflect on its inherent mortality. Necker's body, physically marked by illness, itself became the mark – or stigma – of social malaise, through an almost messianic process that could absolve her of her sin and enable her, finally, to claim divine grace. On an intimate and personal level, Necker's final gesture served as a recuperative act of fidelity and pious devotion, not only to the memory of her mother, but also to God.

Dying was a state that Madame Necker understood intimately. As she observed in a letter to her close friend Paul Moultou, 'Never have I had more need of courage to bear the weight of my existence: it seems to me that through my extended sufferings I have already come to know eternity'.[10] As a result of her frequent illnesses, she conceived of herself as a frail body prone to weakness and always on the verge of death. Hers was a dying body, whose journey into decline and decay was clearly discernible. At the same time, through her charity work, hers was a public body, physically marked by the sufferings of those whose causes she championed and prominently displayed for all to behold.

Death was a popular and controversial topic of discussion during the eighteenth century. In the medical profession, death was seen as the antithesis of life.[11] In the words of one doctor, Paul-Jacques Malouin, as found in the *Encyclopédie*, if life could be defined through movement – respiration and the circulation of blood – then death could be understood as the point of absolute stillness.[12] However, even as the medical profession propagated this oppositional perspective, another, more fluid understanding of death gained equal currency. Louis de Jaucourt, in another *Encyclopédie* entry, posited death as an imperceptible process which began at the moment of birth, thus envisioning life as an inevitable and drawn-out process of dying:

> Little by little this life increases and expands; it acquires consistency and, in the context of its growth, develops and strengthens itself; as soon as it begins to wither, the quantity of life diminishes; finally, while it gives in, it dries up and collapses; life withers, narrows and is reduced almost to nothing. We begin life by degrees and we finish by dying in the same way we began to live.[13]

Jaucourt's definition was heavily informed by the perspectives of Necker's close friend the Comte de Buffon, who offered a similarly biologically determinist view of human life: death, he maintained, was a lengthy and almost imperceptible process that began at the point at which the body reached maturity.[14] Taking each aspect of the body in turn, Buffon painted a picture of inevitable dissolution, in which the glory and beauty of youth slowly gave way to physical degeneration and decay. 'The body dies, therefore, little by little and bit by bit', Buffon observed, in such a way that, ultimately, death could be understood only as the final nuance of life.[15] For Buffon and Jaucourt, death and life were inextricably intertwined; each was a natural part of the other and neither was possible on its own.

The very fact that the contradictory perspectives of Malouin and Jaucourt could coexist in the pages of the *Encyclopédie* suggests that meanings and understandings of death were in flux during this period. Historians who have studied French views on death see the eighteenth century as an era of uncertainty, during which attitudes towards death and dying were undergoing tremendous change. Ariès notes a desire to conceal death during this period, an instinct which, he suggests, manifested itself in an indifference to the rituals of death. In contrast to previous centuries during which the ceremonial nature of funeral rituals was upheld, Ariès contends that eighteenth-century mourners practised 'restraint in the outward signs of mourning': not only was there an increased desire to hide the body, but there were no ceremonies, no vigils, no tolling bells, no hired mourners and few candles.[16] In addition to these proofs of indifference, Ariès notes that wills began to include fewer and fewer instructions for funerals and suggests that these changes came from a desire to deny the meaning and relevance of death as a part of everyday life and, in the process, to create the impression of immortality.[17]

A contradictory impulse emerged at the same time: just as death appeared to be losing its meaning as a public event, the physical cadaver began to assume immense importance in the public sphere. An entity still believed to be possessed of inherent sensibility, it appeared to defy the prognostications of the medical profession.[18] As Necker recalled: 'The tomb of the maréchal de Saxe was discussed in *La petite Feuille* and it was said, in that mannered tone of voice so much in vogue at the time: *The countenance of the deceased has so much expression that one could say that it is full of life*'.[19]

This interest in – and fear of – the sensibility of the corpse led to public outrage at instances of perceived corporeal violation, such as the ransacking of graves for medical dissections, the use of cemeteries as grazing spaces and the unhygienic nature of common graves.[20] These concerns also led to a lengthy and contentious debate on the subject of premature burial, an extended discussion in which eighteenth-century society was forced to confront its fear of death through a process of public consideration and reflection. Indeed, Pierre Chaunu observes that the fear of premature burial was a dominant feature of most wills by mid-century.[21]

Madame Necker entered this debate in 1790. Her twenty-two-page treatise on the subject, *Des inhumations précipitées*, is organized into two sections. In the first, Necker outlined the reasons for her strong critique of premature burial, while in the second, she proposed a new law that would help to ensure dignity for the body and the peaceful passage from life to death. Necker's work capped half a century of discussion on this topic, a debate which had begun with the 1742 publication of Jacques-Jean Bruhier's translation of Jacques-Bénigne Winslow's treatise, the *Dissertation sur l'incertitude des signes de la mort et l'abus des enterremens et embaumemens précipités*. Winslow, a doctor in the Faculty of Medicine in Paris and member of the French Royal Academy of Sciences, began his *Dissertation* with a controversial statement: 'Death is certain and it is not. It is certain because it is inevitable. It is uncertain because it is sometimes unclear if the individual is actually dead.'[22] He then offered the reader numerous examples of premature burial, among them a monk who was removed, breathing, from a grave three or four days after his interment (but who had bitten off his hands in the meantime), a woman whose body began to tremble upon the first incision of a caesarean section and a man, fully prepared for burial, who returned to life and complete health upon having water sprinkled into his mouth. Winslow's work painted a horrific tableau of a multitude of bodies rising from their shrouds, their coffins and even their graves, a picture filled with the shrieks and cries of apparently dead individuals dissected prematurely. He used these scenes of horror to deliver a simple message: the conventional signs and proofs of death were insufficient means to prove certain or absolute death. The only certain sign of death was the beginning of the putrefaction of the corpse, a fact which led him to suggest a number of reforms with regard to the dying body.[23] François Thiéry, like Winslow a Parisian doctor, entered the debate in 1787. *La Vie de l'homme respectée et défendue dans ses derniers momens, ou Instruction sur les soins qu'on doit aux morts et à ceux qui paraissent l'être, sur les funérailles et les sepultures* also stressed the uncertainty of death. Death, Thiéry insisted, was a multistage process that progressed from the ambiguous 'état de mort', or apparent death, from which a return to life was not unusual, through to 'la vie réduite au moindre degré' – life reduced to the smallest degree – and finally, real death.[24]

Necker's *Inhumations* directly followed the path laid out by her predecessors: it outlined the uncertainty and ambiguity of death and proposed a series of reforms. Like Winslow, she posited death as uncertain and, like Thiéry, she proposed a multistage palliative model in which the dying individual moved almost insensibly between the stages of *agonie* and *cadavre*, apparent and absolute death:

> Death begun is called *agony*. Apparent death is a hidden and insensitive state of life which follows *agony*, and it is not uncommon for people to recover from this. Death fully achieved is the state of cadaver, but there is an interval between apparent death (believed to be certain) and the cadaverous state. That which is called death, in the first hours, is actually life reduced to the tiniest degree; it is the penultimate state that must be travelled by the inner self; it is, ultimately, an intermediary state between death begun and death completed, and nobody knows how long this uncertain state will last.[25]

In addition to this, Necker argued for an extended waiting period between death and burial, during which the body should not be treated as dead, but rather as sick.[26]

However Madame Necker's work also differed significantly from that of her predecessors in other ways. Not only was it considerably shorter, 22 pages in comparison to Winslow/Bruhier's 372 and Thiéry's 264, but it also differed markedly in tone. Madame Necker was not a medical professional and, therefore, could offer no horrific examples and make no medical claims. Instead, as a woman, she wrote from the position of a sexed and gendered body already medically marked by weakness. Consequently, she took a different point of departure.

From the perspective of a woman of sensibility, she offered a moral reflection on dying, death and premature burial. Drawing on the ideas put forward by her friend and colleague Buffon, Madame Necker defined death as the natural culmination of a lengthy process of dying. She argued that the period of transition itself, an intermediary phase of indeterminate duration, was of profound importance and deserved humanity's care, concern and consideration. For Necker, the dying body offered the possibility for humankind to achieve its greatest potential as 'the protector of the dying'.[27] Just as society took care of its young and its old, so too was it responsible for the care for the dying, those who floated in the space between life and death and who were no longer capable of giving physical signs of their struggles.

In order to provide a corrective to what she perceived as society's lack of concern for bodily remains, Madame Necker outlined a policy proposal in the second section of the work. In a series of thirteen articles, she laid out the basic tenets of corporeal respect as they might be conceived in a judicial framework, mandating the responsibilities and actions of observers – whether doctors, police commissioners or witnesses – and outlining detailed procedures to be followed. Death could be confirmed only after an extended waiting period (minimum forty-eight hours, but with the possibility of extension to seventy-two and potentially further) and even then required certification through a bureaucratic process involving the submission of a signed report to the police commissioner.[28] The body was to be maintained until such time as decomposition became dangerous for the living. Only the doctor could operate on, or otherwise open, the body.[29] In short, Necker proposed a method of social organization which could not only help alleviate the perceived problem of premature burial, but, more importantly, would ensure the dignity of and respect for the dying body. By focusing directly on the period of transition between apparent and actual death, she highlighted the indeterminacy of the final stages of life, emphasizing uncertainty, ambiguity and opacity. In the process, neither death nor life could be clearly defined; instead, each flowed seamlessly into the other. Dying, as a transitional phase, lacked – indeed, in some cases, resisted – clear definition.

Madame Necker's perspectives were, as she herself suggested, shaped by her experiences as the director of the Hospice de charité. While this philanthropic project was a success, there were also failures.[30] Mortality rates remained high and Necker became increasingly distressed at the treatment of the dead body. 'In spite of all my best efforts', she wrote in the introduction to her *Inhumations*, '[I] have been unable to persuade the nuns, so compassionate towards the living, to show enough care and respect for the dead'.[31] Necker's perspectives also arose from a far more personal impulse: her own extended struggle with illness and concomitant experience of corporeal instability.

The *Inhumations*, together with Madame Necker's intricate funerary prep-arations, combine into an elaborate commemorative act, a public project of mourning informed by the fluidity between her private and public selves. Cer-tainly, Necker's funerary rituals and requirements suggest a need to imagine death within the parameters of public display and to claim death as a site of pub-lic mourning and memorialization; in other words, to use the abjection of the corpse as a way of gesturing towards a collective responsibility for dying, death and memory. In the *Inhumations*, for example, she was extremely critical of soci-ety's careless attitude towards the dead, suggesting that this callous negligence could be seen as tantamount to murder. As she pointed out:

> Cessation of movement, complete impassivity, are evidence only of external death, and one is guilty of homicide if one buries the corpse before being assured that com-plete internal death has been absolutely consummated. Our terrible customs seem, however, suited to cause or hasten death.[32]

The society that did not take proper care of its dying members could be con-strued as a murderous one: 'It cannot be overemphasized that the first duty of man is to extend the life of man. The assassin often only hastens death by a few hours.'[33] In Necker's conceptualization, dying, death, mourning and memory were part of a public process of corporeal veneration in which the body came not only to symbolize humankind's physical instability and uncertainty, but also to manifest its moral promise and potential through the enactment of the memory of those who remained behind. Central to such a formulation was the idea of display: just as the sick body displayed its illnesses, so too the dying body functioned as a stage. In this case, however, the performer was humankind, as represented by those present. Madame Necker argued that it was only through society's response to the dead and dying that true virtue could be judged.

The dying body, itself, assumed performative prominence. Such, indeed, was the case with Madame Necker's elaborate – and some would say, excessive and obsessive – burial rituals. Christina Marsden Gillis has observed that while death creates an absence, that very absence creates a need for presence.[34] This relation-ship must also be reciprocal; presence relies on absence. In Necker's case, the public visibility of corporeal abjection, as figured through the rituals performed upon her dead body, enabled a coming to terms with the precariousness of life. 'Dying', Marsden Gillis suggests, 'bridges a no man's land where the unfathomed and the unknowable confront the scientific and the humanistic imagination. While death may be the vanishing point of medical knowledge and representa-tion, it is also a point of mediation.'[35]

Madame Necker's involvement with a key act of eighteenth-century memorialization serves to highlight this relationship. In 1770, she initiated a subscription project and, together with some eighty other members of the

French intelligentsia, commissioned the famed sculptor Jean-Baptiste Pigalle to create a monument to Voltaire.[36] The resulting work, *Voltaire nu*, completed in 1776, provoked a furore. While the work had been designed to commemorate Voltaire's heroic contribution to the Enlightenment, Pigalle chose to render the great thinker as the old, weak and frail being that he had become: a gaunt, emaciated man whose skin hung loosely off his skeleton. As an act of memorialization, it was a curious gesture that depicted greatness in the guise of the everyday. Corporeal decrepitude – in a body that, like Necker's, was marked by illness – rendered Voltaire's literary and philosophical achievements all the more monumental, even as the decaying body undermined this reading by signalling the fundamental commonality of human experience.[37] Madame Necker thought deeply about the nature of death and the process of memorialization during this period. In two letters to Thomas, for example, she imagined her own tomb as a tender and comforting space. 'In my romantic dreams, I like to think that they would erect a monument to my memory among the beautiful trees at St Ouen', she wrote, 'You would write the inscription, and during your quiet walks you would pause to look at it, listening to the sound of the leaves stirred by the wind, to that sound that seems to mimic the murmur of the shadows, so well painted by Virgil.'[38] These words, nostalgic and melancholy, suggest a courting of death and a desire for full communion with the afterlife.

Speculum (of the Other)[39]

Madame Necker's final years were filled with almost continual suffering; at numerous points, she was on the verge of death. But she was also consciously and actively involved in the process of her own dying, to the extent that she appears to have carefully choreographed not only her own final moments, but also those of her husband and, later, those of her daughter. Indeed, this final act, the public staging and memorialization of Suzanne Curchod Necker as cadaver, was most theatrical in nature. During the final years of her life, she laid full claim to her bodily frailty in a performative *tour-de-force* in which the rituals of dying, death, burial and memory converged into a display of specularity. What, however, does a specular death mean? What might it entail? What purpose might such a theatrical gesture have served? Why was Madame Necker, a pious woman so convinced by the promise of eternal life that she once suggested that the body was nothing more than a flawed temporary container for her soul,[40] so concerned with the permanence of that same infirm shell?

The philosophical insights of Luce Irigaray may go some way to helping us answer these questions. In her foundational work, *Speculum of the Other Woman*, Irigaray posits the female body as the speculum that reveals her exclusion from the Western philosophical tradition. The mirror upon which man projects his own image, the female body is also that which, in its concave specularity, imperfectly reflects the contours of the masculine subject. As Irigaray points out:

> the speculum is not necessarily a mirror. It may, quite simply, be an instrument to *dilate* the lips, the orifices, the walls, so that the eye can penetrate the *interior*. So that the eye can enter, to see, notably with speculative intent … [But] What will he, what will they, have *seen* as a result of that dilation? And what will they get out of it?[41]

I use the term specular invoking all of its connotations. According to the *Oxford English Dictionary*, it implies qualities of reflection, transparency or mirroring.[42] That which is specular opens itself up to the external gaze, revealing hidden depths and mysteries. By invoking specularity, I also refer to the speculum, the medical device most commonly used for directing the gaze inside the female body. It is, after all, the speculum – as an instrument or tool – which facilitates and gives access to the specularity of the body. In this sense, speculum and specularity are deeply intertwined: that which is specular can also, by definition, be understood as the speculum – the source of specularity – itself. The death, burial and veneration of Madame Necker can be approached from each of these angles. On the one hand, the specular rituals of memorialization reflected and revealed her deep religious belief and spiritual stance. Necker's conscious self-positioning within the horror of the suffering body suggests a gesture of penitence in which she claimed the sins of her society in a final attempt to absolve herself of sin. The process of dying, by bringing her closer to eternal communion, was redemptive: 'My faults will be erased by this sponge of death'.[43] On the other hand, these rituals, by focusing the gaze on the frail corporeal machine, transformed the body itself into a speculum. The dying body, however, did not reveal itself; rather, as a concave mirror, it imperfectly mimicked the gaze of the spectators, who, in witnessing corporeal decrepitude, were forced to re-evaluate themselves. Like *Voltaire nu*, Madame Necker's embalmed remains transformed the observer into the observed. Such, indeed, was the horror of death. In this sense, Madame Necker's mimetic refusal, which began as a conscious resistance to the elite sociable imperative, had come full circle.

Imagining Exile

When Madame Necker fled France with her family in 1790, she retraced the footsteps of her mother and grandmother before her. Exile, which had haunted her memory and signalled her entry into adulthood, now also marked the end of her life. The Necker family was not alone in their flight. All told, some 150,000 people fled France during the revolutionary period, among them members of all social classes. Like the Huguenot refugees before them, revolutionary *émigrés* faced many dangers. Revolutionary laws imposed between 1791 and 1794 threatened them with the confiscation of their property, the dissolution of their marriages and even death.[44] *Emigrés* faced an uncertain future and many fled in haste, leaving both material goods and family behind.[45] For most, it was, in William Doyle's words: 'a futile sacrifice. None of them ever recovered all they lost and most would have lost less by staying.'[46] They were profoundly unprepared for the difficult realities that awaited them and many were resistant to assimilation in their new situations.[47]

Unlike most *émigrés*, many of whom anticipated temporary exile in foreign climes and returned to France within ten years' of their departure, Madame Necker was both expatriated and repatriated as a result of her flight from Paris. When she left Paris in 1790, she had spent as many years yearning for her homeland, Switzerland, as she had living in it. Even as she had struggled to maintain her religious and cultural alterity, she was, by this time, a true cultural hybrid, with an identity equally informed by the simple Calvinist idyll of her youth and the seductive, intellectual abandon of her Parisian social circle.

At one stage in her life, Madame Necker had eagerly anticipated her return to Vaud. But the Switzerland of her imagination bore little resemblance to the country to which she returned in 1790. The loose assembly of cantons and cities, increasingly politically unstable, was veering towards revolution. Lausanne was overrun with *émigrés* and many of Necker's close friends had died. Etienette Clavel de Brenles, with whom she had shared her excitement and fear of the French capital, died in 1777, a loss closely followed by that of Necker's surrogate mother and confessor, Henriette Réverdil, in 1779. Finally, Paul Moultou, the friend of her youth who intervened on her behalf during her aborted engagement to Edward Gibbon and later encouraged her to travel to Paris, had died in 1787.

On a personal level, too, Madame Necker found herself surprisingly ill at ease in her former home. Even though she had once attributed her illnesses to her Parisian life, they did not abate upon her return to her homeland; if anything, they became worse. According to Germaine de Staël: 'her health suffers terribly from the air and the boredom of this country'.[48] Staël's commentary, while undoubtedly informed by her own ambivalence towards Switzerland, suggests that her mother now possessed a curiously composite identity. Torn between two worlds, Madame Necker had an uncomfortable foothold in each. While nostalgia and duty tethered her to Switzerland and evoked in her a horror of all things French, she nevertheless experienced the significant personal loss of intimate French friends and colleagues, among them Buffon, Thomas and the great Geoffrin, memories that linked her directly to her Parisian life.[49]

From the perspective of Necker's multistage palliative model, these final years can be conceived as the last, indeterminate stage of life and as such, a corollary, of sorts, to her own mother's sufferings and death. Seen in this light, Necker's final years form a curious coda, an extended leave-taking in which she could intimately reflect upon her life, her actions and her beliefs. This leave-taking manifested itself in a series of commemorative gestures and acts. It is through her final letters to her husband, for example, that she acknowledged that she had fulfilled her conjugal duties:

> Virginal and pure when I made my oath to be faithful to you, I kept my vows (in all of their delicacy); and, I don't even need to tell you, it is but a small virtue, to have lived in innocence prior to marriage and to have remained perfectly chaste during the course of a long union.[50]

In so doing, she outlined not only her sexual fidelity, but also her moral and emotional fidelity to the relationship that had formed the centre of her adult experience.[51]

Her relationship with her daughter, however, was more complicated. Germaine is not mentioned in any of the final letters, nor was she considered in the context of Suzanne Necker's elaborate funeral plans, which called only for her husband Jacques's embalmed remains to join his wife's upon his death. This omission is both curious and, at the same time, expected. On the one hand, if Madame Necker was indeed using the rituals of death as a way of taking stock of her life, then it would be obvious to include her reflections on her maternal role. After all, as we have seen, she was clearly aware of – and responsive to – her responsibility to her daughter. On the other, Germaine's personal life, in particular the complexities surrounding her amorous relationship with Louis de Narbonne and her desire to divorce the Baron de Staël, both of which took place during Madame Necker's final illness, was a source of great distress and profound disappointment to her mother. Narbonne, a known libertine, represented the antithesis of all of Madame Necker's careful teachings and she had previously forbidden her daughter to receive him. Germaine, however, took little heed of her mother's concerns and flew headlong into a passionate affair (which ended, predictably, in disaster). Madame Necker was horrified and, in a particularly heated moment, blamed her ill health directly on her daughter's indiscretions. As Germaine recounted with defiance:

> My mother almost died last night in a choking fit. She called me to her bedside. She said to me: 'My daughter, I am dying as a result of the distress that your guilty and very public affair has caused me. You have been punished by his conduct towards you, conduct which undermines everything that my prayers have been unable to stop you from doing. It is only through the care that you give your father that I will forgive you from heaven. Do not bother answering me. Leave; I do not have the energy to argue at this time.'[52]

What can we make of this statement? To a contemporary ear, Madame Necker's words are vindictive and cruel and recall the repressive power and rigid strictures of early Calvinism. This stern and judgemental mother would appear to merit in full the critiques of her daughter's biographers. But to whom are her harsh admonishments directed?

Read in the light of Madame Necker's experiences and beliefs, another picture emerges. Superimposed upon Madame Necker's dying are the spectre of her mother's death, the memory of her own failed filial virtue and the horror of what she understood as her Calvinist culpability. In this sense, Madame Necker's stern rebuke could just as easily be seen to be addressed to herself. On an intimate level, Necker's rituals of dying and death might be conceived as part of the idea of maternal abjection, a way of laying claim, through corporeal sensibility, to her daughter's moral disarray and, from there, making a gesture towards filial – and maternal – atonement.

Such a postulation can also, I believe, be taken a step further. If Madame Necker's illness can be perceived as part of a context of large-scale critical abjection in which she took on expiation of the social and moral ills of elite society through a process of self-stigmatization, then her specular death can be seen as a further extension of that process. This would imply that Madame Necker's body, by reflecting the social illness to which it was prey, was no longer marked, but became the mark, a physical representation of stigma enacted on a public stage. She no longer claimed the stigma; rather, her corpse was itself the stigma. Her abject body represented both the reality of loss that characterized her entire adult life and also the absolute dissipation and excess of the *ancien régime*, thus, on the one hand, symbolizing her active engagement in what she perceived to be a sinful society and, on the other, evoking the promise of purity and redemption.

Such a positioning is inherently political in nature, particularly in the context of the French and Swiss Revolutions, and would appear to be far removed from Necker's own religious beliefs and domestic behaviours. But it does accord with the approach taken by her husband and first biographer, who, in the introduction to the posthumously published *Mélanges*, cited the words of Thomas in order to assert that his wife should be seen as a symbol of morality in a society dedicated to excess: 'She arrived at a purity and elevation of character which has few examples, and which is so far above that of the country and of the contemptible century in which she lives'.[53] More importantly, it accords with the public activities that governed the last decade of Madame Necker's life. Her charity hospital and writings on premature burial and divorce were all overtly political statements in a society on the brink of revolution. From this perspective, her curtain call seems particularly *à propos*. If we understand Suzanne Necker's role, within the context of sensibility, as the mother of humanity – the embodiment of the characteristics of sensibility identified by Jaucourt – and if we take her sick body as the corporeal representation of societal illness, then her role expands. As 'mère de l'humanité', or mother of humanity, Madame Necker both spoke on behalf of *l'humanité souffrante* and claimed her maternal legacy. Her death, therefore, was a martyr's death; her funerary rites, a martyr's rites. Her body, guaranteed to exist in perpetuity, was the stigma itself – the wound and the fissure – a constant and enduring reminder of human frailty and suffering that bore the sins of the world and, by its very abjection, extended absolution.

Madame Necker's tomb is located in a small, wooded burial plot on the grounds of the family château in Coppet, Switzerland. Completely hidden from the public, the small, stone tomb has not been opened since the death of Germaine de Staël. Inside, Necker's carefully embalmed cadaver, now joined by those of her husband and daughter, functions as a symbolic reminder of the emotional power of the dying body. Permanently preserved in the state of illness which marked Madame Necker's adult years, this corpse does not rest, but remains in a position of perpetual suspension, hovering eternally at the point between life and death, *agonie* and *cadavre*. Its abject presence cannot – and must not – be tamed. Instead, it bears witness to corporeal dignity and offers a moving testimony to Suzanne Necker's heartfelt outcry: 'Who could possibly look upon this horrific state and not see himself as the protector of the dying, whomever they might be!'[54] By voluntarily inhabiting the abject, Madame Necker offered a profound re-imagining of the relationship between life and death. As Winslow, through Bruhier, indicated at the beginning of the debate concerning premature burial, death is certain and it is not. The uncertainty of death, as projected through the instability of Suzanne Curchod Necker's ill and dying body, reveals not only the fear of death – as exemplified in the extended discourse on premature burial – but also the potential that exists in illness, defined in the *Encyclopédie* as that ambiguous space between life and death.[55] By consciously living her dying – by laying claim to corporeal abjection – Madame Necker emphasized the inherent dignity of the frail and suffering body and authorized its role as the site for the performance and presentation of the autobiographical self.

Postscript: Sin and Redemption

The dying, death, and burial of Germaine de Staël, in July 1817, function as a curious postscript to Madame Necker's performance of filial and maternal abjection. Like her mother, Staël spent her final years in extreme suffering and pain. Desperate to stave off the loneliness and finality of death, she sought relief through the use of narcotics and refused to sleep, believing that if she did she might never wake. Surrounded by family and close friends, she was in full command of her intellect, but no longer able to write. Death came prematurely: when she died, on 14 July 1817, she was only fifty-one years old. At Madame de Staël's request, her body was transported to Coppet, where it was interred in the tomb that housed the remains of her mother and father.

Her son-in-law, Victor de Broglie, presided over both the preparations and the ceremony, which took place on 28 July 1817. The Necker-Curchod tomb had not been opened since the death of Jacques Necker in 1804. Broglie reported that he found the tomb chamber empty, save for the black marble basin, still half filled with alcohol, which contained the remains of Suzanne and Jacques Necker. Their bodies lay close together, stretched out under a red cloak. Jacques Necker's face, still visible above the cloak, was perfectly preserved.[56]

Madame de Staël was placed at the foot of the basin. As Broglie recalled:

> The procession stopped at the entry to the tomb. Only my brother-in-law and I entered the monument, followed by four men carrying the coffin. It was laid at the foot of the vat. I once again walled in the doorway, which has never since been opened.[57]

The door, permanently closed, was sealed with a *bas-relief* depicting all three members of the family: Germaine de Staël, weeping over her parents' tomb, her mother in heaven, and Jacques, between them, looking to his wife even as he reached back to his daughter.[58]

Madame Necker, we might recall, had specifically requested that her tomb be opened only once after her death: to welcome the embalmed body of her husband, that his remains could mingle with hers, thus extending their marriage into eternity. Through this process, she sought to confirm the strength of the conjugal union, alleviate the burden of moral responsibility and resist the lonely exile of the sinful believer. What purpose, however, might her daughter's final act have served? To speculate further on this, I turn very briefly to Germaine de Staël's heroic novel, *Corinne*. Staël's most famous literary heroine embodied her creator's intellectual and creative desires. With her formidable skill in oratory, creative intellect, boundless passion and determination to live life on her own terms, Corinne *was* Madame de Staël. As Elisabeth Vigée-LeBrun's famous portrait of Staël suggests, Staël, in return, mirrored her heroine. Like Corinne, she confidently asserted herself on the public stage in a virtuoso performance that earned her the adulation of the intelligentsia of her generation. Like Corinne, too, Madame de Staël could confidently assert that she had lived for love.[59]

Unlike Corinne, however, Staël did not die a lonely death. By linking her remains to those of her parents, she inscribed for herself a happier ending, writing in *De l'influence des passions sur le bonheur des individus et des nations*:

> What is most sacred when speaking of morality are the ties between parents and children: both nature and society rest equally on this duty, and the final degree of depravity is to defy that involuntary instinct which, in these relationships, inspires in us all that virtue can demand. Thus there is always a certain happiness attached to these ties, the fulfilment of these duties.[60]

Social responsibility, happiness, duty and virtue: Staël's language recalls the devout moral stance of her mother, who died just two years before this work was published. Given these echoes, it would be tempting to read Madame de Staël's decision to be interred with her parents as an act of closure, a redemptive gesture in which filial rupture could be exchanged for atonement, absolution and grace. There is, however, no evidence to support this conclusion. Biographers suggest, in fact, that Staël turned not to the memory of her mother for comfort, but rather, to her father and to God during her final months, linking her paternal memory with religious devotion in much the same way as Madame Necker had once sought divine communion with her mother.[61] Thus, while Staël's final act may have reunited the earthly remains of the family, it did not bring peace. Instead, the whole family rests – eternally suspended – in that space between Switzerland and France, life and death, sin and redemption.

NOTES

The following abbreviations are used throughout the notes:

BCUL   Bibliothèque cantonale et universitaire de Lausanne.
BGE   Bibliothèque publique de Genève.

Introduction

1. 'Dans la société, c'est le théâtre qui se présente le premier.' S. Curchod Necker, *Mélanges*, ed. J. Necker, 3 vols (Paris: Pougens, 1798), vol. 1, p. 367. I have retained original spellings, where possible, throughout this book.
2. 'Aujourd'hui le théâtre est partout, et chacun se croit en représentation pour faire effet; c'est ce qui corrompt parmi nous le goût des arts comme le goût moral.' A. L. Thomas, *Oeuvres complètes de Thomas, de l'Académie française; précédées d'une notice sur la vie et les ouvrages de l'auteur*, 6 vols (Paris: Verdière & Firmin Didot, 1825), vol. 6, p. 278.
3. J. M. Read, *Historic Studies in Vaud, Berne, and Savoy*, 2 vols (London: Chatto & Windus, 1897), vol. 2, pp. 284–5.
4. P.-G. d'Haussonville, *Le Salon de Madame Necker, d'après des documents tirés des Archives de Coppet*, 2 vols (Paris: Calmann-Lévy, 1882), vol. 1, pp. 97–8; E. Gibbon, *Letters*, ed. J. E. Norton, 3 vols (London: Cassell, 1956), vol. 1, p. 149.
5. Haussonville, *Le Salon de Madame Necker*, vol. 1, pp. 102–10.
6. B. d'Andlau, *La Jeunesse de Madame de Staël (de 1766 à 1786)* (Geneva: Librairie Droz, 1970), p. 47.
7. A. Lilti, *Le Monde des salons: Sociabilité et mondanité à Paris au XVIIIe siècle* (Paris: Fayard, 2005); A. Litli, 'Mondanité et politique: Le salon Necker', *Cahiers staëliens*, 57 (2006), pp. 185–200.
8. See [S. Curchod Necker], *Hospice de charité* (Paris: Imprimerie royale, 1781); [S. Curchod Necker], *Hospice de charité: institutions, règles, et usages de cette Maison* (Paris: Imprimerie royale, 1780), and the prefaces to the two final accounts, in 1789 and 1790, as found in S. Curchod Necker, *Nouveaux mélanges*, ed. J. Necker, 2 vols (Paris: Pougens; Genets, 1801), vol. 2, pp. 299–316; and S. Curchod Necker, *Des inhumations précipitées* (Paris: Imprimerie royale, 1790).
9. S. Curchod Necker, *Réflexions sur le divorce* (Lausanne: Durant, Ravanel, et cie; Paris: P. F. Aubin et Desenne, 1794).
10. In her will, Necker entrusted her husband, Jacques, with all of her papers. C. Dubeau, 'La Lettre et la mère: Roman familial et écriture de la passion chez Suzanne Necker (1737–1794) et Germaine de Staël (1766–1817)' (PhD dissertation, Université Laval, 2007), p.

52. For more on the relationship between Suzanne Necker and her husband, see S. Boon, 'Does a Dutiful Wife Write; or, Should Suzanne Get Divorced? Reflections on Suzanne Curchod Necker, Divorce, and the Construction of the Biographical Subject', *Lumen: Selected Proceedings from the Canadian Society for Eighteenth-Century Studies/Travaux choisis de la Société canadienne d'étude du dix-huitième siècle*, 27 (2008), pp. 59–73.

11. J. Necker, 'Observations de l'éditeur', in Curchod Necker, *Mélanges*, vol. 1, pp. i–xx; Haussonville, *Le Salon de Madame Necker*.

12. P. Deschanel, *Figures des femmes* (Paris: Calmann-Lévy, 1889), pp. 104–75; S. G. Tallentyre, *The Women of the Salons and other French Portraits* (London: Longmans, Green, & Co., 1901); A. Corbaz, *Madame Necker: Humble vaudoise et grande dame* (Lausanne: Librairie Payot, 1945); M. Gambier-Parry, *Madame Necker, her Family and her Friends* (Edinburgh and London: William Blackwood & Sons, 1913).

13. P. Lejeune, *On Autobiography*, ed. P. J. Eakin, trans. K. Leary (Minneapolis, MN: University of Minnesota Press, 1989).

14. G. de Staël, *Mémoires sur la vie privée de mon père* (Paris: Colburn, 1818); A. de Staël-Holstein, *Notice sur M. Necker* (Paris: Treuttel & Würtz, 1820).

15. A.-A. Necker de Saussure, *Sketch of the Life, Character, and Writings of Baroness de Staël-Holstein* (London: Treuttel & Würtz, 1820).

16. C. Dubeau, 'L'Épreuve du salon ou le monde comme performance dans les *Mélanges* et les *Nouveaux Mélanges* de Suzanne Necker', *Cahiers staëliens*, 57 (2006), pp. 201–26; Dubeau, 'La Lettre et la mère'; E. Giddey, 'Suzanne Necker-Curchod et les lettres anglaises', *Revue historique vaudoise* (1981), pp. 49–56; D. Goodman, 'Le Spectateur intérieur: Les journaux de Suzanne Necker', *Littérales*, 17 (1995), pp. 91–100; D. Goodman, 'Suzanne Necker's *Mélanges*: Gender, Writing, and Publicity', in E. C. Goldsmith and D. Goodman (eds), *Going Public: Women and Publishing in Early Modern France* (Ithaca, NY, and London: Cornell University Press, 1995), pp. 211–23; V. Hannin, 'Une ambition de femme au siècle des Lumières: Le cas de Madame Necker', *Cahiers staëliens*, 36 (1985), pp. 5–19; C. Seth, 'Madame Necker: Une vie au service des autres', *Cahiers staëliens*, 57 (2006), pp. 173–83; G. Soumoy-Thibert, 'Les Idées de Madame Necker', *Dix-huitième siècle*, 21 (1989), pp. 357–68. Biographical studies of Madame de Staël include Andlau, *La Jeunesse de Madame de Staël*; C. J. von Leyden, Lady Blennerhassett, *Madame de Staël et son temps*, 2 vols (Paris: Louis Westhausser, 1890); G. de Diesbach, *Madame de Staël* (Paris: Librairie académique Perrin, 1983); M. Fairweather, *Madame de Staël* (London: Constable, 2005); M. Gutwirth, *Madame de Staël, Novelist: The Emergence of the Artist as Woman* (Urbana, IL: University of Illinois Press, 1978); M. Gutwirth, 'Suzanne Necker's Legacy: Breastfeeding as Metonym in Germaine de Staël's *Delphine*', *Eighteenth-Century Life*, 18:2 (2004), pp. 17–40; P. Kohler, *Madame de Staël et la Suisse* (Lausanne: Payot, 1916); J. C. Herold, *Mistress to an Age: A Life of Madame de Staël* (Indianapolis, IN: Bobbs-Merrill, 1958).

17. A. Aimes, 'Le Séjour de Madame Necker à Montpellier: Fondation de l'hôpital Necker de Montpellier', *Histoire des sciences médicales*, 8 (1974), pp. 477–89; G. Benrekassa, 'Diderot et l'honnête femme: De Mme Necker à Eliza Draper', in A.-M. Chouillet (ed.), *Colloque International Diderot (1713–1784)* (Paris: Aux amateurs de livres, 1995), pp. 87–97; J. Faurey, *Madame Necker et la question du divorce* (Bordeaux: J. Bière, 1931); V. Hannin, 'La Fondation de l'hospice de charité: Une expérience médicale au temps du rationalisme expérimentale', *Revue d'histoire moderne et contemporaine*, 31:1 (1984), pp. 116–30; L. Pérol, 'Diderot, Mme Necker et la réforme des hôpitaux', *Studies on Voltaire and the Eighteenth Century*, 311 (1993), pp. 219–33; B. Vadier, 'La Mère de Mme de

Staël et sa parenté au pays de Vaud', *Étrennes helvétiques* (1901), pp. 287–324; J. Whatley, 'Dissoluble Marriage, Paradise Lost: Suzanne Necker's *Réflexions sur le divorce*', *Dalhousie French Studies*, 56 (2001), pp. 144–53.

18. L. Burnand, 'L'Image de Madame Necker dans les pamphlets', *Cahiers staëliens*, 57 (2006), pp. 237–54.

19. Ms.suppl. 717, BGE; and IS1915/xxx/h/1, BCUL. The letters in the Lausanne collection can also be found in F. Golowkin, *Lettres diverses, recueillies en Suisse* (Geneva: J. J. Paschoud, 1821).

20. See A. de Baecque, *Glory and Terror: Seven Deaths under the French Revolution*, trans. C. Mandell (New York: Routledge, 2001); P. Vecchi, 'De la mort à la vie: La taphophobie et l'au-delà au XVIIIe siècle (Jean-Jacques Bruhier et Suzanne Curchod Necker)', in C. Rosso (ed.), *Transhumances culturelles: Mélanges* (Pisa: Editrice Libreria Goliardica, 1985), pp. 119–30.

21. J.-J. Rousseau, *Correspondance complète de Jean-Jacques Rousseau*, ed. R. A. Leigh, 52 vols (Geneva: Institut et musée Voltaire, 1965–95); F. M. A. de Voltaire, *The Complete Works of Voltaire*, ed. T. Besterman et al., 141 vols (Geneva: Institut et musée Voltaire; Toronto: University of Toronto Press, 1968–); Gibbon, *Letters*; Thomas, *Oeuvres complètes*; G. L. Leclerc, Comte de Buffon, *Correspondance générale de Buffon*, ed. H. Nadault de Buffon, 2 vols (Paris: Hachette, 1860).

22. See, for example, E. R. Dashkova, *The Memoirs of Princess Dashkova*, trans. K. Fitzlyon (Durham, NC, and London: Duke University Press, 1995); S. F. Ducrest de Saint Aubin, Comtesse de Genlis, *Mémoires inédits de madame la Comtesse de Genlis, sur le dix-huitième siècle et la révolution française, depuis 1756 jusqu'à nos jours*, 10 vols (Brussels: P. J. de Mat, 1825); A. Morellet, *Mémoires inédits de l'abbé Morellet*, 2 vols (Paris: Baudouin, 1822); H.-L. de Waldner de Freundstein, Baronne d'Oberkirch, *Mémoires de la Baronne d'Oberkirch*, 2 vols (Paris: Charpentier, 1869); F. M., Freiherr von Grimm, *Correspondance littéraire, philosophique et critique*, 16 vols (Paris: Garnier frères, 1877); L. P. de Bachaumont, *Mémoires secrets pour servir à l'histoire de la République des Lettres en France depuis MDCCLXII, ou Journal d'un observateur, contenant les analyses des pièces de théâtre qui ont paru durant cet intervalle, les relations des assemblées littéraires*, 36 vols (London: John Adamson, 1783–9). Libellous works include *Les Deux conversations de Madame Necker, Femme du Directeur des Finances en France* (Geneva: Cruchaut, 1781); *La Galérie des dames françoises* (London, 1798).

23. Madame Necker's correspondence with Thomas can be found in the *Mélanges*, vol. 2, pp. 124–6, 130–8, vol. 3, pp. 157–218. For more on this correspondence, see N. Bérenguier, 'Lettres de Suzanne Necker à Antoine Thomas (1766–1785)', in E. C. Goldsmith and C. H. Winn (eds), *Lettres de femmes: Textes inédits et oubliés du XVIe au XVIIIe siècle* (Paris: Honoré Champion, 2005), pp. 339–78.

24. 'Pardon madame si je me sers d'une main etrangère. Une incomodité moins dangereuse que la précedente mais plus importune ne me permést pas de tenir la plume.' Suzanne Curchod Necker to Etienette Clavel de Brenles, 10 September 1765, IS1915/xxx/h/3, BCUL.

25. Suzanne Curchod Necker to M. de Sévery, 11 October 1792, 25 July 1793, 6 October 1793, 6 December 1793, P. Charrière de Sévery, B117/3192–3195, Archives cantonales vaudoises, Lausanne.

26. In the extant correspondence, there is no mention of illness in 1770, 1774, 1780, 1787, 1789 or 1791.

27. Unfortunately, it is not always possible to access the manuscript version; Necker's extensive correspondence with Georges-Louis LeSage, for example, published early in the nineteenth century, does not indicate whether the letters are signed or unsigned or if they are penned by Necker herself or by a secretary. See P. Prévost (ed.), *Notice sur la vie et les écrits de Georges-Louis LeSage* (Geneva and Paris: J. J. Paschoud, 1805), which includes ten letters from Madame Necker to LeSage.

28. 'Si je ne connaissais, madame, toute l'activité de votre esprit, au milieu même des langueurs et des souffrances, votre lettre du 11 février m'aurait presque fait douter que vous fussiez malade. La vie et la santé sont à chaque ligne.' Thomas, *Oeuvres complètes*, vol. 6, p. 458.

29. See the correspondence in *The Complete Works of Voltaire*.

30. See the correspondence of Thomas and Buffon, as found in Thomas, *Oeuvres complètes*; and Buffon, *Correspondance générale*; the references in G. de Staël, *Correspondance générale*, ed. B. W. Jasinski, 4 vols (Paris: Jean-Jacques Pauvert, 1962–78); and Staël, *Mémoires sur la vie privée de mon père*; and the recollections of A.-A. Necker de Saussure, quoted in E. Causse, *Madame Necker de Saussure et l'éducation progressive*, 2 vols (Paris: Editions 'Je sers', 1930), vol. 1, p. 64.

31. J. Perreault and M. Kadar, 'Introduction: Tracing the Autobiographical: Unlikely Documents, Unexpected Places', in M. Kadar, L. Warley, J. Perreault and S. Egan (eds), *Tracing the Autobiographical* (Waterloo: Wilfrid Laurier University Press, 2005), pp. 1–7, on p. 1.

32. E. Showalter Jr, 'Authorial Self-Consciousness in the Familiar Letter: The Case of Madame de Graffigny', *Yale French Studies*, 71 (1986), pp. 113–30, on p. 122.

33. Ibid.; M.-C. Grassi, 'Naissance de l'intimité épistolaire (1780–1830)', *Littérales*, 17 (1995), pp. 67–76.

34. '[L]'on répète sans cesse, depuis Mme. de Sévigné, [que les femmes] écrivent mieux que les hommes, et qu'elles sentent plus délicatement qu'eux; comme on croit, depuis Locke et Newton, que les Anglois sont un peuple philosophe.' Curchod Necker, *Mélanges*, vol. 3, pp. 391–2.

35. D. Goodman, *Becoming a Woman in the Age of Letters* (Ithaca, NY, and London: Cornell University Press, 2009). See also D. Goodman, 'Letter Writing and the Emergence of Gendered Subjectivity in Eigtheenth-Century France', *Journal of Women's History*, 17:2 (2005), pp. 9–37.

36. B. Didier, 'Ecrire pour se trouver', in M.-F. Silver and M.-L. Girou-Swiderski (eds), *Femmes en toutes lettres: les épistolières du XVIIIe siècle*, Studies on Voltaire and the Eighteenth Century, 2000:04 (Oxford: Voltaire Foundation, 2000), pp. 243–8, on p. 245.

37. 'Dans ses confidences, la femme parle de la difficulté au XVIIIᵉ siècle d'être une femme.' Grassi, 'Naissance de l'intimité épistolaire', p. 74.

38. Goodman, *Becoming a Woman in the Age of Letters*, p. 3.

39. A.C. Vila, 'Sex and Sensibility: Pierre Roussel's *Système physique et moral de la femme*', *Representations*, 52 (1995), pp. 76–93, on p. 81.

40. Curchod Necker, *Nouveaux mélanges*, vol. 1, p. 79.

41. Showalter, 'Authorial Self-Consciousness in the Familiar Letter', p. 115.

42. 'Je respecte trop Mme. de Sévigné pour mettre son ouvrage en parallèle avec ce grand nombre de lettres galantes que notre siècle a produites, et qui, sous prétexte de peindre les vrais sentimens du coeur, en montrent la corruption; car on peut tout contrefaire, excepté la sensibilité; c'est le seul droit que la nature n'ait jamais cédé à l'art.' Curchod Necker, *Mélanges*, vol. 3, p. 424.

43. A. Hunsaker Hawkins, *Reconstructing Illness: Studies in Pathography* (West Lafayette, IN: Purdue University Press, 1999); G. T. Couser, *Recovering Bodies: Illness, Disability, and Life Writing* (Madison, WI: University of Wisconsin Press, 1997), p. 5; G. T. Couser, 'Autopathography: Women, Illness, and Lifewriting', *a/b: Auto/biography Studies*, 6:1 (1991), pp. 65–75.

44. S. Wendell, *The Rejected Body: Feminist Philosophical Reflections on Disability* (New York and London: Routledge, 1996).

45. V. Raoul, C. Canam, A. D. Henderson and C. Paterson, 'Introduction: Aesthetics, Authenticity, and Audience', in V. Raoul, C. Canam, A. D. Henderson and C. Paterson (eds), *Unfitting Stories: Narrative Approaches to Disease, Disability and Trauma* (Waterloo, Ontario: Wilfrid Laurier University Press, 2007), pp. 25–31, on p. 30.

46. J. Kristeva, *Powers of Horror: An Essay on Abjection*, trans. L. S. Roudiez (New York: Columbia University Press, 1982); L. Irigaray, *This Sex Which Is Not One*, trans. C. Porter (Ithaca, NY: Cornell University Press, 1985); L. Irigaray, *Speculum of the Other Woman*, trans. G. C. Gill (Ithaca, NY: Cornell University Press, 1985); H. Cixous, 'Le Rire de la méduse', *L'Arc* (1975), pp. 39–54.

47. T. Laqueur, *Making Sex: Body and Gender from the Greeks to Freud* (Cambridge, MA, and London: Harvard University Press, 1990); L. Schiebinger, *The Mind Has No Sex? Women in the Origins of Modern Science* (Cambridge, MA, and London: Harvard University Press, 1989); L. Steinbrügge, *The Moral Sex: Woman's Nature in the French Enlightenment*, trans. P. E. Selwyn (New York and Oxford: Oxford University Press, 1995).

48. Steinbrügge, *The Moral Sex*, p. 43.

49. See, for example, the models of ideal womanhood proposed in A. L. Thomas, *Essai sur le caractère, les moeurs et l'esprit des femmes dans les différens siècles* (Paris: Moutard, 1772); J.-J. Rousseau, *Julie, ou, La nouvelle Héloïse: Lettres de deux amants habitants d'une petite ville au pied des Alpes*, 2 vols, ed. H. Coulet (Paris: Le livre de poche, 2002); D. Diderot, 'Sur les femmes', in *Oeuvres complètes*, ed. J. Assézat, 20 vols (Paris: Garnier, 1875–7), vol. 1, pp. 251–62; M. Desmahis, 'Femme (*Morale*)', in D. Diderot and J. le Rond d'Alembert (eds), *Encyclopédie, ou dictionnaire raisonné des sciences, des arts et des métiers, par une Société de Gens de lettres* (Paris: Briasson, 1751–72), vol. 6, p. 475, online at University of Chicago, ARTFL Encyclopédie Project (Winter 2008 edn), ed. R. Morrissey, http://encyclopedie.uchicago.edu/.

50. H. Cixous, *Stigmata*, trans. E. Prenowitz et al. (London and New York: Routledge, 1998), p. xiii.

51. See, for example, the work of Micheline Louis-Courvoisier and Séverine Pilloud: S. Pilloud and M. Louis-Courvoisier, 'The Intimate Experience of the Body in the Eighteenth Century: Between Interiority and Exteriority', *Journal of Medical History*, 47 (2003), p. 451–72; S. Pilloud, 'Mettre les maux en mots, médiations dans la consultation épistolaire au XVIIIe siècle: les malades du Dr. Tissot (1728–1797)', *Canadian Bulletin of Medical History/Bulletin canadien d'histoire de la médecine*, 16 (1999), pp. 214–45; S. Pilloud, 'Tourisme médical à Lausanne dans la seconde moitié du XVIIIe siècle', *Revue historique vaudoise*, 114 (2006), pp. 9–23.

52. J. Butler, 'Performative Acts and Gender Constitution: An Essay in Phenomenology and Feminist Theory', *Theatre Journal*, 40:4 (1988), pp. 519–31; J. Butler, *Bodies that Matter: On the Discursive Limits of 'Sex'* (New York and London: Routledge, 1993).

53. Kristeva, *Powers of Horror*, p. 3.

54. Ibid., p. 4.

55. M. Carlson, 'What is Performance?', in H. Bial (ed.) *Performance Studies Reader*, 2nd edn (London and New York: Routledge, 2004), pp. 70–5, on p. 72; italics added.
56. E. Striff, 'Introduction: Locating Performance Studies', in E. Striff (ed.), *Performance Studies* (Houndmills: Palgrave Macmillan, 2003), pp. 1–13, on p. 1.
57. M. Carlson, *Performance: A Critical Introduction* (London: Routledge, 1996), p. 6.

1 'She Will Never Acquire the Art of Pleasing'

1. '[M]adame Necker n'avait aucun des agréments d'une jeune Française. Dans ses manières, dans son langage, ce n'était ni l'air ni le ton d'une femme élevée à l'école des arts, formée à l'école du monde. Sans goût dans sa parure, sans aisance dans son maintien, sans attrait dans sa politesse, son esprit comme sa contenance, était trop ajusté pour avoir de la grâce.' J.-F. Marmontel, *Oeuvres complètes*, 7 vols (Paris: Verdière, 1818–20), vol. 2, p. 130.
2. 'Ici, je suis contrainte à cacher les mouvemens les plus naturels, pour éviter le reproche de pédanterie: je fais continuellement à mon coeur et à ses émotions une sorte de violence; et au moment où je suis en liberté, je trouve qu'il a perdu son élasticité accoutumée.' Curchod Necker, *Mélanges*, vol. 1, p. 151.
3. A. Alison, *Some Account of my Life and Writings: An Autobiography*, ed. Lady Alison, 2 vols (Edinburgh: W. Blackwood & Sons, 1883), vol. 1, p. 6, n. 1.
4. Mademoiselle de Lespinassy, *Essai sur l'éducation des demoiselles* (Paris: Hochereau, 1764), p. 47. See also: P. Constant, *Un monde à l'usage des demoiselles* (Paris: Gallimard, 1987); M. Sonnet, *L'Éducation des filles au temps des Lumières* (Paris: Le Cerf, 1987).
5. Gutwirth, 'Suzanne Necker's Legacy', p. 30.
6. '[C]umulera les images et épithètes désobligeantes, assurant une meilleure postérité à ses maladresses qu'à ses succès.' Dubeau, 'L'Épreuve du salon', p. 208.
7. 'Les devoirs, les convenances du grand monde, une vigilance perpétuelle sur soi et autour de soi, une sensibilité qui se contraignait et se refoulait souvent en silence et avec douleur, tout contribua à user Mme Necker avant l'âge.' C. A. de Sainte-Beuve, *Causeries du lundi*, 15 vols (Paris: Garnier frères, 1851–62), vol. 4, pp. 194–5.
8. See, for example, L. Junot, Duchesse d'Abrantès, *Histoire des salons de Paris: Tableaux et portraits du grand monde, sous Louis XVI, le Directoire, le Consulat et l'Empire, la Restauration, et le règne de Louis-Philippe Ier*, 6 vols (Paris: Ladvocat, 1837–8); L.-E.-C.-A. d'Osmond, Comtesse de Boigne, *Mémoires de la Comtesse de Boigne née d'Osmond* (Paris: Plon-Nourrit, 1908); L.-E. Vigée-Lebrun, *The Memoirs of Elisabeth Vigée-Lebrun*, trans. S. Evans (London: Camden Press, 1989); H. L. Dillon, Marquise de La Tour du Pin, *Mémoires de la Marquise de La Tour du Pin: Journal d'une femme de cinquante ans, 1778–1846*, ed. C. de L. Beaufort (Paris: Mercure de France, 2002); Genlis, *Mémoires inédits*.
9. Sainte-Beuve, *Causeries du lundi*; E. de Goncourt and J. de Goncourt, *La Femme au XVIIIe siècle* (Paris: Firmin-Didot, 1887), and E. de Goncourt and J. de Goncourt, *Histoire de la société française pendant la révolution* (Paris: Didier, 1864).
10. Haussonville, *Le Salon de Madame Necker*; P. M. M. Henri, Comte de Ségur, *Le Royaume de la rue Saint-Honoré: Madame Geoffrin et sa fille* (Paris: Calmann-Lévy, 1897); P. M. M. Henri, Comte de Ségur, *Julie de Lespinasse* (Paris: Calmann-Lévy, 1905).
11. See, for example, J. Aldis, *Madame Geoffrin: Her Salon and her Times, 1750–1777* (New York and London: G. P. Putnam's Sons and Methuen & Co., 1905); H. Clergue, *The Salon: A Study of French Society and Personalities in the Eighteenth Century* (New York: G. P. Putnam's & Sons, 1907); A. C. Kors, *D'Holbach's Coterie: An Enlightenment in*

Paris (Princeton, NJ: Princeton University Press, 1976); Ségur, *Le Royaume de la rue Saint-Honoré.*

12. J. Habermas, *The Structural Transformation of the Public Sphere: An Inquiry into a Category of Bourgeois Society*, trans. J. T. Burger Cambridge, MA; MIT Press, 1991); D. Goodman, *The Republic of Letters: A Cultural History of the French Enlightenment* (Ithaca, NY, and London: Cornell University Press, 1994). See also the following works by D. Goodman: 'Enlightenment Salons: The Convergence of Female and Philosophic Ambitions', *Eighteenth-Century Studies*, 22:3 (1989), pp. 329–50; 'Policing Society: Women as Political Actors in the Enlightenment Discourse', in H. E. Bödeker and L. Steinbrügge (eds), *Conceptualising Women in Enlightenment Thought/Conceptualiser la femme dans la pensée des Lumières* (Berlin: Berlin Verlag Arno Spitz GmbH, 2001), pp. 129–41; 'Public Sphere and Private Life: Toward a Synthesis of Current Historiographical Approaches to the Old Regime', *History and Theory*, 31:1 (1992), pp. 1–20; and 'Suzanne Necker's *Mélanges*'.

13. See the following works by J. T. Pekacz: *Conservative Tradition in Pre-Revolutionary France: Parisian Salon Women* (New York: Peter Lang, 1999); 'The French Salon of the Old Regime as a Spectacle', *Lumen: Selected Proceedings from the Canadian Society for Eighteenth-Century Studies/Travaux choisis de la société canadienne d'étude du dix-huitième siècle*, 22 (2001), pp. 83–102; 'Gender as Political Orientation: Parisian Salonnières and the Querelle des Bouffons', *Canadian Journal of History/Annales canadiennes d'histoire*, 32 (1997), pp. 405–14; 'Salon Women and the Quarrels about Opera in Eighteenth-Century Paris', *European Legacy: Towards New Paradigms*, 1:4 (1996), pp. 1608–14; and 'The Salonnières and the Philosophes in Old Regime France: The Authority of Aesthetic Judgement', *Journal of the History of Ideas* 60:2 (1999), pp. 277–97. The recent work of Steven D. Kale relies on the Pekacz model: see *French Salons: High Society and Political Sociability from the Old Regime to the Revolution of 1848* (Baltimore, MD: Johns Hopkins University Press, 2004); 'Women, the Public Sphere, and the Persistence of Salons', *French Historical Studies*, 25:1 (2002), pp. 115–48; and 'Women, Salons, and the State in the Aftermath of the French Revolution', *Journal of Women's History*, 13:4 (2002), pp. 54–80.

14. Pekacz, 'The French Salon of the Old Regime as a Spectacle', p. 87.

15. Dubeau, 'L'Épreuve du salon'.

16. Pekacz, *Conservative Tradition*, p. 12.

17. S. McKay, 'The "Salon de la Princesse": "Rococo" Design, Ornamented Bodies and the Public Sphere', *Revue d'art canadienne/Canadian Art Review*, 21:1–2 (1994), pp. 71–84.

18. Suzanne Curchod Necker to Henriette Réverdil, 15 July 1766, ms.suppl. 717, f. 11, BGE.

19. 'Imaginez-vous que depuis deux ans je suis alternativement ménagère et femme du monde, que j'étois si ignorante sur le premier de ces objets qu'il a exercé toutes mes facultés, et si gauche sur le second qu'il a captivé toute mon attention, si vous joignez à cela un attachement et des devoirs nouveaux, vous verrez que je n'ai pu sauver que mon coeur du naufrage de mes idées.' Suzanne Curchod Necker to Etienette Clavel de Brenles, 11 June 1766, IS1915/xxx/h/1, BCUL. The new duties to which she refers are those of motherhood: her daughter, Anne-Louise-Germaine, was born on 22 April 1766.

20. 'Je n'ai pas un moment à moi; les détails de ma maison sont énormes pour une tête inepte comme la mienne et si je ny mettois le plus grand ordre nous serions ruinez. Suzanne Curchod Necker to Henriette Réverdil, July and September 1766, ms.suppl. 717, f. 14, BGE.

21. 'On n'ose parler. Mme Necker intimide les plus intrépides ... On dirait que [Madame Necker] s'est imposé un grand rôle dont elle ne sort jamais; elle parle de vertu, de décence, de sentiment, non par un effusion de son propre coeur, mais par les idées qu'elle s'est formé de ce qui doit être; et je crois que son caractère à elle est parfaitement inconnu, et qu'elle n'a jamais eu ... un moment d'abandon.' A. A. Necker de Saussure, reporting in 1787, quoted in Causse, *Madame Necker de Saussure*, vol. 1, p. 64.

22. H. Walpole, *Correspondence of Horace Walpole*, 3 vols (London: Henry Colburn, 1837), vol. 3, p. 130.

23. '[M]adame Necker n'avait aucun des agréments d'une jeune Française.' Marmontel, *Oeuvres complètes*, vol. 2, p. 130.

24. 'M. Necker ne me plut point ... Madame Necker est bien pis encore. En dépit des grandes positions qu'elle a occupées, c'est une institutrice, et rien de plus. Elle est pédante et prétentieuse au delà de tout ... Elle est belle, et elle n'est point agréable; elle est bienfaisante, et elle n'est point aimée; son corps, son esprit, son coeur, manquent de grâce. Dieu, avant de la créer, la trempa en dedans et en dehors dans un baquet d'empois. Elle n'aura jamais l'art de plaire.' Oberkirch, *Mémoires*, vol. 1, pp. 253–4.

25. 'Ils ne s'ennuyèrent point; mais ils ennuyèrent les autres et se mirent à s'adorer, à se complimenter, à s'encenser sans cesse.' Ibid., vol. 1, p. 254.

26. Bachaumont, *Mémoires secrets*, vol. 16, p. 100.

27. P. d'Ortigue de Vaumorière, *The Art of Pleasing in Conversation: In French and English. Written by the Famous Cardinal Richelieu*, 2 vols (London: J. Darby, 1722), vol. 1, p. 5.

28. '[S]on amitié vive pour tous les hommes distingués, sa charité, sa bonté, son humanité, qui la firent nommer la mère des pauvres.' 'Necker (Madame)', in A. V. Arnault et al. (eds), *Biographie nouvelle des contemporains, ou Dictionnaire historique et raisonné de tous les hommes qui, depuis la Révolution française, ont acquis de la célébrité par leurs actions, leurs écrits, leurs erreurs ou leurs crimes, soit en France, soit dans les pays étrangers*, 20 vols (Paris: Librairie historique, 1820–5), vol. 15, p. 31.

29. '[C]ulte de son époux.' Sainte-Beuve, *Causeries du lundi*, vol. 4, p. 195.

30. E. Lairtullier, *Les Femmes célèbres de 1789 à 1795, et leur excellence dans la révolution*, 2 vols (Paris: Chez France, à la librairie politique, 1840), vol. 1, pp. 111, 107, 114.

31. 'Necker, Suzanne', in H. G. Adams (ed.), *A Cyclopaedia of Female Biography consisting of Sketches of all Women who have been Distinguished by Great Talents, Strength of Character, Piety, Benevolence, or Moral Virtue of any kind; forming a Complete Record of Womanly Excellence or Ability* (London: Groombridge & Sons, 1857), p. 576.

32. 'Mais ... votre conduite à été très bonne et très sage [et] ... vous ne vous este pas attiré la moindre condamnation du public ni le plus peti ridicule, que de plus, madame, toute les fois que j'ai eu l'honneur de vous voir, vous m'aves marqué amitié estime et confiance, en voilà bien sufisament pour avoir effacée en moi les mauvaise impressions que votre trop d'amour pour l'esprit dépouillé de raison et de vertus m'avoit donnée.' Quoted in Haussonville, *Le Salon de Madame Necker*, vol. 1, p. 262.

33. 'Je sai que le sejour de Paris, en faisant eclater sur un plus grand Theatre votre gout et vos talens, n'a point étouffé votre franchise Helvetique.' Gibbon, *Letters*, vol. 2, p. 126.

34. Haussonville, *Le Salon de Madame Necker*, vol. 1, pp. 116–17; Lilti, *Le Monde des salons*, pp. 369–77; Marmontel, *Oeuvres complètes*, vol. 2, p. 132.

35. Haussonville, *Le Salon de Madame Necker*, vol. 2, pp. 9–14; Andlau, *La Jeunesse de Madame de Staël*, pp. 109–10; G. de Staël, 'Mon Journal', *Cahiers staëliens*, 28 (1980), pp. 55–79; and D. Johnson-Cousin, 'Le Théâtre de Necker: A propos d'inédits des Archives de Coppet', *Revue de la société d'histoire du théâtre*, 32:3 (1980), pp. 220–31.

36. See, for example, her correspondence with Madame de Brenles, IS1915/xxx/h/1 and IS1915/xxx/h/3, BCUL.

37. 'Depuis que je suis à Paris, monsieur, je n'ai pus me livrer à cet abandon de pensées et de sentiment qui me rend votre correspondance si précieuse. Ici je suis contrainte à cacher les mouvemens les plus naturels, pour éviter le reproche de pédanterie: je fais continuel-lement à mon coeur et à ses émotions une sorte de violence; et au moment où je suis en liberté, je trouve qu'il a perdu son élasticité accoutumée. Je ne puis m'empêcher de juger ce pays avec sévérité.' Curchod Necker, *Mélanges*, vol. 1, p. 151.

38. 'Ah! Madame, quelle différence des momens que je passois auprès de vous dont le souve-nir me dédommage encore de la futilité de mes occupations actuelles. Le seul avantage de ce pays est de former le goût, mais c'est au dépens du génie; on tourne une phrase en mille manières, on compare l'idée par tous ses rapports ... On disserte à perte de vue, et l'on finit par dire: 'Cela est de mauvais gout'.' Suzanne Curchod Necker to Etienette Clavel de Brenles, 7 November 1765, IS1915/xxx/h/1, BCUL.

39. Suzanne Curchod Necker to Etienette Clavel de Brenles, 1765, IS1915/xxx/h/1, BCUL.

40. 'Je ne puis bien vous rendre l'impression que me fait Paris; ce n'est plus qu'une illusion, qu'un monde imaginaire peuplé d'êtres fantastiques.' Curchod Necker, *Mélanges*, vol. 3, p. 212.

41. 'Il y a vingt ans, si vous vous en souvenez, que me trouvant, pour la première fois, au milieu des plus beaux esprits de l'Europe, j'entendis traiter de chimères toutes les idées sur lesquelles j'avois fait reposer mon bonheur, ainsi que l'explication des phénomènes de ce monde; je gardai chèrement mes opinions au milieu de ce torrent d'incrédulité.' Ibid., vol. 3, pp. 212–13.

42. Suzanne Curchod Necker to Etienette Clavel de Brenles, 7 June 1765, and Suzanne Cur-chod Necker to Etienette Clavel de Brenles and Jacques Abram Elie Daniel Clavel de Brenles, 17 December 1767, IS1915/xxx/h/1, BCUL.

43. 'Mon âme [est] sans cesse électrisée par de nouveaux objets et par de nouveaux goûts.' Suzanne Curchod Necker to Etienette Clavel de Brenles, 28 June 1768, IS1915/xxx/h/1, BCUL.

44. Suzanne Curchod Necker to Etienette Clavel de Brenles, 12 December 1768, IS1915/xxx/h/1, BCUL.

45. 'Nous ressemblons à ces gourmands dont le palais blasé est dégouté de tous les alimens et ne peut cependant revenir à des mets simples et salutaires; la finesse du goût est prodi-gieusement perfectionnée tant pour le corps que pour l'esprit, et nous réalisons au moral et au physique l'histoire du Sybarite, que le pli d'une feuille de rose empêchoit de dormir.' Suzanne Curchod Necker to Etienette Clavel de Brenles, 6 April 1773, IS1915/xxx/h/1, BCUL.

46. 'Ce qu'on appeloit franchise en Suisse, devenoit égoïsme à Paris; négligence des petites choses, étoit ici manque aux bienséances.' Suzanne Curchod Necker to Etienette Clavel de Brenles, 31 August 1771, IS1915/xxx/h/1, BCUL.

47. 'Dans ce moment ma position est bien différente, j'étois pauvre alors, incertaine de mon sort; mais j'avois des accès de joie dont je ne suis plus susceptible et je cherche vainement dans les plus brillantes assemblées, quelques traces de la vive impression que j'éprouvai alors.' Suzanne Curchod Necker to Etienette Clavel de Brenles, 4 September 1768, IS1915/xxx/h/1, BCUL.

48. 'Je vis dans un pays, Madame, où l'on ne peut répondre que de son coeur ... vous m'avez appris à faire un usage mille fois plus précieux, et quand il seroit possible que le tourbil-lon où je vis étourdit ma sensibilité, vos lettres charmantes me rappelleroient bientôt

toutes les délices de l'amitié.' Suzanne Curchod Necker to Etienette Clavel de Brenles, 12 December 1768, IS1915/xxx/h/1, BCUL.

49. N. Faret, N., *L'Honneste homme, ou L'Art de plaire à la cour* (Paris: T. du Bray, 1630).

50. D. Diderot, 'Bienséance', in Diderot and d'Alembert (eds), *Encyclopédie*, vol. 2, p. 245.

51. Ibid., vol. 2, p. 245.

52. L. de Jaucourt, 'Civilité, politesse, affabilité', in Diderot and d'Alembert (eds), *Encyclopédie*, vol. 3, p. 497; anon., 'Politesse', in Diderot and d'Alembert (eds), *Encyclopédie*, vol. 12, p. 916.

53. '[Revêtu] de la douceur, de la modestie, & de la justice que l'esprit cherche, & dont la société a besoin pour être paisible & agréable.' Anon., 'Politesse', in Diderot and d'Alembert (eds), *Encyclopédie*, vol. 12, p. 916.

54. '[L]'homme au-dehors comme il devroit être intérieurement.' Jaucourt, 'Civilité, politesse, affabilité', in Diderot and d'Alembert (eds), *Encyclopédie*, vol. 3, p. 497.

55. 'Le désir de plaire renferme donc le désir d'être aimé.' F.-A. Paradis de Moncrif, *Essais sur la nécessité et sur les moyens de plaire* (Paris: Prault, 1738), p. 17.

56. Curchod Necker, *Nouveaux mélanges*, vol. 1, p. 34.

57. Curchod Necker, *Mélanges*, vol. 1, pp. 279, 296.

58. 'La propreté ne consiste pas seulement dans des vêtemens ou dans des meubles propres; mais elle se montre par le grand arrangement des choses qui nous entourent. Cet ordre averti l'imagination que rien n'a été négligé.' Ibid. vol. 2, p. 72.

59. '[T]out cela est désagréable, de mauvais ton et de mauvais grâce.' Curchod Necker, *Nouveaux mélanges*, vol. 2, p. 270.

60. See, for example, Curchod Necker, *Mélanges*, vol. 1, pp. 36, 311–13, 315.

61. P. Goring, *The Rhetoric of Sensibility in Eighteenth-Century Culture* (Cambridge: Cambridge University Press, 2005). See also D. C. Stanton, *The Aristocrat as Art: A Study of the Honnête Homme and the Dandy in Seventeenth and Nineteenth-Century French Literature* (New York: Columbia University Press, 1980).

62. J. Bentham, *Panopticum; or, The Inspection-House*, 3 vols (London: R. Baldwin, 1791).

63. 'Glaces mouvantes.' R. de Bary, *L'Esprit de cour, ou Les Conversations galantes* (Paris, 1662), p. 29.

64. 'Vous ne devez pas vous considérer parce que je vous estime, vous devez vous considérer parce que vous estes estimable ... il est temps que vous scachiez par vos propres observations que vous meritez bien qu'on vous observe.' Ibid., p. 30.

65. Ibid., p. 31.

66. 'On disoit de Mme. De Lauzun: Elle s'est modelée sur le caractère qu'on lui a donné d'abord dans le monde, et c'est pour cela qu'elle est parfaite.' Curchod Necker, *Nouveaux mélanges*, vol. 1, p. 78.

67. M. Merleau-Ponty, *Basic Writings*, ed. T. Baldwin (London: Routledge, 2004), p. 81; italics in original.

68. 'Vous m'avez écrit une lettre délicieuse; vous faites passer à votre plume la flamme qui anime vos rôles, tout est pour vous les matériaux de la vie. Je l'ai lue seule cette lettre, d'abord avec attendrissement, ensuite je l'ai rendue avec orgueil à toute ma société. Sans cesse je m'en vois entourée, on me dit, Contez-nous encore un peu de ce grand homme, Comment jouoit-il Hamlet? le Roi Lear? Sir John Brute? Je conte, et l'on pleure ou l'on rit.' D. Garrick, *The Private Correspondence of David Garrick with the most Celebrated Persons of his Time*, ed. J. Boaden, 2 vols (London: Henry Colburn & Richard Bentley, 1832), vol. 2, p. 624.

69. Ibid., vol. 2, p. 625.

70. M. M***, *Discours sur les hommes; ou nouvelle apologie des femmes* (Paris, 1755).
71. 'La femme a été créée pour charmer l'Homme, elle le charme, & la nature est contente.' Ibid., p. 26.
72. Ibid., p. 10.
73. 'Nous trouverons que sa face est le Miroir de son esprit, & que la Beauté mesme n'est que l'image de son corps.' F. de Grenaille, *Les plaisirs des dames* (Paris: Gervais Clousier, 1641), p. 64.
74. '[Mademoiselle de Lespinasse] les avait pris çà et là dans le monde, mais si bien assortis, que, lorsqu'ils étaient là, ils s'y trouvaient en harmonie comme les cordes d'un instrument monté par une habile main. En suivant la comparaison, je pourrais dire qu'elle jouait de cet instrument avec un art qui tenait du genie; elle semblait savoir quel son rendrait la corde qu'elle allait toucher; je veux dire que nos esprits et nos caractères lui étaient si bien connus, que, pour les mettre en jeu, elle n'avait qu'un mot à dire. Nulle part la conversation n'était plus vive, plus brillante, ni mieux réglée que chez elle.' Marmontel, *Oeuvres complètes*, vol. 1, p. 472.
75. D. Goodman, 'Julie de Lespinasse: A Mirror for the Enlightenment', in F. M. Keener and S. E. Lorsch (eds), *Eighteenth-Century Women and the Arts* (New York: Greenwood Press, 1988), pp. 3–10; J.-N. Pascal, 'La Muse de l'*Encyclopédie*: Julie de Lespinasse', in R. Bonnel and C. Rubinger (eds), *Femmes savantes et femmes d'esprit: Women Intellectuals of the French Eighteenth Century* (New York: Peter Lang, 1994), pp. 243–65.
76. 'Une société de personnes spirituelles et polies, réunies pour s'entretenir ensemble et s'instruire, dans une conversation agréable, par la communication mutuelle de leurs idées et de leurs sentiments, m'a toujours paru la plus heureuse représentation de l'espèce humaine et de la perfection sociale. Là, chacun apporte son desir et ses moyens de plaire, sa sensibilité, son imagination, son expérience, le tout embelli par la politesse et contenu par la décence; là, se montre un instinct mutuel d'affections bienveillantes ... là, sans règlement, sans contrainte, s'exerce une douce police, fondée sur le respect qu'inspirent les uns aux autres les hommes réunis, sur le besoin qu'ils on d'être bien ensemble.' J. Delille, 'La Conversation: Poème en trois chants', in *Oeuvres de J. Delille*, ed. L.-G. Michaud, 2 vols (Paris: Lefèvre, 1844), vol. 2, p. 195.
77. 'On a regardé la politesse comme une servitude; et son origine au contraire se trouve dans les ménagemens de la force pour la foiblesse, pour la vieillesse, pour les femmes, pour les enfans, etc. La politesse est conforme à ce principe d'égalité dont on nous parle si souvent; elle est le rempart de ceux qui ne peuvent passe [*sic*] défendre, et c'est même ce qui en fait l'éloge et le mérite.' Curchod Necker, *Nouveaux mélanges*, vol. 2, p. 291.
78. '[L]es expressions du visage, du geste, de la voix, sont un second langage.' Paradis de Moncrif, *Essais*, p. 45.
79. 'Personne n'a plus senti que moi, qu'il faut être né dans ce pays pour y réussir par les agrémens.' Suzanne Curchod Necker to Etienette Clavel de Brenles, 1775, IS1915/xxx/h/1, BCUL. A similar comment appears in her *Mélanges*, vol. 2, pp. 91–2.
80. *Dictionnaire de l'Académie françoise*, 4th edn, 2 vols (Paris: Bernard Brunet, 1762), vol. 1, p. 529.
81. Haussonville, *Le Salon de Madame Necker*, vol. 2, pp. 5–6.
82. Curchod Necker, *Mélanges*, vol. 1, p. 22.
83. 'Remplir mes devoirs, voilà donc ma première passion et mon premier soin.' Quoted in Andlau, *La Jeunesse de Madame de Staël*, p. 42.
84. 'Un des grands principes de l'usage du monde, c'est de paroître bien avec toutes les personnes qu'on rencontre, soit qu'on les aime, soit qu'on ne les aime pas; car si l'on y fait

attention, il est possible de rapprocher toutes les maximes de la politesse, des préceptes de l'Evangile; les unes sont l'image et les autres la réalité.' Curchod Necker, *Mélanges*, vol. 2, p. 11.

85. See Burnand, 'L'Image de Madame Necker dans les pamphlets'.
86. See, for example, *Les Deux conversations de Madame Necker*.
87. Bachaumont, *Mémoires secrets*, vol. 15, p. 188.
88. Lilti, *Le Monde des salons*, p. 370.

2 Embodied Faith

1.   'Pour moi, je vous l'avoue, je ne dis pas avec les philosophes, *Je pense, donc je suis*; je dis, *Je pense, donc Dieu est*. Cette idée est inséparable du sentiment de mon être; elle comprend tout pour moi, elle satisfait tous mes goûts, elle répond à tous mes penchans: je n'ai plus de curiosité, le mot de l'énigme est trouvé; je n'ai plus de désir, tous mes voeux sont remplis; je n'ai plus d'incertitude, ma route est tracée.' Curchod Necker, *Mélanges*, vol. 2, p. 160; italics in original.
2.   J. Calvin, *Institutes of the Christian Religion* (1559), ed. J. T. McNeill, trans. F. L. Battles, 2 vols (Philadelphia, PA: Westminster Press, 1960), vol. 1, p. 847.
3.   See, for example, letters of Suzanne Curchod Necker to [Jean-André] De Luc, April 1778, ms. 2465, f. 136, BGE; Suzanne Curchod Necker to Georges-Louis LeSage, 14 July 1793, ms.suppl. 514, Papiers Georges-Louis LeSage fils, f. 79, BGE.
4.   'Mon cher ami, Pouvez-vous me soupçonner un instant? J'ai reçu mes sentimens avec l'existence et vous voudriez que je les abandonnasse dans le temps où mon bonheur en est le fruit? ... Je vis, il est vrai, au milieu d'un grand nombre d'athées; mais leurs argumens n'ont jamais même effleuré mon esprit, et, s'ils ont été jusqu'à mon coeur, ce n'a été que pour le faire frémir d'horreur.' Quoted in Haussonville, *Le Salon de Madame Necker*, vol. 1, p. 164. See also similar assurances in Suzanne Curchod Necker to Henriette Réverdil, 10 September [1768], ms.suppl. 717, f. 31, BGE.
5.   '[N]otre premier soin doit être de le consacrer à Dieu.' Curchod Necker, *Mélanges*, vol. 2, p. 146.
6.   Curchod Necker, *Nouveaux mélanges*, vol. 2, p. 118.
7.   W. Monter, 'Protestant Wives, Catholic Saints, and the Devil's Handmaid: Women in the Age of Reformations', in R. Bridenthal, C. Koonz and S. Stuard (eds) *Becoming Visible: Women in European History* (Boston, MA: Houghton Mifflin, 1987), pp. 203–19, on p. 205.
8.   With apologies to Mary McCarthy. M. McCarthy, *Memories of a Catholic Girlhood* (Orlando, FL: Harcourt, 1957).
9.   'Protestant et marchand, conseiller de ville en 1585 et consul en 1588.' A. de Coston, *Histoire de Montélimar*, 4 vols (Montélimar: Bourron, 1886), vol. 3, p. 378.
10. 'Mes relations avec Made. Necker ont en quelque sorte précédé sa naissance & la mienne puisque nos Parens ont déjà rempli réciproquement les devoirs de l'amitié dans toute leur entendue.' Elie-Salomon-François Réverdil to Jacques Necker, 29 August 1798, ms.suppl. 728, f. 129, BGE.
11. 'Vous êtes – oserais-je le dire? – oui, vous êtes savante. Faut-il s'étonner après cela si le beau sexe sonne l'alarme?' Quoted in E. Ritter, *Notes sur Madame de Staël* (Geneva: H. Georg, 1899), pp. 51–2.
12. 'Lorsque j'étudiois en belles-lettres, à Lausanne, M. Darney, notre professeur, nous disoit que vous étiés une exception de votre sexe par vos lumières, et vous proposoit pour notre

modèle. Lorsque vous passiés dans les rues, toujours entourée d'un cortège d'admirateurs, j'entendois le public qui disoit: "Voilà la belle Curchod!" et je courois aussitôt sur votre passage, où je demeurois le plus longtemps qu'il m'étoit possible.' Quoted in Haussonville, *Le Salon de Madame Necker*, vol. 1, pp. 26–7.

13. H. Rosenblatt, *Rousseau and Geneva: From the First Discourse to the Social Contract, 1749–1762* (Cambridge: Cambridge University Press, 1997), p. 19.

14. Ibid.

15. J. Calvin, *The Letters of John Calvin*, trans. J. Bonnet, 4 vols (New York: Burt Franklin, 1972).

16. J. R. Watt, 'Women and the Consistory in Calvin's Geneva', *Sixteenth Century Journal*, 24:2 (1993), pp. 429–39; and E. M. Wengler, 'Women, Religion, and Reform in Sixteenth-Century Geneva' (PhD dissertation, Boston College, 1999).

17. *The iudgement of the synode holden at Dort, concerning the fiue Articles* (London: John Bill, 1619).

18. M. I. Klauber, *Between Reformed Scholasticism and Pan-Protestantism: Jean-Alphonse Turretin (1671–1737) and Enlightened Orthodoxy at the Academy of Geneva* (Selinsgrove, PA: Susquehanna University Press, 1994), p. 10.

19. Ibid., p. 111.

20. J. Watt, *Choosing Death: Suicide and Calvinism in Early Modern Geneva* (Kirksville, MO: Truman State University Press, 2001), pp. 284–6.

21. J. Necker, *De l'importance des opinions réligieuses* (Liège: C. Pomteux, 1788); H. Grange, *Les idées de Necker* (Paris: C. Klincksieck, 1974).

22. Rosenblatt, *Rousseau and Geneva*, p. 11.

23. '[L]a SOCIÉTÉ … n'est point l'ouvrage de l'homme: c'est Dieu lui-même qui en est l'auteur … [La société], qui par les secours que les hommes tirent les uns des autres, leur procure toutes les connoissances, toutes les commodités & les douceurs qui font la sûreté, le Bonheur & l'agrément de la vie! Il est vrai que tous ces avantages supposent que les hommes, bien loin de se nuire, vivent dans une bonne intelligence, & entretiennent cette union par des offices réciproques.' J.-J. Burlamaqui, *Principes du droit naturel*, 2 vols (Geneva: Barrillot, 1748), vol. 1, pp. 56–7.

24. Rosenblatt, *Rousseau and Geneva*, p. 24.

25. C. Renevey-Fry et al. (eds), *En attendant le prince charmant: L'Éducation des jeunes filles à Genève, 1740–1970* (Geneva: Service de la recherche en éducation et Musée d'ethnographie, 1997), p. 35. See also H. Rosenblatt, 'On the "Misogyny" of Jean-Jacques Rousseau: The *Letter to d'Alembert* in Historical Context', *French Historical Studies*, 25:1 (2002), pp. 91–114.

26. Renevey-Fry et al. (eds), *En attendant le prince charmant*, p. 36.

27. 'On trouve en elle la Femme sensée; la vraye Chrétienne; la femme éclairée; l'Epouse, la Mère, la Parente, l'Amie consacrée à ses Devoirs; la Femme d'ordre et active; la Femme forte et courageuse; la Femme du Monde dont les manières nobles et engageantes sont un modelle; et pour tout dire la Vertue modeste; qui, contente de l'acquit de ses Devoirs fuit l'éclat, cherche bien moins l'approbation publique que celle de son propre coeur, et de mériter la tendresse d'un digne Mari.' Quoted in ibid., p. 35.

28. Gibbon, *Letters*, vol. 1, p. 161.

29. Magdeleine Curchod to Henriette Réverdil, undated, ms.suppl. 363, ff. 26–7, BGE.

30. 'Je m'en prenois à toi de toutes les contrariétés de ma vie, parce que de toi seule dépendoit mon bonheur.' Quoted in Haussonville, *Le Salon de Madame Necker*, vol. 1, p. 88.

31. 'Il n'y a rien qui puisse tenir lieu du devoir ou qui dédommage de la crainte d'avoir diminué le bonheur de celle qui nous donne la vie.' Suzanne Curchod Necker to Élie-Salomon-François Réverdil, 21 October 1770, ms.suppl. 725, f. 1, BGE.

32. 'Je vous assure que malgré les charmes que le monde et ma situation me presentent, je cherche Dieu comme le souverain bien ainsi que vous me le conseillés.' Suzanne Curchod Necker to Henriette Réverdil, 10 September [1768], ms.suppl. 717, f. 31, BGE; underlining in original.

33. 'Puisse-t-elle voir du haut des cieux mon coeur enflamé encore du desir de lui plaire.' Suzanne Curchod Necker to Henriette Réverdil, February 1765, ms.suppl. 717, f. 2, BGE.

34. 'Dieu, veuille bénir nos soins, il me semble que ma chére mére les approuve du haut des cieux; et que j'oserai me présenter devant elle au moment ou je la rejoindrai.' Suzanne Curchod Necker to Henriette Réverdil, undated, ms.suppl. 717, f. 8, BGE.

35. 'Les infortunés de cette communion qui sont isolées au milieu des Catholiques.' Suzanne Curchod Necker to Henriette Réverdil, 15 July 1766, ms.suppl. 717, f. 12, BGE.

36. B. C. Lane, 'Spirituality as the Performance of Desire: Calvin on the World as a Theatre of God's Glory', *Spiritus: A Journal of Christian Spirituality*, 1:1 (2001), pp. 1–30, on p. 1.

37. Ibid., p. 1.

38. Ibid., pp. 9–10.

39. '[J]e voudrois bien mon cher ange qu'il te fut possible de faire parvenir jusqu'a moi; ma bible si tu en trouvez une dans mes livres ou en cas du contraire une Bible que tu m'achéterois avec un nouveau Testament le tout de la plus nouvelle version; tu y joindrois aussi une traduction en prose des pseaumes ... c'est un large en 4to mais trez mince couvert de carton qui doit être dans la caisse je voudrois encore le catechism d'Osterwald ... et en un mot les livres de piété que peuvent m'etre necessaires pour l'instruction de ma petite qui commence à parler et à comprendre.' Suzanne Curchod Necker to Sophie and Henriette Réverdil, 10 September [1768], ms.suppl. 717, f. 30, BGE.

40. 'Née moi même sans fortune.' Suzanne Curchod Necker to an unidentified correspondent, 17 May, DO 32/51, BGE.

41. References to Bellami are scattered throughout Necker's correspondence with Réverdil.

42. J. A. Fatio to Suzanne Curchod Necker, undated, ms.suppl. 716, ff. 24–5, BGE.

43. See numerous references in letters of Suzanne Curchod Necker to Henriette Réverdil, ms.suppl. 717, ff. 1–201, BGE.

44. 'Les effets du mauvais sang qu'elle a recue.' Suzanne Curchod Necker to Henriette Réverdil, 8 June 1774, ms.suppl. 717, f. 124, BGE.

45. 'L'on vient donc de publier cette loi dangereuse qui autorise et favorise le divorce; ce n'étoit pas assez des divisions attachées à l'esprit de parti, il falloit encore disjoindre les époux, isoler les enfans, et combattre toutes les affections naturelles; c'est cependant leur réunion qui forme la Patrie et qui la protége; ce sont les rameaux d'un arbre sacré, qu'on ne peut en séparer successivement sans laisser sa tige chauve et déshonorée.' Curchod Necker, *Réflexions sur le divorce*, p. 5.

46. J. Witte Jr and R. M. Kingdon, *Sex, Marriage, and Family in John Calvin's Geneva, Volume 1: Courtship, Engagement, and Marriage* (Grand Rapids, MI, and Cambridge: William B. Eerdmans Publishing Company, 2005), pp. 31–2.

47. Calvin, *Institutes of the Christian Religion*, vol. 2, p. 1481.

48. C. J. Blaisdell, 'The Matrix of Reform: Women in the Lutheran and Calvinist Movements', in R. L. Greaves (ed.), *Triumph Over Silence: Women in Protestant History* (Westport, CT: Greenwood Press, 1985), pp. 13–44, on p. 28.

49. Curchod Necker, *Réflexions sur le divorce*, p. 6.

50. Witte and Kingdon, *Sex, Marriage, and Family*, pp. 47–50.

51. Calvin, *The Letters*, vol. 4, p. 71.

52. Watt, 'Women and the Consistory', p. 436.

53. Reprinted numerous times, most recently in 1928 (Paris: A. Michel), the *Réflexions* also represents the longest lasting public display of Madame Necker's Calvinism.

54. 'Combien la religion change le tableau de la vie! les douleurs mêmes du corps sont le présage d'une nouvelle existence: nos défauts et ceux des autres nous offrent un double moyen d'exercer nos vertus; ainsi le paradis est déjà dans notre pensée.' Curchod Necker, *Mélanges*, vol. 1, p. 93.

55. 'Je t'adore et je m'élève jusqu'à toi. Mon amour fait évanouir la distance qui nous sépare; il est immense comme elle.' Quoted in Haussonville, *Le Salon de Madame Necker*, vol. 2, p. 15.

56. 'Que laisserai-je d'ailleurs ... une machine à demi usée qui semble m'avertir chaque jour de l'instant du départ, qui se refuse à tous mes sentiments et qui m'en suggère souvent de contraires à ma raison. Si c'est donc ta volonté; oh! mon Dieu, termine sans douleur une vie que tu as comblée de tes faveurs les plus particulières, mais qui est empoisonnée par des remords, par des souvenirs, par le dédain et l'ingratitude ... Mon Dieu, daigne jeter sur ta créature un regard de bonté et pardonne à la témérité de sa prière.' Quoted in ibid., vol. 2, pp. 18–19.

57. 'Je suis à la source du bonheur mais il s'échappe loin de moi comme un fleuve rapide, et bientôt il va se perdre dans un précipice inconnu.' Quoted in ibid., vol. 2, p. 15.

58. 'Je crains, madame, que vous ne fassiez pas tout ce qu'il faut pour rétablir votre santé. Je crains, pour vous, cette activité de devoir, qui vous dévore, et qui vous fait sans cesse sacrifier vous-même à ceux que vous aimez.' Thomas, *Oeuvres complètes*, vol. 6, p. 260.

59. I. Backus and C. Chimelli, 'Préface', in *La Vraie piété: Divers traités de Jean Calvin et Confession de foi de Guillaume Farel*, ed. I. Backus and C. Chimelli (Geneva: Labor et Fides, 1986), pp. 7–13, on p. 7.

60. Calvin, *Institutes*, vol. 1, p. 690.

61. 'Notre ame est une; elle est faite pour suivre une seule idée, comme notre coeur pour aimer une seule personne.' Curchod Necker, *Nouveaux mélanges*, vol. 2, p. 190.

62. Calvin, *Institutes of the Christian Religion*, vol. 1, p. 847.

63. Ibid., vol. 1, p. 184.

64. '[U]n miroir qui réfléchit l'idée et les idées de la Divinité.' Curchod Necker, *Nouveaux mélanges*, vol. 2, p. 118.

65. '[L]e malheureux, voulant être quelque chose en soi-même, incontinent commença à oublier et méconnaître d'où le bien lui venait, et par outrageuse ingratitude, il entreprit de s'élever et enorgueillir contre son facteur et auteur de toutes ses grâces.' J. Calvin, 'A tous amateurs de Jésus-Christ et de son Évangile, Salut (1535)', in *La Vraie piété*, pp. 25–38, on p. 25.

66. M.-J. Ducommon and D. Quadroni, *Le Refuge Protestant dans le Pays de Vaud (fin XVIIe – début XVIIIe siècle)* (Geneva: Droz, 1991), p. 11.

67. Coston, *Histoire de Montélimar*, vol. 3, pp. 379–80.

68. Ibid., vol. 3, p. 377.

69. Ibid., vol. 3, p. 377.

70. Ibid., vol. 3, p. 381.
71. Letters of Elie-Salomon-François Réverdil to Henriette Réverdil, ms.suppl. 718, ff. 68–79, BGE.
72. 'Mlle Suzanne Curchod, bourgeoise d'Echalens et de Lausanne, ci-devant résident à Crassy, pays de Vaud, comme fille unique et héritière de Louis-Antoine Curchod.' Quoted in Coston, *Histoire de Montélimar*, vol. 3, p. 382.
73. P. Benedict, *The Faith and Fortunes of France's Huguenots, 1600–85* (Aldershot: Ashgate, 2001), p. 94.
74. Ducommon and Quadroni, *Le Refuge Protestant*, pp. 14, 45.
75. 'Exile', in *The Oxford English Dictionary*, 2nd edn (Oxford: Oxford University Press, 1989), online edn.
76. 'Dans un esprit soumis à la volonté divine, l'habitude des souffrances produit toujours quelque changement moral, et trompe les spectateurs, qui supposent la diminution du mal; mais ils ne voient pas qu'on apprend à supporter les persécutions de la douleur, comme celles d'une étrangère dont on va bientôt se séparer.' Curchod Necker, *Nouveaux mélanges*, vol. 2, pp. 7–8.
77. See Lane, 'Spirituality as the Performance of Desire'.
78. Haussonville, *Le Salon de Madame Necker*, vol. 1, p. 87.
79. Curchod Necker, *Nouveaux mélanges*, vol. 2, p. 118.
80. Calvin, *Institutes of the Christian Religion*, vol. 1, p. 847.
81. '[P]ar les secours que les hommes tirent les uns des autres, leur procure toutes les connoissances, toutes les commodités & les douceurs qui font la sûreté, le Bonheur & l'agrément de la vie!' Burlamaqui, *Principes du droit naturel*, vol. 1, p. 57.
82. 'Celui qui se présente le premier est l'état de FAMILLE. Cette société est la plus naturelle & la plus ancienne de toutes, & elle sert de fondement à la *Société Nationale*: car un Peuple ou une *Nation* n'est qu'un composé de plusieurs Familles.' Ibid., vol. 1, p. 59; italics in original.
83. '[J]'ai besoin de l'air natal.' Suzanne Curchod Necker to Etienette Clavel de Brenles, June 1765, IS1915/xxx/h/1, BCUL.
84. 'Le système de quelques philosophes tend à éteindre tous les intérêts en refroidissant tous les sentimens: religion, piété, respect filial, amour conjugal, amour de la patrie, tous les intérêts de la vie se trouvent détruits dans leur livres, excepté celui de boire froid et de manger chaud, etc., qui ne peut pas produire beaucoup de grands hommes.' Curchod Necker, *Nouveaux mélanges*, vol. 2, p. 118.
85. 'Pour qui sait penser, ce monde est partout un miroir qui réfléchit l'idée et les idées de la Divinité.' Ibid., vol. 2, p. 118.

3 Filial Duty and the Maternal Body

1. S. de Beauvoir, *The Second Sex*, trans. H. M. Parshley (New York: Knopf, 1989), p. 281.
2. 'Permettez Madame que je finisse en vous assurant de mon plus tendre attachement; ce sera la dernière lettre que j'aurai l'honneur de vous écrire avant que j'ai doublé mon être ou pour mieux dire avant que j'aye mis au jour un nouveau coeur pour vous aimer; je sens que mon enfant doit avoir les sentiments de sa mére.' Suzanne Curchod Necker to Etienette Clavel de Brenles, 1766, IS1915/xxx/h/1, BCUL.
3. Watt, 'Women and the Consistory', p. 434.
4. Elisabeth M. Wengler points out that some women found ways around this. Wengler, 'Women, Religion and Reform'.

5. J. L. Thompson, *John Calvin and the Daughters of Sarah* (Geneva: Librairie Droz, 1992), p. 17.

6. Watt, 'Women and the Consistory'.

7. R. L. Greaves, 'Introduction', in Greaves (ed.), *Triumph Over Silence*, pp. 3–12, on p. 4.

8. N. L. Roelker, 'The Appeal of Calvinism to French Noblewomen in the Sixteenth Century', *Journal of Interdisciplinary History*, 2:4 (1972), pp. 391–418, on p. 407.

9. Monter, 'Protestant Wives', p. 205.

10. R. A. Mentzer, 'Morals and Moral Regulation in Protestant France', *Journal of Interdisciplinary History*, 32:1 (2000), pp. 1–20, on p. 9.

11. J. Necker, *Compte rendu au Roy* (Paris: Imprimerie royale, 1781), p. 103.

12. Necker, 'Observations de l'éditeur.'

13. Ibid., p. xviii.

14. 'J'ai désiré l'*Hospice* afin de le joindre au *Compte rendu* et de renfermer dans un même volume les deux ouvrages les plus intéressans que j'aie jamais lus et que je puisse jamais lire. J'ai vu dans l'un la justice, la vérité, le courage, la dignité, la raison, le génie employer toutes leurs forces pour refréner la tyrannie des hommes puissans; et dans l'autre la bienfaisance et la pitié tendre leurs mains secourables à la partie de l'espèce humaine la plus à plaindre, les maladies indigens.' Quoted in Haussonville, *Le Salon de Madame Necker*, vol. 2, p. 135.

15. M. Linton, 'Virtue Rewarded? Women and the Politics of Virtue in 18th-Century France. Part I', *History of European Ideas*, 26 (2000), pp. 35–49; M. Linton, 'Virtue Rewarded? Women and the Politics of Virtue in 18th-Century France. Part II', *History of European Ideas*, 27 (2001), pp. 51–65.

16. '[M]ais enfin, qu'est-ce que la vertu? en deux mots c'est *l'observation constante des lois qui nous sont imposées, sous quelque rapport que l'homme se considère.*' Romilly, 'Vertu, (*Ord. encyclop. Mor. Polit.*)', in Diderot and d'Alembert (eds), *Encyclopédie*, vol. 17, p. 176; italics in original.

17. L. de Jaucourt, 'Vertu, (*critiq. Sacrée*)', 'Vertu, (*Mythol.*)' and 'Vertu, (*lang. franç.*)', in Diderot and d'Alembert (eds), *Encyclopédie*, vol. 17, p. 185.

18. Linton, 'Virtue Rewarded? Part I', p. 36.

19. C. Blum, *Rousseau and the Republic of Virtue: The Language of Politics in the French Revolution* (Ithaca, NY: Cornell University Press, 1986), p. 50.

20. Ibid., p. 47.

21. Linton, 'Virtue Rewarded? Part II', p. 55.

22. I am indebted here to ideas put forward in unpublished work of Dena Goodman, 'Germaine de Staël's Dilemmas: Writing, Gender and Publicity' (unpublished manuscript).

23. J.-J. Rousseau, 'Jean-Jacques Rousseau, citoyen de Genève, à M. d'Alembert', in *Oeuvres complètes de J. J. Rousseau*, 25 vols (Paris: Dalibon, 1826), vol. 2, p. 154–5.

24. J. Weber, *Mémoires de Weber, concernant Marie-Antoinette, archiduchesse d'Autriche et reine de France et de Navarre; avec des notes et des éclaircissemens historiques, par Mm. Berville et Barrière*, ed. S.-A. Berville and F. Barrière (Paris: Baudouin frères, 1822), pp. 270–2.

25. E. Badinter, *Émilie, Émilie: L'Ambition féminine au XVIIIe siècle* (Paris: Flammarion, 1983).

26. 'Elle a tant travaillé à paraître ce qu'elle n'était pas qu'on ne sait plus ce qu'elle est en effet. Ses défauts mêmes ne lui sont peut-être pas naturels, ils pourraient tenir à ses prétentions; son impolitesse et son inconsidération, à l'état de princesse; sa sécheresse et ses distrac-

tions, à celui de savante; son rire glapissant, ses grimaces et ses contorsions, à celui de jolie femme.' Grimm, *Correspondance littéraire*, vol. 11, p. 436–7.

27. 'Une femme si chrétienne, une âme si élevée, devoit avoir naturellement de la modestie et de la sincérité; mais l'ambition démesurée d'une célébrité éclatante n'altéra que trop, à cet égard, son goût et son caractère. Pour obtenir des louanges, combien n'en a-t-elle pas prodigué à des ouvrages qu'elle n'aimait point, et à des hommes qu'elle ne pouvoit estimer!' S. F. Ducrest de Saint Aubin, Comtesse de Genlis, *De l'influence des femmes sur la littérature française, comme protectrices des lettres et comme auteurs; ou précis de l'histoire des femmes françaises les plus célèbres* (Paris: Maradin, 1811), p. 303.

28. Haussonville, *Le Salon de Madame Necker*, vol. 2, p. 5.

29. Ibid.

30. '[J]e n'ai reconnu les vertus que pour me convaincre que je n'avois point.' Suzanne Curchod Necker to Elie-Salomon-François Réverdil, 30 November 1772, ms.suppl. 725, f. 8, BGE.

31. S. Curchod Necker, 'Portrait de M. Necker', in *Mélanges*, vol. 2, pp. 372–404.

32. 'Heureuses les femmes qui ont su cacher long-temps leur mérite par la simplicité et la modestie, et qui ont appris leur secret au public avant de le savoir elles-mêmes! Heureuses celles qui ont su se faire aimer, avant de faire naître l'envie, et qui ont jugé de bonne heure que l'exemple donné en silence est le plus utile de tous!' Curchod Necker, *Mélanges*, vol. 1, p. 377.

33. 'On aime plus la vertu quand on la pratique que quand on la peint; cet exercice continuel de la vertu semble appeler plus souvent la présence divine, et donne ainsi aux petites choses un caractère de grandeur et une sort d'étendue.' Ibid., vol. 1, p. 266.

34. Ibid., vol. 1, p. 88.

35. Ibid., vol. 2, p. 21.

36. 'Il est impossible de s'exagérer les jouissances que donne l'exercice de ses devoirs.' Ibid., vol. 1, p. 22.

37. 'On ne se refroidit point sur ses devoirs en les multipliant; cet exercice continuel de la vertu semble appeler plus souvent la présence divine, et donne ainsi aux petites choses un caractère de grandeur et une sorte d'étendue.' Ibid., vol. 1, p. 284.

38. 'Fixons donc notre attention sur ce travail secret qui se fait en nous; nous apprendrons à mieux connoître l'agent qui y préside.' Ibid., vol. 1, p. 364.

39. 'La vertu est [le secret] du bonheur.' Ibid., vol. 1, p. 179.

40. 'La vertu dépend de nos efforts, que l'Être suprême favorise toujours; elle nous donne l'espoir de rejoindre ceux qui ne vivent plus pour nous: l'accomplissement de tous nos devoirs augmente chaque jour la tendresse et l'estime des personnes que nous aimons; une âme toujours saine et un régime exact, fortifie la santé; et quand on obtiendroit la jeunesse, la beauté et les talens, il faudroit toujours les perdre par la vieillesse et par la mort. La vertu seule nous procure tous les dons joints à l'immortalité.' Ibid., vol. 3, p. 60.

41. *The iudgement of the synode holden at Dort*, p. 4.

42. Curchod Necker, *Mélanges*, vol. 1, p. 148.

43. Ibid., vol. 3, p. 105.

44. 'Je ne crois pas pouvoir trop le répéter, ce mélange du vice et de la vertu est extrêmement dangereux; il embellit le vice et diminue les charmes de la vertu.' Ibid., vol. 1, p. 59.

45. See note 2 above.

46. 'Les tourmens des damnés.' Suzanne Curchod Necker to Etienette Clavel de Brenles, 11 June 1766, IS1915/xxx/h/1, BCUL.

47. 'Une espèce de gens bien plus terribles que les furies, inventés exprès pour faire frémir la pudeur et révolter la nature.' Suzanne Curchod Necker to Etienette Clavel de Brenles, 11 June 1766, IS1915/xxx/h/1, BCUL.

48. Calvin, *Institutes of the Christian Religion*, vol. 1, p. 242.

49. 'Nous confessons et nous recongnoissons sans feinctise, deuant ta saincte maiesté, que nous sommes paoures pecheurs, conceuez et nez en iniquité et corruption: enlins à mal faire, inutiles à tout bien.' 'Confession des péchés (1542)', in M.-C. Pitassi, *De l'orthodoxie aux Lumières: Genève 1670–1737* (Geneva: Labor et Fides, 1992), p. 60.

50. 'Notre Seigneur nous monstre, en quelle paoureté et misere nous naissons tous, en nous disant, qu'il nous fault renaistre.' 'Liturgie du baptême (1542)', in ibid., p. 60.

51. 'Nous devons naître de nouveau, si nous voulons entrer dans le Royaume de Dieu.' 'Liturgie du baptême (1724)', in ibid., p. 60.

52. Beauvoir, *The Second Sex*, pp. 517–27.

53. Ibid., p. 179.

54. Cixous, 'Le Rire de la méduse'; Irigaray, *This Sex Which Is Not One*; L. Irigaray, 'The Bodily Encounter with the Mother', in *The Irigaray Reader*, ed. M. Whitford, trans. D. Macey (Oxford and Cambridge, MA: Basil Blackwell, 1991), pp. 34–46; Kristeva, *Powers of Horror*; J. Kristeva, 'Motherhood [according to Giovanni Bellini]', in K. Oliver (ed.), *French Feminism Reader* (Lanham, MD, and Oxford: Rowman & Littlefield Publishers, 2000), pp. 176–80; I. M. Young, *On Female Body Experience: 'Throwing Like a Girl' and Other Essays* (New York: Oxford University Press, 2005).

55. Kristeva, 'Motherhood', p. 178.

56. Haussonville, *Le Salon de Madame Necker*, vol. 1, p. 15.

57. Ibid., vol. 2, p. 287.

58. '[L]a mort de ma mére a altéré ma santé d'une maniére irréparable.' Suzanne Curchod Necker to Henriette Réverdil, 25 June 1768, ms.suppl. 717, f. 28, BGE.

59. 'Thomas, *Oeuvres complètes*, vol. 6, pp. 264–5.

60. Suzanne Curchod Necker to Henriette Réverdil, undated [1765] and 26 September 1776, ms.suppl. 717, ff. 1, 172, BGE.

61. See, for example, Haussonville, *Le Salon de Madame Necker*, vol. 2, p. 5.

62. 'En vain je voudrois confier mes peines; qui m'entendra? Je cherche à te rappeller dans l'illusion du sommeil, je crois te voir, je te parle; mon âme s'épanche dans ton sein; le sein d'une mère, où est-il? ... oh! ma mère, ne rejette pas ton enfant; il a été coupable envers toi, mais combien peu de temps et que de larmes, que de tendresse, que de sentiments, que de transports ont racheté ces instants d'humeur! ... et pendant ces trois années encore où mon caractère s'était altéré, je n'ai pas cessé un instant de t'adorer; pardonne donc, fais grâce; l'Être suprême pardonne à ceux qui l'ont offensé. Dix-sept ans de remords dévorants n'ont-ils point expié mes fautes? Vois ces larmes que je répands par torrents, reçois ton enfant, ne l'éloigne pas de toi, il implore ta pitié.' Quoted in Haussonville, *Le Salon de Madame Necker*, vol. 1, pp. 87–8. Necker refers here to the three years between the death of her father and mother.

63. '[Q]ue vous êtes heureux Monsieur d'embelir comme vous le faites la vie d'une mére respectable; j'adorois la mienne; et je n'ai pû dans sa vieillesse lui donner que des larmes et des regrets; sans ce souvenir toûjours poignant mon sort serait si doux qu'il ne s'écouleroit pas un jour sans me laisser le regret de sa perte et l'espoir du lendemain.' Suzanne Curchod Necker to Elie-Salomon-François Réverdil, 23 March 1770, ms.suppl. 725, ff. 3–4, BGE.

64. 'Puissiez vous Monsieur jouir de toutes les bénédictions que le ciel répand sur les enfants qui ont fait le bonheur de leur mére.' Suzanne Curchod Necker to Elie-Salomon-François Réverdil, 13 February 1779, ms.suppl. 725, f. 13, BGE.

65. '[P]uisse-t-elle voir du haut des cieux mon coeur enflamé encore du désir de lui plaire.' Suzanne Curchod Necker to Henriette Réverdil, undated [1765], ms.suppl. 717, f. 2, BGE.

66. 'Dieu veuille bénir nos soins. il me semble que ma chére mére les approuve du haut des cieux; et que j'oserai me présenter devant elle au moment ou je la rejoindrai.' Suzanne Curchod Necker to Henriette Réverdil, undated, ms.suppl. 717, f. 8, BGE.

67. 'Vous ignorez peut être tout ce que je dois à mdme votre mére, et a mdme votre soeur, elles m'ont recherchées dans mes plus grands malheurs et ne m'ont point abandonnée dans la prospérité.' Suzanne Curchod Necker to Elie-Salomon-François Réverdil, 30 November 1772, ms.suppl. 725, ff. 7–8, BGE.

68. '[M]ère de famille dans toute l'étendue du terme, mère de tous les malheureux; exemple continuel des vertus les plus respectables; amie incomparable.' Suzanne Curchod Necker to Henriette Réverdil, 12 March 1771, ms.suppl. 717, f. 56, BGE.

69. Suzanne Curchod Necker to Henriette Réverdil, 15 December 1777, ms.suppl. 717, ff. 193–4, BGE.

70. Suzanne Curchod Necker to Henriette Réverdil (in the handwriting of Marc-Louis Réverdil), 3 November 1765, ms.suppl. 717, ff. 6–7, BGE.

71. Suzanne Curchod Necker to Henriette Réverdil, 21 September [1771], ms.suppl. 717, ff. 65–7, BGE.

72. 'Votre lettre m'a touchée sensiblement; j'y vois une ame encor douloureusement affectée; mais que les plus sublimes vertus élevent au dessus de ses peines; pour ce qui me concerne j'y vois une bonté inestimable et infatigable; toutes vos expressions tous vos sentiments me rappellent ces natures angeliques dont je ne vois plus ici ny les modeles ny même l'image.' Suzanne Curchod Necker to Henriette Réverdil, 17 June 1773, ms.suppl. 717, f. 100, BGE.

73. 'Je suivrai vos conseils Madame je ne m'obstinerai point contre la nature cependant j'ai lieu de me flatter qu'elle me sera favorable comme en nourrissant je ne cherche qu'a m'acquitter de mon devoir, ce seroit aller à contre fins si je nuisois à mon enfant.' Suzanne Curchod Necker to Henriette Réverdil, [1766], ms.suppl. 717, f. 8, BGE.

74. 'Vous êtes Madame la confidente de ma situation et de mes devoirs secrets.' Suzanne Curchod Necker to Henriette Réverdil, 15 July 1766, ms.suppl. 717, f. 11, BGE.

75. 'C'est dans votre lettre seule que je retrouve le souvenir d'une mére adorée et l'image de sa vertu.' Suzanne Curchod Necker to Henriette Réverdil, 12 March 1771, ms.suppl. 717, f. 59, BGE.

76. 'Permettez moi donc de vous dire Madame qu'à l'aide de vos soins je crois avoir rempli bien au delà la volonté de ma digne mère; et par lâ tous mes devoirs.' Suzanne Curchod Necker to Henriette Réverdil, 26 September 1776, ms.suppl. 717, f. 171, BGE.

77. 'J'ai pour la mémoire de mon pére le même respect que pour celle de ma mére; et je les confonds tous les deux dans mon coeur, quoique avec un sentiment différent; l'un est un souvenir doux qui me retrace des vertus sans tâche, et qui me console dans les peines de la vie; l'autre me rappelle une perte irréparable et ne se présente à moi que pour me faire éprouver des déchirements.' Suzanne Curchod Necker to Henriette Réverdil, 21 September 1771, ms.suppl. 717, ff. 65–6, BGE.

78. '[Q]uand je ne fais pas assez je crois entendre l'ame de ma chére mére qui se plaint de ma négligence.' Suzanne Curchod Necker to Henriette Réverdil, 9 March 1767, ms.suppl. 717, f. 18, BGE.

79. E. Badinter, *The Myth of Motherhood: An Historical View of the Maternal Instinct*, trans. R. De Garis (London: Souvenir Press, 1981), p. 117.

80. See I. Brouard-Arends, *Vies et images maternelles dans la littérature du dix-huitième siècle* (Oxford: Voltaire Foundation, 1991); I. Brouard-Arends, 'Entre nature et histoire: Dire la maternité au siècle des Lumières', in O. B. Cragg and R. Davison (eds), *Sexualité, mariage et famille au XVIIIe siècle* (Montréal: Les presses de l'université Laval, 1998), pp. 233–9; J. J. Popiel, 'Making Mothers: The Advice Genre and the Domestic Ideal, 1760–1830', *Journal of Family History*, 29:4 (2004), pp. 339–50; C. Duncan, 'Happy Mothers and Other New Ideas in French Art', *Art Bulletin*, 55 (1973), pp. 570–83; M. H. Darrow, 'French Noblewomen and the New Domesticity', *Feminist Studies*, 5:1 (1979), 41–65.

81. Badinter, *The Myth of Motherhood*, p. 148.

82. M. Jacobus, 'Incorruptible Milk: Breast-Feeding and the French Revolution', in S. E. Melzer and L. W. Rabine (eds), *Rebel Daughters: Women and the French Revolution* (New York and Oxford: Oxford University Press, 1992), pp. 54–75.

83. B. d'Argis, 'Mère, s.f. (*Jurisprud.*)', in Diderot and d'Alembert (eds), *Encyclopédie*, vol. 10, p. 379.

84. Andlau, *La Jeunesse de Madame de Staël*, p. 17.

85. 'Je nourris moi-même, et malgré vos soupçons, c'est avec un grand succès.' Suzanne Curchod Necker to Etienette Clavel de Brenles, 11 June 1766, IS1915/xxx/h/1, BCUL. For more on Madame Necker's experiences with breastfeeding, see Gutwirth, 'Suzanne Necker's Legacy'.

86. M.-H. Huet, *Monstrous Imagination* (Cambridge, MA: Harvard University Press, 1993).

87. Jacobus, 'Incorruptible Milk'.

88. N. Senior, 'Aspects of Infant Feeding in Eighteenth-Century France', *Eighteenth-Century Studies*, 16:4 (1983), pp. 367–88, on p. 373.

89. J.-J. Rousseau, *Emile*, trans. B. Foxley (London: J. M. Dent & Sons Ltd., 1974), p. 13. For more on wetnursing and the maternal body, see S. Boon, 'Maternalising the (Female) Breast: A Comparison of Marie-Angélique Anel Le Rebours' *Avis aux mères qui veulent nourrir leurs enfans* (1767) and La Leche League International's *The Womanly Art of Breastfeeding* (1963)', *LIMINA*, 15 (2009).

90. Senior, 'Aspects of Infant Feeding', p. 381.

91. Roze de l'Epinoy, *Avis aux mères qui veulent allaiter* (Paris: P.-F. Didot, le jeune, 1785), p. 42.

92. 'Pour avoir un goût parfait, faut-il être né dans un pays ou dans une société, à Paris par exemple, où l'on reçoive les principes du goût avec le lait et par l'autorité?' Curchod Necker, *Mélanges*, vol. 2, p. 91.

93. For more on this, see the article 'Nourrice s.f. (*Médec.*)', in Diderot and d'Alembert (eds), *Encyclopédie*, vol. 11, pp. 260–1.

94. E. L. Bergmann, 'Language and "Mother's Milk": Maternal Roles and the Nurturing Body in Early Modern Spanish Texts', in N. J. Miller and N. Yavneh (eds), *Maternal Measures: Figuring Caregiving in the Early Modern Period* (Aldershot: Ashgate, 2000), pp. 105–20, on p. 106.

95. Badinter, *The Myth of Motherhood*, p. 177.

96. Ibid., p. 180.

97. 'Je fus obligée de travailler durement sur ma frêle machine pour me rendre propre à nourrir, et je supprime des détails qui exigèrent tout le courage de la tendresse maternelle, épreuves douloureuses dont je conserve encore des traces et qui se prolongèrent pendant

quatre mois d'une nourriture pénible mais où l'instinct maternel me dédommageait de toutes les souffrances.' Quoted in Andlau, *La Jeunesse de Madame de Staël*, p. 47.

98. '[J]'ai eu ... le chagrin amer, d'être obligée de discontinuer les fonctions de nourrice, après avoir surmonté toutes les peines et toutes les souffrances de cet état pendant près de quatre mois, ma petite fille s'affoiblissoit à vue d'oeil, et moi aussi.' Suzanne Curchod Necker to Etienette Clavel de Brenles, 19 November 1766, IS1915/xxx/h/1, BCUL.

99. Gutwirth, 'Suzanne Necker's Legacy', p. 36.

100. 'Une contrainte perpétuelle, voilà ce que représentait probablement la mère pour l'enfant gaie et spontanée', and 'un devoir, comme les pauvres ou la toilette'. Andlau, *La Jeunesse de Madame de Staël*, pp. 36–7.

101. Diesbach, *Madame de Staël*; Fairweather, *Madame de Staël*; Gutwirth, *Madame de Staël, Novelist*; Kohler, *Madame de Staël et la Suisse*; Herold, *Mistress to an Age*.

102. '[P]eu de femmes semblent moins faites pour procréer que Mme Necker.' Diesbach, *Madame de Staël*, p. 19.

103. Ibid., p. 38; Fairweather, *Madame de Staël*, p. 33.

104. Gutwirth, *Madame de Staël, Novelist*, p. 31.

105. D. Goodman, 'Filial Rebellion in the Salon: Madame Geoffrin and her Daughter', *French Historical Studies*, 16:1 (1989), pp. 28–47.

106. '[U]ne sorte de complicité' and 'un accord secret'. Andlau, *La Jeunesse de Madame de Staël*, p. 45.

107. Fairweather, *Madame de Staël*, p. 37.

108. '[U]ne grosse Flamande.' Suzanne Curchod Necker to Henriette and Sophie Réverdil, 1766, ms.suppl. 717, f. 16, BGE.

109. Suzanne Curchod Necker to Henriette and Sophie Réverdil, 10 September [1768], ms.suppl. 717, f. 30, BGE.

110. Curchod Necker, *Nouveaux mélanges*, vol. 1, p. 76.

111. Suzanne Curchod Necker to Etienette Clavel de Brenles, 12 December 1768, IS1915/xxx/h/1, BCUL.

112. Andlau, *La Jeunesse de Madame de Staël*, p. 25.

113. See letters from Suzanne to Germaine Necker as found in Haussonville, *Le Salon de Madame Necker*, vol. 2, pp. 40–4.

114. 'On conçoit que pendant le dîner nous ne dîmes rien; nous écoutions; mais il fallut voir comment Mlle Necker écoutait! Ses regards suivaient les mouvements de ceux qui parlaient et avaient l'air d'aller au-devant de leurs idées. Elle n'ouvrait pas la bouche et semblait pourtant parler à son tour, tant ses traits mobiles avaient d'expression. Elle était au fait de tout, saisissait tout, comprenait tout, même les sujets politiques qui à cette époque faisaient déjà un des grands intérêts de la conversation.' C. Rilliet Huber, 'Notes sur l'enfance de Madame de Staël', *Occident et cahiers staëliens*, 2:1 (1933), pp. 41–7, on p. 43. See also C. Rilliet Huber, 'Notes sur l'enfance de Madame de Staël (suite et fin)', *Occident et cahiers staëliens*, 2:2 (1934), pp. 140–6.

115. Rilliet Huber, 'Notes sur l'enfance de Madame de Staël', p. 43.

116. B. Craveri, 'Madame de La Ferté-Imbault (1715–1791) et son monde', *Revue d'histoire littéraire de la France*, 105:1 (2005), pp. 95–110; B. Craveri, *The Age of Conversation*, trans. T. Waugh (New York: New York Review of Books, 2005), pp. 303–12; Goodman, 'Filial Rebellion in the Salon'.

117. 'Madame Necker l'avait fort mal élevée, en lui laissant passer dans son salon les trois quarts de ses journées, avec la foule des beaux-esprits de ce temps, qui tous entouraient mademoiselle Necker; et tandis que sa mère s'occupait des autres personnes, et surtout

des femmes qui venaient la voir, les beaux-esprits dissertaient avec mademoiselle Necker sur les passions et sur l'amour. La solitude de sa chambre et de bons livres auraient mieux valu pour elle.' Genlis, *Mémoires inédits*, vol. 3, p. 296.

118. 'Le but [du livre] est de prouver l'utilité des passions, c'était la doctrine des encyclopédistes, qui entourèrent l'enfance et la jeunesse de madame de Staël. Il faut pardonner à sa mémoire ces principes pernicieux, on les lui avait inspirés dès le berceau.' Ibid., vol. 5, p. 326.

119. S. F. Ducrest de Saint Aubin, Comtesse de Genlis, *Adèle et Théodore, ou Lettres sur l'éducation*, 3 vols (Paris: Imprimerie M. Lambert, 1782).

120. Rilliet Huber, 'Notes sur l'enfance de Madame de Staël', p. 43.

121. Andlau, *La Jeunesse de Madame de Staël*, pp. 121–4, 148–52.

122. Ibid., pp. 48–9.

123. Rilliet Huber, 'Notes sur l'enfance de Madame de Staël', p. 43.

124. [Curchod Necker], *Hospice de charité*, p. 3.

125. The Edict of Toleration was signed in November 1787 and came into force in January 1788.

126. Such a reading is given credence by the work of Jean-Denis Bredin, who concentrates on presenting the Necker family as a self-congratulatory and mutually adoring triptych of reciprocal virtue. See J.-D. Bredin, *Une singulière famille: Jacques Necker, Suzanne Necker et Germaine de Staël* (Paris: Fayard, 1999).

127. Pekacz, 'The French Salon of the Old Regime as a Spectacle', p. 87.

128. 'Ma fille n'a pas besoin de moi pour être heureuse. Ses goûts et les miennes diffèrent, et bientôt elle cessera même de me regretter.' Quoted in Haussonville, *Le Salon de Madame Necker*, vol. 2, p. 18.

129. 'Il y a un tel degré de vertu qui nous rend indifférens à toutes les gloires, excepté à celle d'avoir des enfans qui nous ressemblent.' Curchod Necker, *Mélanges*, vol. 1, p. 88.

130. See a 1794 letter from Germaine de Staël to Narbonne, in which she recounts a conversation with her mother during which Madame Necker blames Staël's ill-advised liaison with Narbonne for her failing health (Staël, *Correspondance générale*, vol. 2, p. 253).

4 Performing Pathology

1. 'Il est certain que l'exercice et l'enthousiasme de la vertu exaltent les ames, et je crois que chaque action honnête délie un des chainons qui attachent l'ame à la foiblesse du corps; je sens, je l'avoue, que le moi dépend absolument de ma santé, et mon coeur seul n'en est pas esclave.' Suzanne Curchod Necker to Etienette Clavel de Brenles, Paris, 13 February 1770, IS1915/xxx/h/1, BCUL.

2. 'On a dit que la médecine étoit la théologie du corps.' Curchod Necker, *Mélanges*, vol. 2, p. 135.

3. '[D]e fort bonne heure, elle fut soumise à des angoisses nerveuses tellement pénibles, que, par degrés, elle perdit le sommeil; et le jour, obligée de céder à un mouvement d'agitation, elle se tenoit debout, même en société, et n'obtenoit un peu de repos que dans le bain.' Necker, 'Observations de l'éditeur', p. xii.

4. Abrantès, *Histoire des salons de Paris*, vol. 1, pp. 102, 104.

5. 'Elle était belle pourtant, si l'on pouvait l'être avec cette pâleur de mort qui couvrait son visage, et dont le regard éternel de ses yeux confirmait la triste vérité.' Ibid., vol. 1, p. 83.

6. Fairweather, *Madame de Staël*, p. 68.

7. See Suzanne Curchod Necker to Etienette Clavel de Brenles, 7 November 1765, 12 December 1768, IS1915/xxx/h/1; Seth, 'Madame Necker', p. 174; A. L. Thomas's 1784 and 1785 letters to Madame Necker (Thomas, *Oeuvres complètes*, vol. 6, pp. 404–27, 434–6, 440–6, 453–66, 470–4, 503); and Staël, *Correspondance générale*, vol. 1, pp. 117–31.

8. O. d'Haussonville, 'Un projet de lettre de Mme Necker à Louis XVI', *Cahiers staëliens*, 20 (1976), pp. 3–8.

9. Fairweather, *Madame de Staël*, p. 47; Herold, *Mistress to an Age*, p. 51.

10. See Louise Florence Pétronille Tardieu d'Esclavelles d'Épinay to Guillaume-Antoine de Luc, 7 October 1758, DO 16/56, BGE. J. de Lespinasse, *Lettres* (1809; Paris: La Table Ronde, 1997); see also F. B. Sturzer, 'Love and Disease: The Contaminated Letters of Julie de Lespinasse', *Studies on Voltaire and the Eighteenth Century*, 2000:8 (2000), pp. 3–16.

11. Magdeleine Curchod to Henriette Réverdil, undated, ms.suppl. 363, BGE.

12. Andlau, *La Jeunesse de Madame de Staël*, p. 29.

13. D. M. Vess, *Medical Revolution in France, 1789–1796* (Gainesville, FL: Florida State University Press, 1975), p. 11.

14. M. Ramsey, *Professional and Popular Medicine in France, 1770–1830* (Cambridge: Cambridge University Press, 1988), p. 69.

15. Ibid., p. 62.

16. '[L]e plus étendu, le plus nombreux, le plus riche & le plus effrayant de tous nos hôpitaux ... une longue enfilade de salles contiguës, où l'on rassemble les malades de toute espèce, & où l'on en entasse souvent trois, quatre, cinq & six dans un même lit; les vivans à côté des moribonds & des morts; l'air infecté des exhalaisons de cette multitude de corps mal sains, portant des uns aux autres les germes pestilentiels de leurs infirmités; & le spectacle de la douleur & de l'agonie de tous côtés offert & reçu. Voilà *l'hôtel-Dieu*.' D. Diderot, 'Hôtel-Dieu', in Diderot and d'Alembert (eds), *Encyclopédie*, vol. 8, p. 319; italics in original.

17. J. Tenon, *Mémoires sur les hôpitaux de Paris* (Paris: Chez Royez, libraire, 1788), p. 278.

18. S.-A.-A.-D. Tissot, *Avis au peuple sur sa santé*, 2 vols (Paris: P.-F. Didot le jeune, 1782). For more on Tissot, see A. Emch-Dériaz, *Tissot: Physician of the Enlightenment* (New York: Peter Lang, 1992).

19. A. Emch-Dériaz, 'L'Enseignement clinique au XVIIIe siècle: L'Exemple de Tissot', *Canadian Bulletin of Medical History/Bulletin canadien d'histoire de la médecine*, 4 (1987), pp. 145–64; on p. 162, n. 43.

20. 'Il faut beaucoup d'attention et d'habitude, pour bien juger de l'état d'un malade qu'on ne voit pas, lors même qu'on est instruit aussi-bien qu'on peut l'être de loin, mais cette difficulté est fort augmentée, et même changée en impossibilité, quand l'information n'est pas exacte ... C'est pour prévenir cet inconvénient, que je joins ici une liste des questions auxquelles il faut pouvoir répondre.' Tissot, *Avis au peuple sur sa santé*, vol. 2, p. 325.

21. D. B. Weiner, *The Citizen-Patient in Revolutionary and Imperial Paris* (Baltimore, MD: Johns Hopkins University Press, 1993), p. 31.

22. Ibid., p. 31.

23. T. D. Murphy, 'The French Medical Profession's Perception of its Social Function between 1776 and 1830', *Journal of Medical History*, 23 (1979), pp. 259–78, on p. 260.

24. Weiner, *The Citizen-Patient*, pp. 37, 40.

25. 'On se croit et on se sent presque Médecin et philosophe aprèz vous avoir lû et heureusement on est en même tems plus vertueux et mieux pourtant.' Suzanne Curchod Necker

to Samuel-Auguste-André-David Tissot, undated, ms.suppl. 1909, f. 292, Fonds Eynard, BGE.

26. [Curchod Necker], *Hospice de charité: Institutions*, p. ii.

27. 'Ces monumens d'humanité sont devenus, en plusieurs endroits, des monumens d'indifférence & presque de barbarie.' Curchod Necker, *Nouveaux mélanges*, vol. 2, p. 301.

28. For more insight into Necker's hospital reform and the history of the Hospice de charité, see R. Gervais, *Histoire de l'Hôpital Necker, 1778–1885* (Paris: A. Davy, 1885); J. R. Cotinat, 'La Fondation et les débuts de l'hôpital Necker à Paris (Hospice de la Charité): Son fonctionnement sous l'Ancien Régime' (Thesis of Medicine, University of Paris, 1974), work summarized in M. Poisvert, 'Les Débuts de l'hôpital Necker', *Histoire des sciences médicales*, 7 (1973), pp. 315–26; L. S. Greenbaum, 'Jacques Necker and the Reform of the Paris Hospitals before the French Revolution', *Eighteenth-Century Life*, 9:1 (1984), pp. 1–15; Aimes, 'Le Séjour de Madame Necker à Montpellier'; Pérol, 'Diderot, Mme Necker et la réforme des hôpitaux'; Hannin, 'La Fondation de l'hospice de charité'; and S. Boon, 'Performing the Woman of Sensibility: Suzanne Necker and the *Hospice de charité*', *Journal for Eighteenth-Century Studies*, 32:2 (2009), pp. 235–54.

29. [Curchod Necker], *Hospice de charité: Institutions*, p. 21.

30. Curchod Necker, *Nouveaux mélanges*, vol. 2, pp. 302–3.

31. See [Curchod Necker], *Hospice de charité*; [Curchod Necker], *Hospice de charité: Institutions*; and the prefaces to the two final accounts, which are included in Curchod Necker, *Nouveaux mélanges*, vol. 2, pp. 299–316. See also the account written in 1788 by the first doctor of the hospice: F. Doublet, *Hospice de charité, année 1788* (Paris: Imprimerie Royale, 1789).

32. '[D]isposition tendre & délicate de l'âme, qui la rend facile à être émue, à être touchée ... la sensibilité est la mère de l'humanité, de la générosité; elle sert de mérite, secourt l'esprit, & entraîne la persuasion à sa suite.' L. de Jaucourt, 'Sensibilité (morale)', in Diderot and d'Alembert (eds), *Encyclopédie*, vol. 15, p. 52.

33. '[S]ont l'autel vivant, destiné par un dieu de bonté à recevoir les seules offrandes et le seul hommage qui puisse atteindre jusqu'à lui.' Curchod Necker, *Nouveaux mélanges*, vol. 2, p. 312.

34. Ibid., vol. 2, p. 311.

35. Necker, *Compte rendu au Roy*, p. 103.

36. 'Vous allez quelquefois à l'Hôtel-Dieu servir le manger aux malades & aux autres pauvres; & c'est ordinairement aux grandes fêtes. Je voudrois que ce fût un peu plus souvent: mais ne vous gênez point. Quand je dis souvent, je n'entends qu'une fois le mois.' J. J. Duguet, *Conduite d'une dame chrétienne pour vivre saintement dans le monde*, 3rd edn (Paris: Jacques Estienne, 1730), p. 161.

37. For more on the Montpellier project, see Aimes, 'Le Séjour de Madame Necker à Montpellier'.

38. For more information on the development of the charitable imperative in late eighteenth- and early nineteenth-century Paris, see C. Duprat, '*Pour l'amour de l'humanité*: Le Temps des philanthropes. La Philanthropie parisienne des Lumières à la monarchie de Juillet*, 2 vols (Paris, France: Éditions du C. T. H. S., 1993), vol. 1.

39. 'Maladie', in Diderot and d'Alembert (eds), *Encyclopédie*, vol. 9, p. 929.

40. Curchod Necker, *Des inhumations précipitées*, p. 7.

41. 'Peut-on voir, sans être ému de compassion, des hommes entassés dans un même lit, abandonnés à une mal-propreté qui révolte les sens les plus grossiers, & constraints à respirer

un air corrompu qui détruit l'effet de tous les remèdes?' [Curchod Necker], *Hospice de charité: Institutions*, p. 3.

42. 'Hygiène', in Diderot and d'Alembert (eds), *Encyclopédie*, vol. 8, pp. 385–8.

43. '[L]es passions de l'âme.' Ibid., vol. 8, p. 386.

44. [Curchod Necker], *Hospice de charité: Institutions*, p. 4.

45. In her preface to the 1781 accounts, Madame Necker expressed her discouragement at the number of obstacles to the project's success and commended the parish priests for their persistence. See [Curchod Necker], *Hospice de charité*, p. 5.

46. See M. E. Winston, *From Perfectibility to Perversion: Meliorism in Eighteenth-Century France* (New York: Peter Lang, 2005); and M. E. Winston, 'Medicine, Marriage, and Human Degeneration in the French Enlightenment', *Eighteenth-Century Studies*, 38:2 (2005), pp. 263–81.

47. S.-A.-A.-D. Tissot, *Essai sur les maladies des gens du monde* (Lausanne: François Grasset & Comp., 1770), pp. 12, 25.

48. See [Curchod Necker], *Hospice de charité*. For more details surrounding the hospice as a rational experiment, see Hannin, 'La Fondation de l'hospice de charité'.

49. L. Jordanova, *Nature Displayed: Gender, Science and Medicine, 1760–1820* (London and New York: Addison Wesley Longman, 1999), p. 149.

50. 'C'est de votre santé que le frère et la sœur s'occupent dans ce moment beaucoup plus que de la leur. Vous avez à réparer cinq années de peines et de travaux, qui vous ont ôté autant de forces qu'ils vous ont laissé de gloire.' Thomas, *Oeuvres complètes*, vol. 6, p. 262.

51. J.-P. Peter, 'Entre femmes et médecins: Violence et singularités dans les discours du corps et sur le corps d'après les manuscrits médicaux de la fin du XVIIIe siècle', *Ethnologie française*, 6:3–4 (1976), pp. 341–8, on p. 343.

52. See B. Duden, *The Woman Beneath the Skin: A Doctor's Patients in Eighteenth-Century Germany*, trans. T. Dunlap (Cambridge, MA: Harvard University Press, 1991); and Pilloud, 'Mettre les maux en mots'.

53. '[M]a maladie me devient chère par l'intérêt que vous daignez y prendre.' Suzanne Curchod Necker to Etienette Clavel de Brenles, 7 November 1765, IS1915/xxx/h/1, BCUL.

54. The correspondence between Rousseau and Tissot can be found in A. François, 'Correspondance de Jean-Jacques Rousseau et du médecin Tissot', *Annales de la société Jean-Jacques Rousseau*, 7 (1911), pp. 19–40.

55. 'Mettez, Monsieur, cette maladie dans vos registres si vous jugez qu'elle en vaille la peine, et puisse-t-elle vous fournir quelques reflexions instructives soit pour la conservation de cette courte et misérable vie humaine, soit pour apprendre de plus en plus aux hommes à ne l'estimer que ce qu'elle vaut.' Ibid., p. 36.

56. '[Le tourisme médical] génère ... une véritable vie de cour ou de salon, où il est de bon ton d'être vu en compagnie des grands du monde.' Pilloud, 'Tourisme médical à Lausanne', p. 23.

57. Pilloud and Louis-Courvoisier, 'The Intimate Experience of the Body'.

58. See also B. Duden, *Disembodying Women: Perspectives on Pregnancy and the Unborn*, trans. L. Hoinacki (Cambridge, MA, and London: Harvard University Press, 1993).

59. 'Ma maladie est intérieure, il n'y a que moi qui la sente, j'ai cru aussi qu'il n'y avoit que moi qui put la décrire; c'est pourqoui je ne prends point pour interprete quelque docteur de la faculté, qui en se servant de termes de l'art, m'expliqueroit peut-être moins bien que ne fera mon foible jargon.' Cited in Pilloud, 'Mettre les maux en mots', p. 231.

60. '[V]ieux malade de Ferney.' Voltaire signed many of his letters to the Clavel de Bren-les family this way. See, for example, the letters contained in dossier IS1915/xxx/h/1, BCUL.

61. 'La privation des yeux n'ôte rien à l'esprit de société, rend l'âme plus attentive, et aug-mente même l'imagination.' Voltaire, *The Complete Works*, vol. 124, p. 220.

62. D. Dawson, 'Voltaire's Complaint: Illness and Eroticism in *La Correspondance*', *Litera-ture and Medicine*, 18:1 (1999), pp. 24–38, on p. 34.

63. 'Le patient doit être pensé autrement: un personnage qui ... constitue une figure dynamique, en interaction à la fois avec son propre passé, avec son entourage, avec les professionnels de la santé, et avec le savoir médical de son temps.' P. Rieder and V. Barras, 'Écrire sa maladie au siècle des Lumières', in V. Barras and M. Louis-Courvoisier (eds), *La médecine des Lumières: tout autour de Tissot* (Geneva and Paris: Georg Editeur, 2001), pp. 202–22, on p. 205.

64. '[L]e temps et la santé me manquent tous les jours, ma sensibilité seule est inépuisable.' Suzanne Curchod Necker to Etienette Clavel de Brenles, 6 April 1773, IS1915/xxx/h/1 BCUL.

65. See E. A. Williams, *A Cultural History of Medical Vitalism in Enlightenment Montpellier* (Aldershot: Ashgate, 2003); E. A. Williams, *The Physical and the Moral: Anthropology, Physiology and Philosophical Medicine in France, 1750–1850* (Cambridge: Cambridge University Press, 1994); E. A. Williams, 'Hysteria and the Court Physician in Enlighten-ment France', *Eighteenth-Century Studies*, 35:2 (2002), pp. 247–55.

66. Williams, *A Cultural History of Medical Vitalism*, p. 235.

67. D. Diderot, *Rameau's Nephew and D'Alembert's Dream*, trans. L. W. Tancock (Har-mondsworth: Penguin, 1966), p. 214.

68. P. Pomme, *Traité des affections vapoureuses des deux sexes*, 2nd edn (Lyon: Benoit Duplain, 1765); J. Raulin, *Traité des affections vapoureuses du sexe* (Paris: Jean-Thomas Hérissant, 1758); P. Roussel, *Système physique et moral de la femme ou Tableau philosophique de la constitution, des moeurs et des fonctions propres au sexe* (Paris: Vincent, 1775).

69. '[M]alade parce que femme.' Peter, 'Entre femmes et médecins', p. 342.

70. For more on the relationships between sensibility and illness, see the work of Anne C. Vila, in particular 'Beyond Sympathy: Vapors, Melancholia, and the Pathologies of Sensibility in Tissot and Rousseau', *Yale French Studies*, 92 (1997), pp. 88–101; *Enlight-enment and Pathology: Sensibility in the Literature and Medicine of Eighteenth-Century France* (Baltimore, MD: Johns Hopkins University Press, 1998); 'Reading the "Sensi-ble" Body: Medicine, Philosophy, and Semiotics in Eighteenth-Century France', in R. Mitchell and P. Thurtle (eds), *Data Made Flesh: Embodying Information* (New York: Routledge, 2004), pp. 27–45; and 'Sex and Sensibility'.

71. See, for example, Pomme, *Traité des affections vapoureuses*, pp. 15–16.

72. '[M]a foiblesse tient je crois a une maladie de femme assez commune dans ce pays et inconnuë dans le nôtre.' Suzanne Curchod Necker to Henriette Réverdil, 21 September [1771], ms.suppl. 717, f. 67, BGE.

73. '[L]es maladies des femmes excedent de plus de deux cents celles qui sont particulieres aux hommes.' Raulin, *Traité des affections vapoureuses*, p. viii.

74. 'La sensibilité attachée à l'essence des femmes, ou à des constitutions particulieres qui en sont plus susceptibles que d'autres, fait que leurs fibres portées quelquefois au dern-ier point de délicatesse, sont affectées par le moindre accident; c'est-là la source d'une infinité de symptômes vapoureux & souvent des vapeurs les plus violentes.' Ibid., p. xix.

75. 'Dès la bavette jusques à la vieillesse la plus avancée, elles les lisent avec une si grande ardeur, qu'elles craignent de se distraire un moment, ne prennent aucun mouvement, & souvent veillent très tard pour satisfaire cette passion, ce qui ruine absolument leur santé; sans parler de celles qui sont elle-mêmes auteurs, & ce nombre s'accroît tous les jours.' S.-A.-A.-D. Tissot, *De la santé des gens de lettres* (Lausanne: François Grasset & Comp.; Lyon: Benoit Duplain, 1758), pp. 183–4.

76. 'Une fille qui a dix ans lit au lieu de courir, doit être à vingt une femme à vapeurs & non point une bonne nourrice.' Ibid., p. 184.

77. F. Azouvi, 'Woman as a Model of Pathology in the Eighteenth Century', *Diogènes*, 115 (1981), pp. 22–36, on p. 24.

78. 'Cette matrice peut tout produire – le meilleur et le pire. Les monstres y fructifient presqu'aussi couramment que d'innocentes vies y sont tragiquement broyées.' Peter, 'Entre femmes et médecins', p. 343. Pierre Pomme reminded his readers that excessive sensibility threatened not only women's health and well-being, but also, potentially, that of their children. Pomme, *Traité des affections vapoureuses*, p. 17.

79. Williams, *A Cultural History of Medical Vitalism*, p. 233.

80. 'Plus sensible[s] que robuste[s].' Roussel, *Système physique et moral de la femme*, p. 27.

81. Ibid., p. 36.

82. J.-A. Venel, *Essai sur la santé et sur l'éducation médicinale des filles destinées au mariage* (Yverdon: Chez la Société Littéraire & Typographique, 1776).

83. Steinbrügge, *The Moral Sex*.

84. '[J]oignent à une raison vraiment cultivée une ame forte, & relévent par des vertus, leurs sentiments de courage et d'honneur.' Thomas, *Essai sur le caractère*, p. 205.

85. Azouvi, 'Woman as a Model of Pathology', p. 35.

86. '[J]'ai eu la fièvre en route, j'en avois le germe depuis deux jours.' Suzanne Curchod Necker to Etienette Clavel de Brenles, 20 May 1767, IS1915/xxx/h/1, BCUL.

87. '[J]'ai eu Monsieur cette nuit un accès de toux qui ma jettée dans un grand accablement, je suis hors d'état aujourdhui de recevoir aucune visite.' Suzanne Curchod Necker to David Levade, undated, ms.fr. 301, f. 40, BGE.

88. Suzanne Curchod Necker to Etienette Clavel de Brenles, 7 November 1765, 10 December 1765, April 1766, IS1915/xxx/h/1, BCUL; *Dictionnaire de l'Académie françoise*, vol. 1, pp. 757, 929, 918, vol. 2, p. 13. It is perhaps worth observing that the same source also suggests that 'foiblesse' can, on a political level, refer to a weak state (vol. 1, p. 757).

89. 'Je porte encore l'empreinte de mes anciennes douleurs.' Suzanne Curchod Necker to Etienette Clavel de Brenles, 7 June 1765, IS1915/xxx/h/1, BCUL.

90. Suzanne Curchod Necker to an unidentified correspondent, 25 February, IS1508, BCUL.

91. Suzanne Curchod Necker to Etienette Clavel de Brenles, 25 April 1768, 28 June 1768, IS1915/xxx/h/1, BCUL.

92. '[U]n nouvel accident [qui] avoit fait craindre que ma langueur ne devint très-dangereuse.' Suzanne Curchod Necker to Etienette Clavel de Brenles, 4 September 1768, IS1915/xxx/h/1, BCUL.

93. Suzanne Curchod Necker to Etienette Clavel de Brenles, 12 December 1768, IS1915/xxx/h/1, BCUL.

94. Staël, *Correspondance générale*, vol. 1, p. 134.

95. See note 58 to Chapter 2, above.

96. 'Je suis trez persuadée que la mort de ma mére a altéré ma santé d'une manière irréparable, car dans ce moment ou tout tourne au gré de mes désirs je n'ai presque pas deux heures

de bien être.' Suzanne Curchod Necker to Henriette Réverdil, 25 June 1768, ms.suppl. 717, f. 28, BGE.

97. Haussonville, *Le Salon de Madame Necker*, vol. 2, p. 287.

98. Madame Necker attributes her illnesses to the death of her mother and to her need for 'l'air natal'. Suzanne Curchod Necker to Etienette Clavel de Brenles, June 1765, IS1915/xxx/h/1, BCUL.

99. L. de Jaucourt, 'Hemvé, sub. Masc. (*Médecine*)', in Diderot and d'Alembert (eds), *Encyclopédie*, vol. 8, pp. 129–30.

100. 'Le *hemvé* ... ne devient une peine d'esprit, que parce qu'il est réellement une peine de corps. L'eau, l'air différent de celui auquel on est habitué, produisent des changemens dans une frêle machine.' Ibid., vol. 8, p. 129.

101. 'J'ai eu des moments où j'aurois désiré qu'il m'arrivât quelqu'accident effrayant pour jouir davantage de l'intérêt que vous prenez à ma vie; mais je réprimois ce souhait bizarre dans la crainte de la perdre au moment où vous la rendiez si heureuse.' Suzanne Curchod Necker to Etienette Clavel de Brenles, 18 July 1767, IS1915/xxx/h/1, BCUL.

102. Suzanne Curchod Necker to Etienette Clavel de Brenles, 18 July 1767, IS1915/xxx/h/1, BCUL. 'J'ai souffert cruellement pour vous.' Suzanne Curchod Necker to Jacques Abram Elie Daniel Clavel de Brenles and Etienette Clavel de Brenles, 17 December 1767, IS1915/xxx/h/1, BCUL. '[P]our [cette] santé si précieuse à mon coeur, et dont la certitude fait la douceur de ma vie.' Suzanne Curchod Necker to Etienette Clavel de Brenles, 20 January 1768, IS1915/xxx/h/1, BCUL.

103. Suzanne Curchod Necker to an unidentified correspondent, undated, DO 32/51, BGE.

104. 'Pardon Madame si je me sers d'une main etrangere. Une incomodité moins dangereuse que la precedente, mais plus importune ne me permést pas de tenir la plume; il me semble que c'est une nouvelle separation que je méts entre vous & moi, toutes les privations que jeprouve me font trop connoitre que l'éloignement comme la mort ajoute encore à l'amitié.' Suzanne Curchod Necker to Etienette Clavel de Brenles, Paris, 10 December 1765, IS1915/xxx/h/1, BCUL.

105. 'Combien la religion change le tableau de la vie! les douleurs mêmes du corps sont le présage d'une nouvelle existence: nos défauts et ceux des autres nous offrent un double moyen d'exercer nos vertus; ainsi le paradis est déjà dans notre pensée, malheureux qui se tourmente pour en deviner les plaisirs, et à qui sa piété ne les a pas fait goûter d'avance.' Curchod Necker, *Mélanges*, vol. 1, p. 93.

106. Fairweather, *Madame de Staël*, p. 47.

107. '[H]abitation passagère.' Curchod Necker, *Mélanges*, vol. 1, p. 141.

108. Calvin, *The Letters*, vol. 4, p. 331.

109. 'Tout est passager sur la terre: à peine, dans notre foiblesse, pouvons-nous discerner les tems; et si l'on a dit qu'ils sont tous présens à l'Etre suprême dans son immensité, on peut le dire aussi de nous dans notre petitesse.' Curchod Necker, *Mélanges*, vol. 1, p. 71.

110. 'Quoiqu'il en soit, et quelque parti que vous preniez, j'apprendrai avec transport que vous quittez Paris, si vous pouvez le quitter, si les circonstances nouvelles ne vous y enchaînent pas de nouveau, si votre vie n'est pas destinée à être un sacrifice perpetuel de vous-même au bien que vous voulez faire, et au bonheur des autres.' Thomas, *Oeuvres complètes*, vol. 6, p. 269.

111. Tissot, *Essai sur les maladies des gens du monde*, p. 48.

112. 'J'ai pensé à la faiblesse de votre santé, à ce Paris qui vous rappelle, et où vous aller mener une vie si différente de celle qui vous convient. Ah! le séjour de la campagne était si nécessaire à votre repos! Vous allez chercher des agitations nouvelles ... vous avez eu [la gloire]

de ... mettre [la vertu] en action dans un pays et dans un siècle où presque tout le monde la met en paroles.' Thomas, *Oeuvres complètes*, vol. 6, pp. 264–5.

113. 'Je vous vois au milieu du tourbillon d'un monde inquiet, environnée de mouvements orageux, pressée d'importunités ennuyeuses, conserver votre caractère inaltérable de bonté, de dignité, et ne pas perdre ce sublime repos, cette tranquillité si rare qui ne peut appartenir qu'à des âmes fermes et pures que la bonne conscience et la noble intention rendent invulnérables.' Buffon, *Correspondance générale*, vol. 1, p. 375.

114. See, for example, Thomas *Oeuvres complètes*, vol. 6, p. 503.

115. 'Jamais je n'ai eu plus besoin de courage pour supporter le poids de mon existence: il me semble que mes longues angoisses m'ont déjà fait connoître l'éternité.' Curchod Necker, *Mélanges*, vol. 1, p. 148.

116. '[L]e sentiment et le besoin de l'infini, qui vous appelle.' Thomas, *Oeuvres complètes*, vol. 6, p. 270.

117. '[V]ous anticipez un peu trop sur la vie immortelle, et vous oubliez que vous êtes sur la terre, comme vous le faites oublier aux autres, par vos sentiments et vos idées.' Ibid., vol. 6, p. 405.

118. Staël, *Correspondance générale*, vol. 2, p. 253. I return to this statement in the next chapter.

119. 'J'ai toujours aimé les pensées tristes: ce goût avoit quelque chose de plus piquant lorsque j'étois plus jeune; je me promenais souvent alors dans les asiles de la mort; je sentois, sans me l'avouer, qu'ils alloient renfermer bientôt ce que j'avois de plus cher, et qu'il s'écouleroit un long intervalle avant que je pusse rejoindre ces précieuses cendres.' Curchod Necker, *Mélanges*, vol. 3, p. 173.

120. Staël, *Correspondance générale*, vol. 1, p. 414.

121. M. J. Holroyd Stanley, Baroness of Alderley, *The Girlhood of Maria Josepha Holroyd, Lady Stanley of Alderley: Recorded in Letters of a Hundred Years Ago, from 1776 to 1796* (London, England: Longmans, Green, & Co., 1896), p. 64.

122. Staël, *Correspondance générale*, vol. 3, p. 222.

123. Ibid., vol. 3, p. 224.

124. Ibid., vol. 2, p. 285.

5 Specular Death

1. 'Les moucherons s'assemblèrent un jour sur un champignon; l'un d'eux, appesanti par l'âge, parla ainsi aux plus jeunes: Ecoutez-moi; j'ai une longue expérience; j'ai vu le lever de l'aurore et je vois la fin du monde. C'étoit la nuit qui s'approchoit.' Curchod Necker, *Mélanges*, vol. 2, p. 12.

2. 'La mort est certaine, & elle ne l'est pas.' J.-B. Winslow, *Dissertation sur l'incertitude des signes de la mort et l'abus des enterremens et embaumemens précipités*, trans. J.-J. Bruhier (Paris: Morel, 1742), p. 41.

3. 'Je ne m'étonne plus du courage des martirs, il me paroit bien clair à présent que le calme de la conscience fait la seule force de l'homme.' Suzanne Curchod Necker to Jacques Abram Elie Daniel Clavel de Brenles, 12 December 1769, IS1915/xxx/h/1, BCUL.

4. 'Madame Necker, morte depuis peu, a demandé qu'on la mît dans un cercueil de plomb avec un couvercle de verre et dans l'esprit de vin.' *Sans Culotte*, [2 August 1794].

5. See P.-G. d'Haussonville, *Madame de Staël et M. Necker d'après leur correspondance inédite* (Paris: Calmann-Lévy, 1925), p. 61; and Staël, *Correspondance générale*, vol. 3, pp. 1–2.

6. 'Tu feras faire dans le mur une porte de fer dont toi seul auras la clef, porte qui servira à passer ton corps quand tu ne seras plus et à le porter sur le même lit pour mêler tes cendres avec les miennes, et en observant les mêmes précautions, avec cette différence seulement que tu ordonneras qu'on ferme la porte de fer un mois après ta mort afin que nous restions seuls ensemble ... souviens-toi que nous devons être unis sur la terre et dans le ciel, et exécute mes dernières volontés. Ce coeur, qui fut à toi et qui bat encore pour toi, mérite que tu respectes ses deux faiblesses: la crainte d'être ensevelie sans être morte et celle d'être séparée de toi.' Quoted in Haussonville, *Le Salon de Madame Necker*, vol. 2, pp. 293–4.

7. See J. M. de M. de Norvins, *Mémorial de J. de Norvins: Souvenirs d'un historien de Napoléon*, 3 vols (Paris: Plon, 1896), vol. 1, pp. 88–9; Haussonville, *Madame de Staël et M. Necker*, p. 65; Staël, *Correspondance générale*, vol. 2, p. 524, n. 4. Two of these letters can be found in Staël-Holstein, *Notice sur M. Necker*, pp. 327–30.

8. P. Ariès, *The Hour of Our Death*, trans. H. Weaver (New York: Alfred A. Knopf, 1981), p. 386.

9. 'Ci-gît qui dans son agonie / N'imagina rien de plus beau / Que d'être placée au tombeau / Comme une pêche en l'eau-de-vie.' 'Le Corps de Mme de Staël est-il conservé dans l'alcool?', *Mercure de France*, 15 March 1927.

10. 'Jamais je n'ai eu plus besoin de courage pour supporter le poids de mon existence: il me semble que mes longues angoisses m'ont déjà fait connoître l'éternité.' Curchod Necker, *Mélanges*, vol. 1, p. 148.

11. P.-J. Malouin, 'Mort (médecine)', in Diderot and d'Alembert (eds), *Encyclopédie*, vol. 10, pp. 718–27.

12. '[L]'immobilité parfaite.' Ibid., vol. 10, p. 718.

13. 'Peu-à-peu cette vie s'augmente & s'étend; elle acquiert de la consistance, à mesure que le corps croît, se développe & se fortifie; dès qu'il commence à dépérir, la quantité de vie diminue; enfin lorsqu'il se courbe, se désseche & s'affaisse, la vie décroît, se resserre, se réduit presque à rien. Nous commençons de vivre par degrés, & nous finissons de mourir, comme nous commençons de vivre.' Ibid., vol. 10, p. 716.

14. G. L. Leclerc, Comte de Buffon, *Histoire naturelle générale et particulière*, 21 vols (Paris: Imprimerie du Roy, 1749–89), vol. 2, pp. 557–603.

15. 'Le corps meurt donc peu à peu et par parties', in ibid., vol. 2, pp. 567, 578.

16. Ariès, *The Hour of Our Death*, p. 325.

17. Ibid., p. 326.

18. See Baecque, *Glory and Terror*; and A. de Baecque, *The Body Politic: Corporeal Metaphor in Revolutionary France, 1770–1800*, trans. C. Mandell (Stanford, CA: Stanford University Press, 1997).

19. 'On parloit, dans la *petite Feuille*, du tombeau du maréchal de Saxe, et l'on disoit avec ce ton précieux à la mode: *La figure de la mort a tant d'expression, qu'on pourroit dire qu'elle est pleine de vie.*' Curchod Necker, *Mélanges*, vol. 1, p. 208; italics in original.

20. See Ariès, *The Hour of Our Death*, p. 368; and P. Ariès, *Western Attitudes towards Death: From the Middle Ages to the Present*, trans. P. M. Ranum (Baltimore, MD, and London: Johns Hopkins University Press, 1977), pp. 69–70. See also S. Camet, 'La Mort, spectacle parisien à la fin du XVIIIe siècle', in G. Jacquin (ed.) *Le Récit de la mort: Écriture et histoire* (Rennes: Presses universitaires de Rennes, 2003), pp. 109–23.

21. P. Chaunu, *La Mort à Paris XVIe, XVIIe et XVIIIe siècles* (Paris: Fayard, 1978), pp. 437–8.

22. 'La mort est certaine, & elle ne l'est pas. Elle est certaine, puisqu'elle est inévitable, elle ne l'est pas, puisqu'il est quelquefois incertain qu'on soit mort.' Winslow, *Dissertation sur l'incertitude des signes de la mort*, p. 41.

23. Ibid., p. 85.

24. F. Thiéry, *La Vie de l'homme respectée et défendue dans ses derniers momens, ou Instruction sur les soins qu'on doit aux morts et à ceux qui paraissent l'être, sur les funérailles et les sépultures* (Paris: Debure l'aîné, 1787), pp. 42–3.

25. 'La mort commencée se nomme *agonie*. La mort apparente est encore un état de vie caché & insensible, qui succède à l'agonie, & il n'est pas rare que l'on en revienne. La mort entièrement achevée, est l'état de cadavre; mais il est un intervalle entre la mort apparente & qu'on croit certaine, & l'état de cadavre. Ce qu'on nomme la mort dans les premières heures, est la vie réduite au moindre degré possible; c'est l'avant-dernier terme que doit parcourir la vie intérieure; c'est enfin un état intermédiaire entre la mort commencée & la mort complette, & personne ne sait quelle sera la durée de cet état incertain.' Curchod Necker, *Des inhumations précipitées*, p. 9; italics in original.

26. Ibid., p. 11.

27. '[L]e protecteur des mourans.' Ibid., p. 7.

28. Ibid., p. 12.

29. Ibid., p. 21.

30. Doublet, *Hospice de charité*, pp. 27–41.

31. 'Malgré tous mes efforts, [je] n'ai jamais pu obtenir des Religieuses les plus compatissantes pour les vivans, assez de soin & de respect pour les morts.' Curchod Necker, *Des inhumations précipitées*, p. i.

32. 'La cessation du mouvement, l'impassibilité totale, ne sont qu'une mort extérieure, & l'on est coupable d'homicide, si l'on ensevelit le corps avant d'être assuré que la mort intérieure & complette soit absolument consommée. Nos terribles usages semblent cependant propres à causer ou accélérer la mort intérieure.' Ibid., p. 8.

33. 'L'on ne peut trop le répéter, le premier des devoirs des hommes est de prolonger la vie des hommes. L'assassin ne fait souvent que hâter la mort de quelques heures.' Ibid., p. 10.

34. C. Marsden Gillis, '"Seeing the Difference": An Interdisciplinary Approach to Death, Dying, Humanities and Medicine', *Journal of Medical Humanities*, 27 (2005), pp. 105–15.

35. Ibid., p. 113.

36. For more on this project, see Grimm, *Correspondance littéraire*, vol. 9, pp. 14–17.

37. For an alternative reading, see D. Goodman, 'Pigalle's *Voltaire nu*: The Republic of Letters Represents Itself to the World', *Representations*, 16 (1986), pp. 86–109, on p. 104.

38. 'J'aime à penser, dans mes rêves romanesques, qu'on m'élèvera un monument parmi les beaux arbres de Saint-Ouen: vous en ferez l'inscription; et dans vos promenades solitaires, vous le regarderez, vous prêterez un moment l'oreille au bruit des feuilles agitées par les vents, à ce bruit qui semble imiter le murmure des ombres, si bien peint par Virgile.' Curchod Necker, *Mélanges*, vol. 3, p. 174.

39. Irigaray, *Speculum of the Other Woman*.

40. Curchod Necker, *Mélanges*, vol. 1, p. 141.

41. Irigaray, *Speculum of the Other Woman*, pp. 144–5.

42. 'Specular', *The Oxford English Dictionary*.

43. '[M]es défauts seront effacés par cette éponge de la mort.' Curchod Necker, *Mélanges*, vol. 3, p. 174.

44. R. Davison, 'Time and Exile: The Case of Mme la Marquise de Lage de Volude', *Lumen: Selected Proceedings from the Canadian Society for Eighteenth-Century Studies/Travaux choisis de la société canadienne d'étude du dix-huitième siècle*, 18 (1999), pp. 69–82, on p. 71.

45. See La Tour du Pin, *Mémoires*; Vigée-Lebrun, *The Memoirs*.

46. W. Doyle, 'Introduction', in K. Carpenter and P. Mansel (eds) *The French Émigrés in Europe and the Struggle against Revolution, 1789–1814* (Houndmills: MacMillan Press, 1999), pp. xv–xxii, on p. xxi.

47. K. Carpenter, 'London: Capital of the Emigration' and T. C. Sosnowski, 'French Émigrés in the United States', both in Carpenter and Mansel (eds), *The French Émigrés in Europe and the Struggle against Revolution, 1789–1814*, pp. 43–67, on p. 46; pp. 139–50, on pp. 139–40.

48. '[S]a santé souffre extrêmement de l'air et de l'ennui de ce pays.' Staël, *Correspondance générale*, vol. 1, p. 384. Staël's letter to her husband, dated at Coppet, 11 November 1790, again makes reference to air quality (ibid., vol. 1, p. 389).

49. See ibid., vol. 1, p. 437.

50. 'Vierge et pure, quand je fis le serment de t'être fidèle, j'ai tenu mon serment, dans toute sa délicatesse; et, je n'ai pas besoin de te le dire, c'est un foible mérite, que celui d'avoir vécu dans l'innocence avant de se marier, et d'être restée parfaitement chaste dans le cours d'une longue union.' Staël-Holstein, *Notice sur M. Necker*, pp. 329–30.

51. For more on the relationship between Suzanne Curchod Necker and her husband, see Boon, 'Does a Dutiful Wife Write'.

52. 'Ma mère avait faillie mourir pendant la nuit d'un étouffement horrible. Elle m'a fait demander. Elle m'a dit: "Ma fille, je meurs de la douleur que m'a causée votre coupable et public attachement. Vous en êtes punie par la conduite de son objet envers vous: elle rompt ce que mes prières n'ont pu vous faire abandonner. Ce sont les soins que vous rendrez à votre père qui vous obtiendront mon pardon dans le ciel. Ne me répondez rien. Sortez: je n'ai pas la force de disputer dans ce moment."' Staël, *Correspondance générale*, vol. 2, p. 253.

53. '[E]lle est parvenue à une pureté et à une élévation de caractère qui a peu d'exemples, et qui est si fort au-dessus du pays et du siècle méprisable où elle vit.' Necker, 'Observations de l'éditeur', pp. xvii–xviii.

54. 'Qui peut réfléchir sur cet état affreux, & ne pas se regarder comme le protecteur des mourans, quels qu'ils puissent être!' Curchod Necker, *Des inhumations précipitées*, p. 7.

55. 'Maladie', in Diderot and d'Alembert (eds), *Encyclopédie*, vol. 9, p. 929.

56. V. de Broglie, *Souvenirs, 1785–1870, du feu duc de Broglie*, ed. A. de Broglie, 4 vols (Paris: Calmann-Lévy, 1886), vol. 1, p. 384.

57. 'Le cortège s'arrêta à l'entrée de l'enclos. Il ne pénétra dans le monument que mon beau-frère et moi; suivis de quatre hommes qui portaient le cercueil. Il fut déposé au pied de la cuve. Je fis mûrer de nouveau la porte d'entrée qui depuis n'a plus été ouverte.' Ibid., vol. 1, p. 384.

58. Haussonville, *Le Salon de Madame Necker*, vol. 2, pp. 302–3.

59. G. de Staël, *Corinne, or Italy*, trans. A. H. Goldberger (New Brunswick, NJ: Rutgers University Press, 1987), p. 419.

60. Ce qu'il y a de plus sacré dans la morale, ce sont les liens des parents et des enfants: la nature et la société reposent également sur ce devoir, et le dernier degré de la dépravation est de braver l'instinct involontaire qui, dans ces relations, nous inspire tout ce que la vertu peut commander. Il y a donc toujours un bonheur certain attaché à de tels liens, l'accomplissement de ses devoirs.' G. de Staël, *Oeuvres complètes de madame la Baronne de Staël-Holstein*, 3 vols (Paris: Firmin Didot, 1871), vol. 1, p. 154.

61. Fairweather, *Madame de Staël*, pp. 463, 466.

WORKS CITED

Manuscripts

Archives cantonales vaudoises, Lausanne, B117/3192–3195.

Bibliothèque publique de Genève

ms.fr. 301.

ms.suppl. 363; 514; 716; 717; 718; 725; 728; 1909.

DO 16/56; 32/51.

ms. 2465.

Bibliothèque cantonale et universitaire de Lausanne, IS1915/xxx/h/1; 3.

Primary Sources

Abrantès, L. Junot, Duchesse d', *Histoire des salons de Paris: Tableaux et portraits du grand monde, sous Louis XVI, le Directoire, le Consulat et l'Empire, la Restauration, et le règne de Louis-Philippe Ier*, 6 vols (Paris: Ladvocat, 1837–8).

Alderley, M. J. Holroyd Stanley, Baroness of, *The Girlhood of Maria Josepha Holroyd, Lady Stanley of Alderley: Recorded in Letters of a Hundred Years Ago, from 1776 to 1796* (London: Longmans, Green, & Co., 1896).

Alison, A., *Some Account of my Life and Writings: An Autobiography*, ed. Lady Alison, 2 vols (Edinburgh: W. Blackwood & Sons, 1883).

Bachaumont, L. P. de, *Mémoires secrets pour servir à l'histoire de la République des Lettres en France depuis MDCCLXII, ou Journal d'un observateur, contenant les analyses des pièces de théâtre qui ont paru durant cet intervalle, les relations des assemblées littéraires*, 36 vols (London: John Adamson, 1783–9).

Bary, R., de, *L'Esprit de cour, ou Les Conversations galantes* (Paris, 1662).

Bentham, J., *Panopticum; or, The Inspection-House*, 3 vols (London: R. Baldwin, 1791).

Boigne, L.-E.-C.-A. d'Osmond, Comtesse de, *Mémoires de la Comtesse de Boigne née d'Osmond* (Paris: Plon-Nourrit, 1908).

Broglie, V. de, *Souvenirs, 1785–1870, du feu duc de Broglie*, ed. A. de Broglie, 4 vols (Paris: Calmann-Lévy, 1886).

Buffon, G. L. Leclerc, Comte de, *Histoire naturelle générale et particulière*, 21 vols (Paris: Imprimerie du Roy, 1749–89).

—, *Correspondance générale de Buffon*, ed. H. Nadault de Buffon, 2 vols (Paris: Hachette, 1860).

Burlamaqui, J.-J., *Principes du droit naturel*, 2 vols (Geneva: Barrillot, 1748).

Calvin, J., *Institutes of the Christian Religion* (1559), ed. J. T. McNeill, trans. F. L. Battles, 2 vols (Philadelphia, PA: Westminster Press, 1960).

—, *The Letters of John Calvin*. trans. J. Bonnet, 4 vols (New York: Burt Franklin, 1972).

—, 'A tous amateurs de Jésus-Christ et de son Évangile, Salut (1535)', in *La vraie piété: Divers traités de Jean Calvin et Confession de foi de Guillaume Farel*, ed. I. Backus and C. Chimelli (Geneva: Labor et Fides, 1986), pp. 25–38.

'Le Corps de Mme de Staël est-il conservé dans l'alcool?', *Mercure de France*, 15 March 1927.

Curchod Necker, S., *Des inhumations précipitées* (Paris: Imprimerie royale, 1790).

—, *Réflexions sur le divorce* (Lausanne: Durant, Ravanel et cie; Paris: P. F. Aubin et Desenne, 1794).

—, *Mélanges*, ed. J. Necker, 3 vols (Paris: Pougens, 1798).

—, *Nouveaux mélanges*, ed. J. Necker, 2 vols (Paris: Pougens; Genets, 1801).

[Curchod Necker, S.], *Hospice de charité: Institutions, règles, et usages de cette Maison* (Paris: Imprimerie royale, 1780).

[—], *Hospice de charité* (Paris: Imprimerie royale, 1781).

Dashkova, E. R., *The Memoirs of Princess Dashkova*, trans. K. Fitzlyon (Durham, NC, and London: Duke University Press, 1995).

Delille, J., *Oeuvres de J. Delille*, ed. L.-G. Michaud, 2 vols (Paris: Lefèvre, 1844).

Les Deux conversations de Madame Necker, Femme du Directeur des Finances en France (Genève: Cruchaut, 1781).

Dictionnaire de l'Académie françoise, 4th edn, 2 vols (Paris: Bernard Brunet, 1762).

Diderot, D., *Oeuvres complètes*, ed. J. Assézat, 20 vols (Paris: Garnier, 1875–7).

—, *Rameau's Nephew and d'Alembert's Dream*, trans. L. W. Tancock (Harmondsworth: Penguin, 1966).

Diderot, D., and J. L. Rond d'Alembert (eds), *Encyclopédie, ou dictionnaire raisonné des sciences, des arts et des métiers, par une Société de Gens de lettres*, 28 vols (Paris: Briasson, 1751–72), online at University of Chicago, ARTFL Encyclopédie Project (Winter 2008 edn), ed. R. Morrissey, http://encyclopedie.uchicago.edu/.

Doublet, F., *Hospice de charité, année 1788* (Paris: Imprimerie Royale, 1789).

Duguet, J. J., *Conduite d'une dame chrétienne pour vivre saintement dans le monde*, 3rd edn (Paris: Jacques Estienne, 1730).

Faret, N., *L'Honneste homme, ou L'Art de plaire à la cour* (Paris: T. du Bray, 1630).

La Galérie des dames françoises (London, 1798).

Garrick, D., *The Private Correspondence of David Garrick with the most Celebrated Persons of his Time*, ed. J. Boaden, 2 vols (London: Henry Colburn & Richard Bentley, 1832).

Genlis, S. F. Ducrest de Saint Aubin, Comtesse de, *Adèle et Théodore, ou Lettres sur l'éducation*, 3 vols (Paris: M. Lambert, 1782).

—, *De l'influence des femmes sur la littérature française, comme protectrices des lettres et comme auteurs; ou précis de l'histoire des femmes françaises les plus célèbres* (Paris: Maradin, 1811).

—, *Mémoires inédits de Madame la Comtesse de Genlis, sur le dix-huitième siècle et la révolution française, depuis 1756 jusqu'à nos jours*, 10 vols (Brussels: P. J. de Mat, 1825).

Gibbon, E., *Letters*, ed. J. E. Norton, 3 vols (London: Cassell, 1956).

Golowkin, F., *Lettres diverses, recueillies en Suisse* (Geneva: J. J. Paschoud, 1821).

Grenaille, F. de, *Les plaisirs des dames* (Paris: Gervais Clousier, 1641).

Grimm, F. M., Freiherr von, *Correspondance littéraire, philosophique et critique*, 16 vols (Paris: Garnier frères, 1877).

The iudgement of the synode holden at Dort, concerning the fiue Articles (London: John Bill, 1619).

La Tour du Pin, H. L. D., Marquise de, *Mémoires de la Marquise de La Tour du Pin: Journal d'une femme de cinquante ans, 1778–1846*, ed. C. de L. Beaufort (Paris: Mercure de France, 2002).

Lespinasse, J. de, *Lettres* (1809; Paris: La Table Ronde, 1997).

Lespinassy, Mlle de, *Essai sur l'éducation des demoiselles* (Paris: Hocherau, 1764).

M***, M., *Discours sur les hommes; ou nouvelle apologie des femmes* (Paris, 1755).

Marmontel, J.-F., *Oeuvres complètes*, 7 vols (Paris: Verdière, 1818–20).

Morellet, A., *Mémoires inédits de l'abbé Morellet*, 2nd edn, 2 vols (Paris: Baudoin, 1822).

Necker, J., *Compte rendu au Roy* (Paris: Imprimerie royale, 1781).

—, *De l'importance des opinions réligieuses* (Liège: C. Pomteux, 1788).

—, 'Observations de l'éditeur', in S. Curchod Necker, *Mélanges*, ed. J. Necker, 3 vols (Paris: Pougens, 1798), vol. 1, pp. i–xx.

Necker de Saussure, A.-A., *Sketch of the Life, Character, and Writings of Baroness de Staël-Holstein* (London: Treuttel & Würtz, 1820).

Norvins, J. M. de M. de, *Mémorial de J. de Norvins: Souvenirs d'un historien de Napoléon*, 3 vols (Paris: Plon, 1896).

Oberkirch, H.-L. de Waldner de Freundstein, Baronne d', *Mémoires de la Baronne d'Oberkirch*, 2 vols (Paris: Charpentier, 1869).

Paradis de Moncrif, F.-A., *Essais sur la nécessité et sur les moyens de plaire* (Paris: Prault, 1738).

Pomme, P., *Traité des affections vapoureuses des deux sexes*, 2nd edn (Lyon: Benoit Duplain, 1765).

Prévost, P. (ed.), *Notice sur la vie et les écrits de Georges-Louis LeSage* (Geneva and Paris: J. J. Paschoud, 1805).

Raulin, J., *Traité des affections vapoureuses du sexe* (Paris: Jean-Thomas Hérissant, 1758).

Rilliet Huber, C., 'Notes sur l'enfance de Madame de Staël', *Occident et cahiers staëliens*, 2:1 (June 1933), pp. 41–7.

—, 'Notes sur l'enfance de Madame de Staël (suite et fin)', *Occident et cahiers staëliens*, 2:2 (1934), pp. 140–6.

Rousseau, J.-J., *Oeuvres complètes de J. J. Rousseau*, 25 vols (Paris: Dalibon, 1826).

—, *Correspondance complète de Jean-Jacques Rousseau*, ed. R. A. Leigh, 52 vols (Geneva: Institut et musée Voltaire, 1965–95).

—, *Emile*, trans. B. Foxley (London: J. M. Dent & Sons Ltd., 1974).

—, *Julie, ou, La nouvelle Héloïse: Lettres de deux amants habitants d'une petite ville au pied des Alpes*, 2 vols, ed. H. Coulet (Paris: Le livre de poche, 2002).

Roussel, P., *Système physique et moral de la femme ou Tableau philosophique de la constitution, des moeurs et des fonctions propres au sexe* (Paris: Vincent, 1775).

Roze de l'Epinoy. *Avis aux mères qui veulent allaiter* (Paris: P.-F. Didot, le jeune, 1785).

Sans Culotte, 15 Thermidor, l'an II de la Liberté et de l'Egalité (2 Aout ère arabienne), [2 August 1794].

Staël, G. de, *Mémoires sur la vie privée de mon père* (Paris: Colburn, 1818).

—, *Oeuvres complètes de madame la Baronne de Staël-Holstein*, 3 vols (Paris: Firmin Didot, 1871).

—, *Correspondance générale*, ed. B. W. Jasinski, 4 vols (Paris: Jean-Jacques Pauvert, 1962–78).

—, 'Mon Journal', *Cahiers staëliens*, 28 (1980), pp. 55–79.

—, *Corinne, or Italy*, trans. A. H. Goldberger (New Brunswick, NJ: Rutgers University Press, 1987).

Staël-Holstein, A. de, *Notice sur M. Necker* (Paris: Treuttel & Würtz, 1820).

Tenon, J., *Mémoires sur les hôpitaux de Paris* (Paris: Chez Royez, libraire, 1788).

Thiéry, F., *La Vie de l'homme respectée et défendue dans ses derniers momens, ou Instruction sur les soins qu'on doit aux morts et à ceux qui paraissent l'être, sur les funérailles et les sépultures* (Paris: Debure l'aîné, 1787).

Thomas, A. L., *Essai sur le caractère, les moeurs et l'esprit des femmes dans les différens siècles* (Paris: Moutard, 1772).

—, *Oeuvres complètes de Thomas, de l'Académie française; précédées d'une notice sur la vie et les ouvrages de l'auteur*, 6 vols (Paris: Verdière & Firmin Didot, 1825).

Tissot, S.-A.-A.-D., *De la santé des gens de lettres* (Lausanne: François Grasset & Comp.; Lyon: Benoit Duplain, 1758).

—, *Essai sur les maladies des gens du monde* (Lausanne: François Grasset & Comp., 1770).

—, *Avis au peuple sur sa santé*, 2 vols (Paris: P.-F. Didot le jeune, 1782).

Vaumorière, P. d'Ortigue de, *The Art of Pleasing in Conversation: In French and English. Written by the Famous Cardinal Richelieu*, 2 vols (London: J. Darby, 1722).

Venel, J.-A., *Essai sur la santé et sur l'éducation médicinale des filles destinées au mariage* (Yverdon: Chez la Société Littéraire & Typographique, 1776).

Vigée-Lebrun, L.-E., *The Memoirs of Elisabeth Vigée-Lebrun*, trans. S. Evans (London: Camden Press, 1989).

Voltaire, F. M. A. de, *The Complete Works of Voltaire*, ed. T. Besterman et al., 141 vols (Geneva: Institut et musée Voltaire; Toronto: University of Toronto Press, 1968–).

Walpole, H., *Correspondence of Horace Walpole*, 3 vols (London: Henry Colburn, 1837).

Weber, J., *Mémoires de Weber, concernant Marie-Antoinette, archiduchesse d'Autriche et reine de France et de Navarre; avec des notes et des éclaircissemens historiques, par Mm. Berville et Barrière*, ed. S.-A. Berville and F. Barrière (Paris: Badouin frères, 1822).

Winslow, J.-B., *Dissertation sur l'incertitude des signes de la mort et l'abus des enterremens et embaumemens précipités*, trans. J.-J. Bruhier (Paris: Morel, 1742).

Secondary Sources

Adams, H. G. (ed.), *A Cyclopaedia of Female Biography consisting of Sketches of all Women who have been Distinguished by Great Talents, Strength of Character, Piety, Benevolence, or Moral Virtue of any kind; forming a Complete Record of Womanly Excellence or Ability* (London: Groombridge & Sons, 1857).

Aimes, A., 'Le Séjour de Madame Necker à Montpellier: Fondation de l'hôpital Necker de Montpellier', *Histoire des sciences médicales*, 8 (1974), pp. 477–89.

Aldis, J., *Madame Geoffrin: Her Salon and her Times, 1750–1777* (New York and London: G. P. Putnam's Sons and Methuen & Co., 1905).

Andlau, B. d', *La Jeunesse de Madame de Staël (de 1766 à 1786)* (Paris and Geneva: Librairie Droz, 1970).

Ariès, P., *Western Attitudes towards Death: From the Middle Ages to the Present*, trans. P. M. Ranum (Baltimore, MD, and London: Johns Hopkins University Press, 1977).

—, *The Hour of Our Death*, trans. H. Weaver (New York: Alfred A. Knopf, 1981).

Arnault, A. V., et al., *Biographie nouvelle des contemporains, ou Dictionnaire historique et raisonné de tous les hommes qui, depuis la Révolution française, ont acquis de la célébrité par leurs actions, leurs écrits, leurs erreurs ou leurs crimes, soit en France, soit dans les pays étrangers*, 20 vols (Paris: Librairie historique, 1820–5).

Azouvi, F., 'Woman as a Model of Pathology in the Eighteenth Century', *Diogènes*, 115 (1981), pp. 22–36.

Backus, I., and C. Chimelli, 'Préface', in *La Vraie piété: Divers traités de Jean Calvin et Confession de foi de Guillaume Farel*, ed. I. Backus and C. Chimelli (Geneva: Labor et Fides, 1986), pp. 7–13.

Badinter, E., *The Myth of Motherhood: An Historical View of the Maternal Instinct*, trans. R. de Garis (London: Souvenir Press, 1981).

—, *Émilie, Émilie: L'Ambition féminine au XVIIIe siècle* (Paris: Flammarion, 1983).

Baecque, A. de, *The Body Politic: Corporeal Metaphor in Revolutionary France, 1770–1800*, trans. C. Mandell (Stanford, CA: Stanford University Press, 1997).

—, *Glory and Terror: Seven Deaths under the French Revolution*, trans. C. Mandell (New York: Routledge, 2001).

Beauvoir, S. de, *The Second Sex*, trans. H. M. Parshley (New York: Knopf, 1989).

Benedict, P., *The Faith and Fortunes of France's Huguenots, 1600–85* (Aldershot: Ashgate, 2001)

Benrekassa, G., 'Diderot et l'honnête femme: De Mme Necker à Eliza Draper', in A.-M. Chouille (ed.), *Colloque International Diderot (1713–1784)* (Paris: Aux amateurs de livres, 1995), pp. 87–97.

Bérenguier, N., 'Lettres de Suzanne Necker à Antoine Thomas (1766–1785)', in E. C. Goldsmith and C. H. Winn (eds), *Lettres de femmes: Textes inédits et oubliés du XVIe au XVIIIe siècle* (Paris: Honoré Champion, 2005), pp. 339–78.

Bergmann, E. L., 'Language and "Mother's Milk": Maternal Roles and the Nurturing Body in Early Modern Spanish Texts', in N. J. Miller and N. Yavneh (eds), *Maternal Measures: Figuring Caregiving in the Early Modern Period* (Aldershot: Ashgate, 2000), pp. 105–20.

Blaisdell, C. J., 'The Matrix of Reform: Women in the Lutheran and Calvinist Movements', in R. L. Greaves (ed.), *Triumph Over Silence: Women in Protestant History* (Westport, CT: Greenwood Press, 1985), pp. 13–44.

Blennerhassett, C. J. von Leyden, Lady, *Madame de Staël et son temps*, 2 vols (Paris: Louis Westhausser, 1890).

Blum, C., *Rousseau and the Republic of Virtue: The Language of Politics in the French Revolution* (Ithaca, NY: Cornell University Press, 1986).

Boon, S., 'Does a Dutiful Wife Write; or, Should Suzanne Get Divorced? Reflections on Suzanne Curchod Necker, Divorce, and the Construction of the Biographical Subject', *Lumen: Selected Proceedings from the Canadian Society for Eighteenth-Century Studies/ Travaux choisis de la Société canadienne d'étude du dix-huitième siècle*, 27 (2008), pp. 59–73.

—, 'Last Rites, Last Rights: Corporeal Abjection as Autobiographical Performance in Suzanne Curchod Necker's *Des inhumations précipitées* (1790)', *Eighteenth-Century Fiction*, 21:1 (2008), pp. 89–107.

— 'Maternalising the (Female) Breast: A Comparison of Marie-Angélique Anel Le Rebours' *Avis aux mères qui veulent nourrir leurs enfans* (1767) and La Leche League International's *The Womanly Art of Breastfeeding* (1963)', LIMINA, 15 (2009).

—, 'Performing the Woman of Sensibility: Suzanne Curchod Necker and the *Hospice de charité*', *Journal for Eighteenth-Century Studies*, 32:2 (2009), pp. 235–54.

Bredin, J.-D., *Une singulière famille: Jacques Necker, Suzanne Necker et Germaine de Staël* (Paris: Fayard, 1999).

Brouard-Arends, I., *Vies et images maternelles dans la littérature du dix-huitième siècle* (Oxford: Voltaire Foundation, 1991).

—, 'Entre nature et histoire: Dire la maternité au siècle des Lumières', in O. B. Cragg and R. Davison (eds), *Sexualité, mariage et famille au XVIIIe siècle* (Montréal, QC: Les presses de l'université Laval, 1998), pp. 233–9.

Burnand, L., 'L'Image de Madame Necker dans les pamphlets', *Cahiers staëliens*, 57 (2006), pp. 237–54.

Butler, J., 'Performative Acts and Gender Constitution: An Essay in Phenomenology and Feminist Theory', *Theatre Journal*, 40:4 (1988), pp. 519–531.

—, *Bodies that Matter: On the Discursive Limits of 'Sex'* (New York and London: Routledge, 1993).

Camet, S., 'La Mort, spectacle parisien à la fin du XVIIIe siècle', in G. Jacquin (ed.), *Le Récit de la mort: Écriture et histoire* (Rennes: Presses universitaires de Rennes, 2003), pp. 109–23.

Carlson, M., *Performance: A Critical Introduction* (London: Routledge, 1996).

—, 'What is Performance?', in H. Bial (ed.) *Performance Studies Reader*, 2nd edn (London and New York: Routledge, 2004), pp. 70–5.

Carpenter, K., 'London: Capital of the Emigration', in K. Carpenter and P. Mansel (eds), *The French Émigrés in Europe and the Struggle against Revolution, 1789–1814* (Houndmills: MacMillan Press, 1999), pp. 43–67.

Causse, E., *Madame Necker de Saussure et l'éducation progressive*, 2 vols (Paris: Editions 'Je sers', 1930).

Chaunu, P., *La Mort à Paris XVIe, XVIIe et XVIIIe siècles* (Paris: Fayard, 1978).

Cixous, H., 'Le Rire de la méduse', *L'Arc* (1975), pp. 39–54.

—, *Stigmata*, trans. E. Prenowitz et al. (London and New York: Routledge, 1998).

Clergue, H., *The Salon: A Study of French Society and Personalities in the Eighteenth Century* (New York: G. P. Putnam's & Sons, 1907).

Constant, P., *Un monde à l'usage des demoiselles* (Paris: Gallimard, 1987).

Corbaz, A., *Madame Necker: Humble vaudoise et grande dame* (Lausanne: Librairie Payot, 1945).

Coston, A. de, *Histoire de Montélimar*, 4 vols (Montélimar: Bourron, 1886).

Cotinat, J. R. 'La Fondation et les débuts de l'hôpital Necker à Paris (Hospice de la Charité) : Son fonctionnement sous l'Ancien Régime' (Thesis of Medicine, University of Paris, 1974).

Couser, G. T., 'Autopathography: Women, Illness, and Lifewriting', *a/b: Auto/biography Studies*, 6:1 (1991), pp. 65–75.

—, *Recovering Bodies: Illness, Disability, and Life Writing* (Madison, WI: University of Wisconsin Press, 1997).

Craveri, B., *The Age of Conversation*, trans. T. Waugh (New York: New York Review of Books, 2005).

—, 'Madame de La Ferté-Imbault (1715–1791) et son monde', *Revue d'histoire littéraire de la France*, 105:1 (2005), pp. 95–110.

Darrow, M. H., 'French Noblewomen and the New Domesticity', *Feminist Studies*, 5:1 (1979), pp. 41–65.

Davison, R., 'Time and Exile: The Case of Mme la Marquise de Lage de Volude', *Lumen: Selected Proceedings from the Canadian Society for Eighteenth-Century Studies/Travaux choisis de la société canadienne d'étude du dix-huitième siècle*, 18 (1999), pp. 69–82.

Dawson, D., 'Voltaire's Complaint: Illness and Eroticism in *La Correspondance*', *Literature and Medicine*, 18:1 (1999), pp. 24–38.

Deschanel, P., *Figures des femmes* (Paris: Calmann-Lévy, 1889).

Didier, B., 'Écrire pour se trouver', in M.-F. Silver and M.-L. Girou-Swiderski (eds), *Femmes en toutes lettres: les épistolières du XVIIIe siècle*, Studies on Voltaire and the Eighteenth Century, 2000:04 (Oxford: Voltaire Foundation, 2000), pp. 243–8.

Diesbach, G. de, *Madame de Staël* (Paris: Librairie académique Perrin, 1983).

Doyle, W., 'Introduction', in K. Carpenter and P. Mansel (eds), *The French Émigrés in Europe and the Struggle against Revolution, 1789–1814* (Houndmills: MacMillan Press, 1999), pp. xv–xxii.

Dubeau, C., 'L'Épreuve du salon ou le monde comme performance dans les *Mélanges* et les *Nouveaux Mélanges* de Suzanne Necker', *Cahiers staëliens*, 57 (2006), pp. 201–26.

—, 'La Lettre et la mère: Roman familial et écriture de la passion chez Suzanne Necker (1737–1794) et Germaine de Staël (1766–1817)' (PhD dissertation, Université Laval, 2007).

Ducommon, M.-J., and D. Quadroni, *Le Refuge Protestant dans le Pays de Vaud (fin XVIIe–début XVIIIe siècle)* (Geneva: Droz, 1991).

Duden, B., *The Woman Beneath the Skin: A Doctor's Patients in Eighteenth-Century Germany*, trans. T. Dunlap (Cambridge, MA: Harvard University Press, 1991).

—, *Disembodying Women: Perspectives on Pregnancy and the Unborn*, trans. L. Hoinacki (Cambridge, MA, and London: Harvard University Press, 1993).

Duncan, C., 'Happy Mothers and Other New Ideas in French Art', *Art Bulletin*, 55 (1973), pp. 570–83.

Duprat, C., *'Pour l'amour de l'humanité': Le Temps des philanthropes. La Philanthropie parisienne des Lumières à la monarchie de Juillet*, 2 vols (Paris: Éditions du C. T. H. S., 1993).

Emch-Dériaz, A., 'L'Enseignement clinique au XVIIIe siècle: L'Exemple de Tissot', *Canadian Bulletin of Medical History/Bulletin canadien d'histoire de la médecine*, 4 (1987), pp. 145–64.

—, *Tissot, Physician of the Enlightenment* (New York: Peter Lang, 1992).

Fairweather, M., *Madame de Staël* (London: Constable, 2005).

Faurey, J., *Madame Necker et la question du divorce* (Bordeaux: J. Bière, 1931).

François, A., 'Correspondance de Jean-Jacques Rousseau et du médecin Tissot', *Annales de la société Jean-Jacques Rousseau*, 7 (1911), pp. 19–40.

Gambier-Parry, M., *Madame Necker, her Family and her Friends* (Edinburgh and London: William Blackwood & Sons, 1913).

Gervais, R., *Histoire de l'Hôpital Necker, 1778–1885* (Paris: A. Davy, 1885).

Giddey, E., 'Suzanne Necker-Curchod et les lettres anglaises', *Revue historique vaudoise* (1981), pp. 49–56.

Goncourt, E. de, and J. de Goncourt, *Histoire de la société française pendant la révolution* (Paris: Didier, 1864).

—, *La Femme au XVIIIe siècle* (Paris: Firmin-Didot, 1887).

Goodman, D., 'Pigalle's *Voltaire nu*: The Republic of Letters Represents Itself to the World', *Representations*, 16 (1986), pp. 86–109.

—, 'Julie de Lespinasse: A Mirror for the Enlightenment', in F. M. Keener and S. E. Lorsch (eds), *Eighteenth-Century Women and the Arts* (New York: Greenwood Press, 1988), pp. 3–10.

—, 'Enlightenment Salons: The Convergence of Female and Philosophic Ambitions', *Eighteenth-Century Studies*, 22:3 (1989), pp. 329–50.

—, 'Filial Rebellion in the Salon: Madame Geoffrin and her Daughter', *French Historical Studies*, 16:1 (1989), pp. 28–47.

—, 'Public Sphere and Private Life: Toward a Synthesis of Current Historiographical Approaches to the Old Regime', *History and Theory*, 31:1 (1992), pp. 1–20.

—, *The Republic of Letters: A Cultural History of the French Enlightenment* (Ithaca, NY, and London: Cornell University Press, 1994).

—, 'Le Spectateur intérieur: Les journaux de Suzanne Necker', *Littérales*, 17 (1995), pp. 91–100.

—, 'Suzanne Necker's *Mélanges*: Gender, Writing, and Publicity', in E. C. Goldsmith and D. Goodman (eds), *Going Public: Women and Publishing in Early Modern France* (Ithaca, NY, and London: Cornell University Press, 1995), pp. 211–23.

—, 'Policing Society: Women as Political Actors in the Enlightenment Discourse', in H. E. Bödeker and L. Steinbrügge (eds), *Conceptualising Women in Enlightenment Thought/ Conceptualiser la femme dans la pensée des Lumières* (Berlin: Berlin Verlag Arno Spitz GmbH, 2001), pp. 129–141.

—, 'Letter Writing and the Emergence of Gendered Subjectivity in Eighteenth-Century France', *Journal of Women's History*, 17:2 (2005), pp. 9–37.

—, *Becoming a Woman in the Age of Letters* (Ithaca, NY, and London: Cornell University Press, 2009).

—, 'Germaine de Staël's Dilemmas: Writing, Gender, and Publicity' (unpublished manuscript).

Goring, P., *The Rhetoric of Sensibility in Eighteenth-Century Culture* (Cambridge: Cambridge University Press, 2005).

Grange, H., *Les idées de Necker* (Paris: C. Klincksieck, 1974).

Grassi, M.-C., 'Naissance de l'intimité épistolaire (1780–1830)', *Littérales*, 17 (1995), pp. 67–76.

Greaves, R. L. 'Introduction', in R. L. Greaves (ed.), *Triumph Over Silence: Women in Protestant History* (Westport, CT: Greenwood Press, 1985), pp. 3–12.

Greenbaum, L. S., 'Jacques Necker and the Reform of the Paris Hospitals before the French Revolution', *Eighteenth-Century Life*, 9:1 (1984), pp. 1–15.

Gutwirth, M., *Madame de Staël, Novelist: The Emergence of the Artist as Woman* (Urbana, IL: University of Illinois Press, 1978).

—, 'Suzanne Necker's Legacy: Breastfeeding as Metonym in Germaine de Staël's *Delphine*', *Eighteenth-Century Life*, 18:2 (2004), pp. 17–40.

Habermas, J., *The Structural Transformation of the Public Sphere: An Inquiry into a Category of Bourgeois Society*, trans. T. Burger (Cambridge, MA: MIT Press, 1991).

Hannin, V., 'La Fondation de l'hospice de charité: Une expérience médicale au temps du rationalisme expérimental', *Revue d'histoire moderne et contemporaine*, 31:1 (1984), pp. 116–30.

—, 'Une ambition de femme au siècle des Lumières: Le cas de Madame Necker', *Cahiers staëliens*, 36 (1985), pp. 5–19.

Haussonville, O. d', 'Un projet de lettre de Mme Necker à Louis XVI', *Cahiers staëliens*, 20 (1976), pp. 3–8.

Haussonville, P.-G. d', *Le Salon de Madame Necker, d'après des documents tirés des Archives de Coppet*, 2 vols (Paris: Calmann-Lévy, 1882).

—, *Madame de Staël et M. Necker d'après leur correspondance inédite* (Paris: Calmann-Lévy, 1925).

Herold, J. C., *Mistress to an Age: A Life of Madame de Staël* (Indianapolis, IN: Bobbs-Merrill, 1958).

Huet, M.-H., *Monstrous Imagination* (Cambridge, MA: Harvard University Press, 1993).

Hunsaker Hawkins, A., *Reconstructing Illness: Studies in Pathography* (West Lafayette, IN: Purdue University Press, 1999).

Irigaray, L., *Speculum of the Other Woman*, trans. G. C. Gill, (Ithaca, NY: Cornell University Press, 1985).

—, *This Sex Which Is Not One*, trans. C. Porter (Ithaca, NY: Cornell University Press, 1985).

—, 'The Bodily Encounter with the Mother', in *The Irigaray Reader*, ed. M. Whitford, trans. D. Macey (Oxford and Cambridge, MA: Basil Blackwell, 1991), pp. 34–46.

Jacobus, M., 'Incorruptible Milk: Breast-Feeding and the French Revolution', in S. E. Melzer and L. W. Rabine (eds), *Rebel Daughters: Women and the French Revolution* (New York and Oxford: Oxford University Press, 1992), pp. 54–75.

Johnson-Cousin, D., 'Le Théâtre de Necker: A propos d'inédits des Archives de Coppet', *Revue de la société d'histoire du théâtre*, 32:3 (1980), pp. 220–31.

Jordanova, L., *Nature Displayed: Gender, Science and Medicine, 1760–1820* (London and New York: Addison Wesley Longman, 1999).

Kale, S. D., 'Women, Salons, and the State in the Aftermath of the French Revolution', *Journal of Women's History*, 13:4 (2002), pp. 54–80.

—, 'Women, the Public Sphere, and the Persistence of Salons', *French Historical Studies*, 25:1 (2002), pp. 115–48.

—, *French Salons: High Society and Political Sociability from the Old Regime to the Revolution of 1848* (Baltimore, MD: Johns Hopkins University Press, 2004).

Klauber, M. I., *Between Reformed Scholasticism and Pan-Protestantism: Jean-Alphonse Turretin (1671–1737) and Enlightened Orthodoxy at the Academy of Geneva* (Selinsgrove, PA: Susquehanna University Press, 1994).

Kohler, P., *Madame de Staël et la Suisse* (Lausane: Payot, 1916).

Kors, A. C., *D'Holbach's Coterie: An Enlightenment in Paris* (Princeton, NJ: Princeton University Press, 1976).

Kristeva, J., *Powers of Horror: An Essay on Abjection*, trans. L. S. Roudiez (New York: Columbia University Press, 1982).

—, 'Motherhood [according to Giovanni Bellini]', in K. Oliver (ed.), *French Feminism Reader* (Lanham, MD, and Oxford: Rowman & Littlefield Publishers, 2000), pp. 176–80.

Lairtullier, E., *Les Femmes célèbres de 1789 à 1795, et leur excellence dans la révolution*, 2 vols (Paris: Chez France, à la librairie politique, 1840).

Lane, B. C., 'Spirituality as the Performance of Desire: Calvin on the World as a Theatre of God's Glory', *Spiritus: A Journal of Christian Spirituality*, 1:1 (2001), pp. 1–30.

Laqueur, T., *Making Sex: Body and Gender from the Greeks to Freud* (Cambridge, MA, and London: Harvard University Press, 1990).

Lejeune, P., *On Autobiography*, ed. P. J. Eakin, trans. K. Leary (Minneapolis, MN: University of Minnesota Press, 1989).

Lilti, A., *Le Monde des salons: Sociabilité et mondanité à Paris au XVIIIe siècle* (Paris: Fayard, 2005).

—, 'Mondanité et politique: Le salon Necker', *Cahiers staëliens*, 57 (2006), pp. 185–200.

Linton, M., 'Virtue Rewarded? Women and the Politics of Virtue in 18th-Century France. Part I', *History of European Ideas*, 26 (2000), pp. 35–49.

—, 'Virtue Rewarded? Women and the Politics of Virtue in 18th-Century France. Part II', *History of European Ideas*, 27 (2001), pp. 51–65.

McCarthy, M., *Memories of a Catholic Girlhood* (Orlando, FL: Harcourt, 1957).

McKay, S., 'The "Salon de la Princesse": "Rococo" Design, Ornamented Bodies and the Public Sphere', *Revue d'art canadienne/Canadian Art Review*, 21:1–2 (1994), pp. 71–84.

Marsden Gillis, C., '"Seeing the Difference": An Interdisciplinary Approach to Death, Dying, Humanities and Medicine', *Journal of Medical Humanities*, 27 (2005), pp. 105–15.

Mentzer, R. A., 'Morals and Moral Regulation in Protestant France', *Journal of Interdisciplinary History*, 32:1 (2000), pp. 1–20.

Merleau-Ponty, M., *Basic Writings*, ed. T. Baldwin (London: Routledge, 2004).

Monter, W., 'Protestant Wives, Catholic Saints, and the Devil's Handmaid: Women in the Age of Reformations', in R. Bridenthal, C. Koonz and S. Stuard (eds), *Becoming Visible: Women in European History* (Boston, MA: Houghton Mifflin, 1987), pp. 203–19.

Murphy, T. D., 'The French Medical Profession's Perception of its Social Function between 1776 and 1830', *Journal of Medical History*, 23 (1979), pp. 259–78.

The Oxford English Dictionary, 2nd edn (Oxford: Oxford University Press, 1989), online edn.

Pascal, J.-N., 'La Muse de l'*Encyclopédie*: Julie de Lespinasse', in R. Bonnel and C. Rubinger (eds), *Femmes savantes et femmes d'esprit: Women Intellectuals of the French Eighteenth Century* (New York: Peter Lang, 1994), pp. 243–65.

Pekacz, J. T., 'Salon Women and the Quarrels about Opera in Eighteenth-Century Paris', *European Legacy: Towards New Paradigms*, 1:4 (1996), pp. 1608–14.

—, 'Gender as Political Orientation: Parisian *Salonnières* and the Querelle des Bouffons', *Canadian Journal of History/Annales canadiennes d'histoire*, 32 (1997), pp. 405–14.

—, *Conservative Tradition in Pre-Revolutionary France: Parisian Salon Women* (New York: Peter Lang, 1999).

—, 'The Salonnières and the Philosophes in Old Regime France: The Authority of Aesthetic Judgement', *Journal of the History of Ideas*, 60:2 (1999), pp. 277–97.

—, 'The French Salon of the Old Regime as a Spectacle', *Lumen: Selected Proceedings from the Canadian Society for Eighteenth-Century Studies/Travaux choisis de la société canadienne d'étude du dix-huitième siècle*, 22 (2001), pp. 83–102.

Pérol, L., 'Diderot, Mme Necker et la réforme des hôpitaux', *Studies on Voltaire and the Eighteenth Century*, 311 (1993), pp. 219–33.

Perreault, J., and M. Kadar, 'Introduction: Tracing the Autobiographical: Unlikely Documents, Unexpected Places', in M. Kadar , L. Warley, J. Perreault and S. Egan (eds), *Tracing the Autobiographical* (Waterloo, Ontario: Wilfrid Laurier University Press, 2005), pp. 1–7.

Peter, J.-P., 'Entre femmes et médecins: Violence et singularités dans les discours du corps et sur le corps d'après les manuscrits médicaux de la fin du XVIIIe siècle', *Ethnologie française*, 6:3–4 (1976), pp. 341–8.

Pilloud, S., 'Mettre les maux en mots, médiations dans la consultation épistolaire au XVIIIe siècle: les malades du Dr. Tissot (1728–1797)', *Canadian Bulletin of Medical History/ Bulletin canadien d'histoire de la médecine*, 16 (1999), pp. 215–45.

—, 'Tourisme médical à Lausanne dans la seconde moitié du XVIIIe siècle', *Revue historique vaudoise*, 114 (2006), pp. 9–23.

Pilloud, S., and M. Louis-Courvoisier, 'The Intimate Experience of the Body in the Eighteenth Century: Between Interiority and Exteriority', *Journal of Medical History*, 47 (2003), pp. 451–72.

Pitassi, M.-C., *De l'orthodoxie aux Lumières: Genève 1670–1737* (Geneva: Labor et Fides, 1992).

Poisvert, M., 'Les Débuts de l'hôpital Necker', *Histoire des sciences médicales*, 7 (1973), pp. 315–26.

Popiel, J. J., 'Making Mothers: The Advice Genre and the Domestic Ideal, 1760–1830', *Journal of Family History*, 29:4 (2004), pp. 339–50.

Ramsey, M., *Professional and Popular Medicine in France, 1770–1830* (Cambridge: Cambridge University Press, 1988).

Raoul, V., C. Canam, A. D. Henderson and C. Paterson , 'Introduction: Aesthetics, Authenticity, and Audience', in V. Raoul, C. Canam, A. D. Henderson and C. Paterson (eds), *Unfitting Stories: Narrative Approaches to Disease, Disability and Trauma* (Waterloo, Ontario: Wilfrid Laurier University Press, 2007), pp. 25–31.

Read, J. M., *Historic Studies in Vaud, Berne, and Savoy*, 2 vols (London: Chatto & Windus, 1897).

Renevey-Fry, C., et al. (eds), *En attendant le prince charmant: L'Éducation des jeunes filles à Genève, 1740–1970* (Geneva: Service de la recherche en éducation et Musée d'ethnographie, 1997).

Rieder, P., and V. Barras, 'Écrire sa maladie au siècle des Lumières', in V. Barras and M. Louis-Courvoisier (eds), *La médecine des Lumières: Tout autour de Tissot* (Geneva and Paris: Georg Editeur, 2001), pp. 202–22.

Ritter, E., *Notes sur Madame de Staël* (Geneva: H. Georg, 1899).

Roelker, N. L., 'The Appeal of Calvinism to French Noblewomen in the Sixteenth Century', *Journal of Interdisciplinary History*, 2:4 (1972), pp. 391–418.

Rosenblatt, H., *Rousseau and Geneva: From the First Discourse to the Social Contract, 1749–1762* (Cambridge: Cambridge University Press, 1997).

—, 'On the "Misogyny" of Jean-Jacques Rousseau: The *Letter to d'Alembert* in Historical Context', *French Historical Studies*, 25:1 (2002), pp. 91–114.

Sainte-Beuve, C. A., *Causeries du lundi*, 15 vols (Paris: Garnier frères, 1851–62).

Schiebinger, L. L., *The Mind Has No Sex? Women in the Origins of Modern Science* (Cambridge, MA, and London: Harvard University Press, 1989).

Ségur, P. M. M. H., Comte de, *Le Royaume de la rue Saint-Honoré: Madame Geoffrin et sa fille* (Paris: Calmann-Lévy, 1897).

—, *Julie de Lespinasse* (Paris: Calmann-Lévy, 1905).

Senior, N., 'Aspects of Infant Feeding in Eighteenth-Century France', *Eighteenth-Century Studies*, 16:4 (1983), pp. 367–88.

Seth, C., 'Madame Necker: Une vie au service des autres', *Cahiers staëliens*, 57 (2006), pp. 173–83.

Showalter Jr, E., 'Authorial Self-Consciousness in the Familiar Letter: The Case of Madame de Graffigny', *Yale French Studies*, 71 (1986), pp. 113–30.

Sonnet, M., *L'Éducation des filles au temps des Lumières* (Paris: Le Cerf, 1987).

Sosnowski, T. C., 'French Émigrés in the United States', in K. Carpenter and P. Mansel (eds), *The French Émigrés in Europe and the Struggle against Revolution, 1789–1814* (Houndmills: MacMillan Press, 1999), pp. 139–50.

Soumoy-Thibert, G., 'Les Idées de Madame Necker', *Dix-huitième siècle*, 21 (1989), pp. 357–68.

Stanton, D. C., *The Aristocrat as Art: A Study of the Honnête Homme and the Dandy in Seventeenth and Nineteenth-Century French Literature* (New York: Columbia University Press, 1980).

Steinbrügge, L., *The Moral Sex: Woman's Nature in the French Enlightenment*, trans. P. E. Selwyn (New York and Oxford: Oxford University Press, 1995).

Striff, E., 'Introduction: Locating Performance Studies', in E. Striff (ed.), *Performance Studies* (Houndmills: Palgrave Macmillan, 2003), pp. 1–13.

Sturzer, F. B., 'Love and Disease: The Contaminated Letters of Julie de Lespinasse', *Studies on Voltaire and the Eighteenth Century*, 2000:8 (2000), pp. 3–16.

Tallentyre, S. G., *The Women of the Salons and other French Portraits* (London: Longmans, Green, & Co., 1901).

Thompson, J. L., *John Calvin and the Daughters of Sarah* (Geneva: Librairie Droz, 1992).

Vadier, B., 'La Mère de Mme de Staël et sa parenté au pays de Vaud', *Étrennes helvétiques* (1901), pp. 287–324.

Vecchi, P., 'De la mort à la vie: La taphophobie et l'au-delà au XVIIIe siècle (Jean-Jacques Bruhier et Suzanne Curchod Necker)', in C. Rosso (ed.), *Transhumances culturelles: Mélanges* (Pisa: Editrice Libreria Goliardica, 1985), pp. 119–30.

Vess, D. M., *Medical Revolution in France, 1789–1796* (Gainesville, FL: Florida State University Press, 1975).

Vila, A. C., 'Sex and Sensibility: Pierre Roussel's *Système physique et moral de la femme*', *Representations*, 52 (1995), pp. 76–93.

—, 'Beyond Sympathy: Vapors, Melancholia, and the Pathologies of Sensibility in Tissot and Rousseau', *Yale French Studies*, 92 (1997), pp. 88–101.

—, *Enlightenment and Pathology: Sensibility in the Literature and Medicine of Eighteenth-Century France* (Baltimore, MD: Johns Hopkins University Press, 1998).

—, 'Reading the "Sensible" Body: Medicine, Philosophy, and Semiotics in Eighteenth-Century France', in R. Mitchell and P. Thurtle (eds), *Data Made Flesh: Embodying Information* (New York: Routledge, 2004), pp. 27–45.

Watt, J. R., 'Women and the Consistory in Calvin's Geneva', *Sixteenth Century Journal*, 24:2 (1993), pp. 429–39.

—, *Choosing Death: Suicide and Calvinism in Early Modern Geneva* (Kirksville, MO: Truman State University Press, 2001).

Weiner, D. B., *The Citizen-Patient in Revolutionary and Imperial Paris* (Baltimore, MD: Johns Hopkins University Press, 1993).

Wendell, S., *The Rejected Body: Feminist Philosophical Reflections on Disability* (New York and London: Routledge, 1996).

Wengler, E. M., 'Women, Religion, and Reform in Sixteenth-Century Geneva' (PhD dissertation, Boston College, 1999).

Whatley, J., 'Dissoluble Marriage, Paradise Lost: Suzanne Necker's *Réflexions sur le divorce*', *Dalhousie French Studies*, 56 (2001), pp. 144–53.

Williams, E. A., *The Physical and the Moral: Anthropology, Physiology, and Philosophical Medicine in France, 1750–1850* (Cambridge: Cambridge University Press, 1994).

—, 'Hysteria and the Court Physician in Enlightenment France', *Eighteenth-Century Studies*, 35:2 (2002), pp. 247–55.

—, *A Cultural History of Medical Vitalism in Enlightenment Montpellier* (Aldershot: Ashgate, 2003).

Winston, M. E., *From Perfectibility to Perversion: Meliorism in Eighteenth-Century France* (New York: Peter Lang, 2005).

—, 'Medicine, Marriage, and Human Degeneration in the French Enlightenment', *Eighteenth-Century Studies*, 38:2 (2005), pp. 263–81.

Witte, J. Jr, and R. M. Kingdon, *Sex, Marriage, and Family in John Calvin's Geneva, Volume 1: Courtship, Engagement, and Marriage* (Grand Rapids, MI, and Cambridge: William B. Eerdmans Publishing Company, 2005).

Young, I. M., *On Female Body Experience: 'Throwing Like a Girl' and Other Essays* (New York: Oxford University Press, 2005).

INDEX